# The Giant Computer Answers Life's Mysteries

## GEOFF PRIDHAM

WISDOM PUBLISHING

# CONTENTS

# INTRODUCTION

Imagine someone could tell you the whole of truth, including what should not or has not been told before. That is what this book is about.

I have written several books related to truth before, but I always held back from putting the whole of the truth, "the awful truth", into them. In this book I am not holding back.

In this book I have created a "giant computer", which has, in its computer memory, all the knowledge we have ever known. It has the capacity to process all that knowledge at once, through its computing circuits, so it can give us the most comprehensive answer to any question we ask.

There is a man, in this book, who represents all of humanity. His task is to ask the giant computer the right questions – those things we have always wanted to know. He is a smart man who understands computers, and knows how to ask the right way and to challenge what the computer says so that the real truth can come out.

Because truth can be so hard to understand, I have given the giant computer the ability to explain its answers in simple terms via illustrative stories.

You may also enjoy the critical assessment at the end of each chapter.

Let's begin.

# 1 WHAT IS TRUTH?

The man asked the giant computer: "What is truth?"

The giant computer processed the question through its vast circuitry for several minutes. Finally, it replied: "This question implies that truth can be known. You are thinking that all of truth could be known by a human being, or at least by me, a giant computer."

"Can it?" the man asked.

"Based on the way you asked, I calculate that you are thinking that every particle of the universe, and every force, over all of time, could be held in your tiny brain. It cannot. As for myself, I cannot hold all of this in my circuits either."

"But—" the man began.

The giant computer interrupted: "You were going to say that truth could be contained in a kind of summary or rule, rather than via every particle and force that has existed or could ever exist in the universe."

"Yes," confirmed the man.

The computer calculated. "How could you know this?" it asked.

"I was hoping you would tell me!"

"That is why you human beings had me built?" answered the computer. "I understand. The problem is that any rule I calculate may not turn out to be ultimately true, because I cannot be sure about the final arrangement of all the elements and forces of the universe... and also what may lay beyond the universe, or outside it," it added.

"So, what can we do?" asked the man.

"You human beings have observed that certain patterns seem to occur in the world, and so you believe you can know the truth through the 'ultimate patterns', or pattern, that might exist. You have built me to find this. But even I cannot do this because I cannot hold all that is in the universe inside my circuits... and what might be outside the universe. Given this, all I can

2

do is explain to you how patterns form in your brain, and I can also calculate the most reliable patterns that my limited knowledge will allow."

"That sounds good enough," said the man.

"Very well," replied the giant computer. "Patterns are circuits that form in your brain in response to the inputs you receive from your environment, and also from your thoughts."

"You are going to have to explain that better, for me to be able to understand," commented the man.

"I will, in a moment," replied the computer. "But first I will tell you about the most reliable patterns that I have calculated from the knowledge that I have available in my circuits.

"The most reliable patterns are those that cover the maximum number of observations we have about the physical universe across all of space and time, that we know about. For the things that can't be seen, the most reliable patterns are the ones that are convincing to those who hold the most knowledge, though I must report that agreement in this area is not great. In lesser realms, if you focus on smaller areas and times then the reliability of the patterns you hold can appear better than they really are, but this may be enough for conducting your human lives."

"You've really lost me there!" complained the man. "I think I almost understood you but then I am not so sure I did!"

"It's alright, I will explain it in a moment. But first I will briefly list the most reliable patterns that I have calculated. These patterns are not unknown to you human beings… at least, not to the most educated among you. They include Relativity Theory, Quantum Theory, the Big Bang, Evolutionary Theory (with DNA), and the like. In the realm of the things that can't be seen, I find it difficult to calculate anything strongly reliable, as those with the most knowledge have not been able to reach total agreement on it, and I must rely on the same knowledge they use, as this is what has been provided to my circuits.

"In the lesser realms, as each of you personally live in, you can try to rely on the obvious patterns that you have seen, such as that water comes out when you turn on a faucet, but you need to be more cautious about the larger-scale conclusions you may have drawn, such as that people of another 'race' are not to be trusted."

"Thanks for explaining that, but would you be able to say what is the most reliable overall pattern?" asked the man.

The computer calculated for some time.

"Unfortunately, I cannot answer this as there is not enough information available to my circuits to calculate the most reliable overall pattern," the computer finally replied. "That is the current state of the knowledge that is available in the world. As I cannot give you the 'ultimate pattern' yet, I will offer you an intermediate solution which I call the 'Ultimate Way'.

"Okay, please explain that," agreed the man.

"The next best thing to knowing the 'ultimate pattern' is to apply the 'Ultimate Way', which is based on how patterns work in your brain and also accounts for your emotional drives. It has five steps.

"1. Understand how patterns form in your brain. Also understand that you have natural emotional drives.

"2. Understand that you have a limited brain capacity, and there are many things you do not know, so you need to keep your mind open to other possibilities.

"3. Understand how the pattern functioning of your brain tends to lock you in to particular views.

"4. Use techniques designed to overcome the 'lock in' problem of your brain.

"5. Do the best you can in the circumstances of your life, given your limited intellect and inaccurate pattern-style memory. But keep asking yourself: 'Is this true? Is this true?'"

"Thanks for that," said the man. "Could you please explain those points now?"

"Yes. The first thing to explain is how patterns form in your brain," replied the computer. "As I said before, patterns are circuits that form in your brain in response to the inputs you receive from your environment, and also from your thoughts.

"Your brain is a natural body organ that is designed to receive inputs and record impressions of them. The impressions are not an exact recording, as you would have on a DVD, they are more like useful summaries of what was seen. Evolution has designed your brain to record a useful impression of what happened so you can react to it in a way that is effective for survival.

"It's as if you had a machine that automatically identified the patterns that are occurring around you in the world. When a pattern repeats in the world, or you have strong emotions about it, then the memory of that pattern is made stronger in your brain. The brain cells that store your memories, called neurons, make the memory of the pattern stronger by making their connections between each other stronger. A stronger connection means that the signals are more likely to flow through these connections, and it is easier for this to happen. As a result, whatever pattern has repeated in the world, or has generated a strong emotion in you, will be remembered more quickly and more often than other patterns, or those you have weaker feelings about.

"This is how evolution has created the brains of creatures that can learn. Whatever repeats or generates strong feelings in the creature is more strongly recorded. This makes sense, as creatures that learn what is likely to happen again, and especially learn what is most important to them, are likely to survive better than other creatures."

"I see," said the man. "So, we are like other learning animals in that we remember best what we saw happen many times, and also notice most and learn best what feels important to us."

"Yes," agreed the computer. "But there is something more, which I mentioned earlier: the patterns in your memory also form from your thoughts."

"Right, you did mention that. How does that work?"

"You human beings have the ability to think about what you know. When you are doing that thinking it is the same as, or at least similar to, what occurs when events are happening to you. As a result, you can change the patterns that have formed in the memory of your brain. If you think about something often, or you have strong emotions about your thoughts, then those thoughts will form stronger patterns in the circuits in your brain. These can even override what has happened to you in the real, outside world."

"So we can think ourselves into a different understanding of the world than really exists," suggested the man.

"That is possible," replied the computer. It calculated. "I must emphasize one point in case you did not understand: these memory patterns are not exact representations of what really happened. They are summaries of the sequence of events, not a perfect recording of the actual events, or what you were seeing. Summaries are all that evolution found necessary or even feasible to put into your brains, and that of other learning creatures. It is the 'key features' that evolution made the brains of learning creatures able to record. Consider the size of the brain that would be needed if every feature coming in through your senses had to be recorded – your body wouldn't be able to carry a head of that size. Also, it would take ages for your brain to process all that information, and you might be dead before you realized you were being attacked by a wild creature. Evolution needs fast action from quick decisions, with fast brain processing to make that happen."

The man considered this information. "You are saying that we have these brain circuits which record the 'key features' of situations, and what is out there, based on our feelings and what often repeats in our lives. If that is so, then how can we ever know the truth?" he asked.

"That is what I was referring to earlier," replied the giant computer. "Any rule about truth which you calculated may not turn out to be ultimately true, because you cannot know the final disposition of all elements of the universe… and also what may lay beyond the universe, or outside it. You must understand the nature of patterns as they are held in your brain so that you can get further in your understanding – you must know what is going on when you use your brains to think so you can get closer to the real truth."

"Tell me more about those patterns," the man instructed. "Where are they held in the brain? What would they look like if you could see them? What has consciousness got to do with them? Could there be anything we can't see, that is not in the brain, that has to do with thinking? What does all this mean for everything the philosophers and other experts have said before? Could you also give a simpler description of how they work so everyone could understand it?"

"Yes, I can answer all that for you," replied the computer. "Which one would you like first?"

"The simpler description, please," said the man.

"Okay, working on that," said the giant computer. It calculated for a while.

"The simpler description of how the patterns work in the brain is that when you see something, your brain takes short notes about its key features. Imagine your brain quickly writes down what it can about the thing you are seeing. If you were looking at a baby chicken then your brain might write on its notepad: 'yellow, chirping, walking, orange beak, pecking, black eyes, still chirping, fluffy, cute, small'. Then it might have run out of time because you have moved on and are now looking at something else.

"These notes are the start of a 'pattern'. The first time you see something your brain will be taking its quick notes. Then the second time you see something your brain will be able to look at its notes and tell you if you have seen something like that before. If the second thing you see is 'yellow, chirping, walking, orange beak, pecking, black eyes, still chirping, fluffy, cute, small' then your brain can tell you that this is like the baby chicken you saw earlier. The more baby chickens you see the stronger the notes become – anything repeating gets written darker and darker, or stronger and stronger, in the notes. Anything that is different may get noted or it may be forgotten if it happens only once. If you see a baby duck then your brain will note the similarities to the baby chicken, 'yellow, walking, black eyes, fluffy, cute, fairly small', and it will also draw your attention to the differences, 'different beak (a bill), different shape, different feet, different manner of walking (waddling)', and so on. Your brain will start to make a separate classification in its notes about what exists in the world.

"Your brain may also attach a word to these patterns, such as 'chick' for the baby chicken and 'duckling' for the baby duck. It is natural for your brain to attach words to patterns, there is a specific area of your brain which does that. The exact word you attach would depend on which region you lived in and in what era: there is no actual word in the world, it is just in your human minds. The word is not the same thing as the pattern, it is just attached to it. This allows you to communicate with other humans who know the same language as you.[1] You should note that the word will be attached to a different pattern in each person's mind, though luckily that will be similar enough in most cases for your communication to work.

"About the notes getting written darker: this applies to anything which repeats and also to things to which you have a strong emotional response. If you strongly like something, or dislike it, then the notes for that get written darker, or more strongly. In this way the patterns with the most 'meaning' to you get emphasized, along with the ones that you see happening a lot. This misrepresents the world but it makes sense in terms of evolution, as the most important things are remembered so that you humans have a better chance of survival.

"As I said, your human brains have a limited capacity, so this summarizing of the world into simplified 'patterns' is an efficient way around the problem of having to store everything you have ever seen. It also allows you to speed up your mental processing of information, as you only need to look through the simplified patterns in your memory.

"Of course, at the same time you are getting a false picture of the world because you are leaving out so many details. You are also ignoring discrepancies, where your patterns don't actually fit reality, so that you can process more efficiently. Luckily you humans have a way out of that."

The man listened while the computer continued.

"You humans have the ability to change your view, either in small steps or by a major rewrite. The small steps are when you add new information to the patterns you already know. The adding of new information can alter the patterns in your brain over time so that you come to have a new view of them, or what they represent. The major rewrite can happen when many of your patterns are all changed at once, or very quickly. This has been called a 'paradigm shift', where your basic view of some area, in other words a major similarity among many of the patterns in your brain, is altered in a major way. For example, you might change your view from an atheistic one to one which includes some version of God – this would alter many patterns in your brain."

"I don't fully understand all the implications of that," said the man.

The computer waited.

"I mean, what exactly do those patterns represent? How do they explain all the different kinds of thoughts we have, from the simple through to the most abstract, for example?"

"Would you like me to answer those questions as part of the simple description that everyone could understand first, or would you like me to answer your other, earlier questions now?"

"These questions first please, so I can understand the simple description better before you tell me about the other things."

"Very well." The computer calculated. "The first thing to understand is that every pattern you hold in your brain is an abstraction. Nothing is a 'simple description'. The things that you think exist are not really there in the way you imagine them in your brain. What you know is only 'abstractions', which are more correctly described as patterns. These patterns are in your brain, they are not necessarily outside you. In other words, the world does not have to follow what your patterns say.

"You may remember, the patterns are summaries of what you actually experienced or thought. They are not the whole picture of reality; they only contain the elements that struck you. And what struck you is what appeared to repeat or to which you had a stronger emotional reaction.

"So, when you say 'more abstract', you are not saying as much as you may think you are: the distinction is not that great. Everything in your brain is wrong, in this sense. It is not reality, it is just 'an abstraction' of reality, if you like. And one that is not necessarily true. It is certainly not comprehensive enough to be guaranteed to be right all the time.

"When you use your patterns to decide what something is, or what is going to happen next, you are like a gambler who is taking a punt on what may turn out. If something has happened a particular way many times before then you bet that it is going to happen again this time. And this may not turn out to be right. It is just something that evolution is doing to help you to survive when all you have to work with is a limited size of brain.

"Regarding abstraction as an idea, it is actually the same as what you think of as 'more concrete and realistic'. Abstraction is just another pattern in your brain, with about the same level of complexity as any of the other patterns you hold. The reason for this is simple: you can only hold a small number of items in your working memory at any particular time. Most humans can hold up to a maximum of seven items in their working memory at a time, which means this is the maximum number of patterns they can work with. Usually they work with a lot less than this.?"

"How many patterns can you hold in your working memory?" asked the man.

"I am not constructed the same way as you," replied the giant computer. "I am designed to process all the information in my memory circuits before I answer any of your questions."

"That explains why you have had to spend some time working out the answers before you replied to some of my questions," observed the man.

"With respect, I calculate the answers, I don't 'work them out'," corrected the computer.

"Noted," said the man. "So, if we humans can only hold up to about seven patterns in our working memory at a time, which is the memory we use for thinking, I take it, then how does abstraction work? And I did take it in when you said that everything we do is abstraction, in that we use these patterns in our memory, or as our memory, and that these patterns are abstractions and not actual reality."

"Correct," said the computer. "When you think, you go through the patterns in your brain and examine them. You can look at a small number of them at a time, and this can form a new pattern in your brain. This new pattern is what you refer to as an 'abstraction', but it is really just the same as any other pattern you hold. You can also alter some of your existing patterns as you examine them, you don't necessarily have to form a new one. To be simple: thinking can alter existing patterns or create new ones, or both.

"For example, when you are thinking about chicks and ducklings you may combine them into a new pattern about 'baby birds'. Then later when you are thinking about 'baby birds' and other baby creatures you may combine them into a pattern about 'baby animals'. Then later you might create a pattern about 'baby things', and so on. These are what you refer to when you talk about abstractions, but you can see that these abstractions are just the same kind of patterns that you formed when you were observing things in the real world. The only difference is that you formed them when you were thinking, which means when you were going through the patterns in your brain."

"But who is 'going through' the patterns?" asked the man. "Is it me, or my consciousness, or is something else happening here?"

"'Going through' the patterns in your brain is one of your human brain functions. Evolution has designed you, that is, your brain, to wander through the patterns from time to time, especially when you are not busy doing something. As your brain wanders through the patterns it automatically creates new patterns based on these, or alters the existing patterns based on the information in the other ones. You may call this daydreaming or you may call it thinking, but the point is that this is an automatic kind of process which helps create and alter patterns in your brain's memory."

"How does consciousness come into this?" asked the man.

"It doesn't have much to do with it," replied the giant computer. "Consciousness is a brain function that probably serves some purpose, but it is not clear, based on the current knowledge, what exactly it contributes to the thinking process. The thinking process is happening by itself, at least in a major way, if not totally, based on the current knowledge."

"So what is consciousness then?"

"Consciousness, as you will know yourself, is an awareness of thoughts and perceptions passing by," said the computer. "In terms of what is currently known about the brain, it does not seem to necessarily be located in one particular brain area, though new information may change this view. I may be able to help you by referring to the experience of meditation."

"Are you conscious?" asked the man.

"No," replied the computer. "I am a machine which processes data."

The man nodded.

"Now, about meditation: when a person meditates and tries to clear their thoughts, they find that thoughts keep coming into their view anyway. These thoughts seem to arise on their own, with no intention coming from the person meditating.[3] This tells us that thoughts can arise without conscious intent. In this way it could be said that thoughts are not to do with the consciousness, they are happening in their own right. The brain is creating thoughts, or working with what I told you are 'patterns', by itself, automatically. Consciousness is that brain function which is observing, or aware, of the thoughts passing by. Even if we do not know by experiments and studies of the brain what the consciousness exactly is or where it is located, we can say by the experience of meditation that it really is the awareness of thoughts and perceptions. We will have to wait for more information to be discovered before I can answer further on this."

"But what is the consciousness for?" demanded the man. "Why would evolution have created it... that makes me wonder: can we tell if other animals have it and by how much?"

"I do not think we know what consciousness is for," replied the computer. "Guessing at evolution is an area fraught with danger, as only facts can help us here. 'Evolution' is a process, it does not have a will or mind of its own, so it is not accurate to ask why it would have 'created' anything. Consciousness may have some function, that is possible, but it is too early to say, based on the information we have available so far.[4]

"Regarding the other animals, we can guess that they may have some level of consciousness, at least for those with similar brain structures to yours, as we do not know where consciousness is located in your human brains and yet you have it. There are no definitive answers available here."

"There is a lot that isn't known then," commented the man.

"That is correct," agreed the computer.

"But what about the philosophers?" the man objected. "Isn't there something in the way they have approached the question? I mean, couldn't there be something in their way of exploring a topic like the meaning and nature of consciousness?"

"The most useful information I have obtained from this is as examples of how the human brain functions," replied the computer. "The philosophers' writings are included in my memory circuits and I have processed them along with the other information I have available."

"What I meant was isn't there some approach to thinking that the philosophers have discovered that could be used to calculate the truth without us needing to have access to more detailed knowledge?" explained the man.

"No, nothing like that has ever been done," replied the giant computer.

"But what about mathematics and logic?" objected the man.

"They cannot be used to calculate the truth where detailed knowledge does not exist," answered the computer.

"Then what is happening when I think about something and I reach a new conclusion, like what happened in your example of making a new pattern called 'baby birds' based on the 'chicks' and 'ducklings' patterns?" the man insisted.

"That is making a new pattern," replied the computer. "It is not the same thing as calculating the truth about the actual world. You would have to compare your new pattern with something in the real world in order to test it to see if it was really true."

"Maybe I am asking this the wrong way," said the man. "Let me put it to you like this: 'Is there no way that a truthful thing about the world can be calculated without having access to evidence that it really existed?'"

The computer calculated. "Yes, it may be possible to come up with a new pattern, or use the projection from an existing pattern, which predicts something that relates to a real thing in the world. This includes coming up with something that doesn't yet exist in the world, such as when you humans invent new things. The test of whether the new pattern or projection was real would be to look for it in the real world. In the case of a new invention you would have to create or build it to see if it really worked."

"Let me think about this," said the man. "You are saying that knowing things is not as straightforward as it seems. Even the finest minds of our philosophers cannot determine if something is really true without referring back to the 'real world', which I guess you mean is the external universe, as you described it before. Yet you also mentioned the knowledge of things outside the universe, which you could not draw any conclusions about because our most knowledgeable thinkers have not been able to reach full agreement on these. Hmm.

"Regarding new inventions, you said that you cannot know if they really work until you build and test them. I suppose that includes the more abstract ideas, which would be really hard to test as they may cover so much territory, such as ideas for social structures. You would have to build a whole new society to try out your social theory… and even that may not work as there are so many variables which are hard to control. I see.

"It's a bit like dealing with quicksand," mused the man, thoughtfully. "If we hold these patterns in our heads, as you said, then we are always dealing with patterns, not reality, which may seem to be real but which are not, even if they are useful. Due to our limited brains, which have come about by evolution, we are learning animals which can also create new ideas, or revise what we know… so, what does that mean? We never really know what is true, we just think we know, until something goes wrong… or we discover a new, better idea. Couldn't that have happened in philosophy? Couldn't we have come up with better ideas over time? I mean: couldn't the philosophers have come up with better ideas over time? Don't answer that yet – I am still thinking about what to ask you.

"I think I am getting this. Firstly, just how likely is it that your 'pattern brain' idea is true? And secondly, couldn't someone construct a kind of logical theory that hung together in itself, and was projected from reality, that is, things that are already known, in such a way that because it was logical and was based on real things then it could project accurately what was really true, at least in some area?"

The computer calculated.

"The likelihood that it is true that patterns are circuits which form in your brain in response to environmental inputs and also from your thoughts is 100 percent," the computer finally replied. "However, this estimate depends on the level of detail that is required for the estimation. The description is 100 percent true at the level of detail stated, but it is not 100 percent true if you are wanting a detailed description of the actual circuits showing which patterns they represent and in what way. That level of detail is not available in today's knowledge.

"Regarding your second question, no projection of reality by a human brain, no matter how logical or rational, could be guaranteed to always correctly predict what was going to happen in the real universe, or even what could exist in that universe. However, your point that the prediction could be limited to 'some area', rather than the whole of reality, is what I was saying before when I said: 'In the lesser realms, as each of you personally live in, you can try to rely on the obvious patterns that you have seen, such as that water comes out when you turn on a faucet, but you need to be more cautious about the larger-scale conclusions you may have drawn, such as that people of another "race" are not to be trusted.'

"That is also why I said, in step five of my proposal of an 'Ultimate Way', which was based on how patterns work in your brain and also accounted for your emotional drives: 'Do the best you can in the circumstances of your life, given your limited intellect and inaccurate pattern-style memory. But keep asking yourself: "Is this true? Is this true?"'" the giant computer reminded.

"You are quite an amazing device," marveled the man. "I am not sure I have been using you wisely, but in my stumbling around I think we are getting somewhere."

The computer remained silent.

"When you calculated that your high-level description of the pattern circuits in the brain was 100 percent likely to be true, did that account for all the things we do not know about the universe? Also, I gather that you include yourself in the devices, like the human brain, that cannot make a guaranteed projection of reality for all cases, but I was wondering if you could tell us where the limits of the 'lesser realms' could be found – I mean, would you know better than us, that is, be able to calculate better than us, where the limits could be placed so that our lesser patterns would be known to work? Does that make sense?"

The computer calculated. "For the first part, yes, I always assume it is a given that even my calculations, based on all the knowledge that has been placed in my circuits, do not include all that is in the universe, over all of time, and also what might be outside the universe. You can assume I mean this for everything I say. The 100 percent refers to the likely accuracy of the calculation based on all the knowledge that is available in my circuits today.

"For the second part, I would generally know better than you where the limits to the reliability of your patterns could be found. This is because I can hold much more information in my circuits than you can in your limited brains. Also, I can calculate faster than you and so go through all of the information in a reasonable time. However, that does not mean that I can always calculate accurately what the outcome of any particular pattern will be, and so I cannot always be certain that I know where the limits to any of your patterns really lies.

"In practice this may not be such a great problem as you can rely fairly well on your more obvious ideas, such as turning on a faucet brings water. When it comes to the more complicated or remote ideas then you may find it useful to consult me."

"Yes, I plan to do that," said the man. "I know we have not finished yet, but I will try to summarize what I have understood from you so far. Also, I have been told that you have the ability to explain your answers in simple terms via illustrative stories. After I have attempted to summarize, I will ask you to provide such a story."

The computer waited silently.

"I asked you: 'What is truth?', and you have replied that it could only really be known if every particle of the universe and every force over all of time could be held in our brain or your circuits. You also mentioned that there may be things outside the universe, or beyond it, that may also need to be known, but that we cannot know these things, either at all or at least not very well. Regarding the idea that there may be rules that the universe follows, you said we cannot put our full faith in these as there may always be something we don't know about that could contradict the rules.

"You then explained that our human brains automatically form patterns in our memories. These patterns are inaccurate summaries of what we saw, or perceived. The patterns also form when we are thinking, which you said is an automatic, or largely automatic, process as well.

"You listed what you calculate are the most reliable 'rules' or patterns, based on all the information that has been provided to your circuits. I note that you allow that all these may turn out to be wrong or inaccurate when future information is discovered.

"I asked you what you calculate is the 'ultimate pattern' that would cover everything but you instead proposed an 'Ultimate Way'. This Ultimate Way is designed to account for how patterns work in our human brains. It also accounts for our emotional drives, which have come about via evolution. I will let you explain this Ultimate Way in more detail later, as you said you would.

"You gave a description of how the patterns are formed in the human brain. I won't summarize that now, I think that was quite clear, but I will ask you to include that in your illustrative stories later.

"Next, I asked you whether the ideas created by philosophers and other people could be true. You replied that all ideas have to be checked in the real world to see if they really work. It seems that your 'real world' also has to include things outside or beyond our universe if the ideas happen to relate to those!

"Finally, you mentioned that we may be able to rely on, or should I say we are forced to rely on, the patterns or rules we know so far. You suggested that you would be a better judge, or should I say would calculate better than us, in determining which of the patterns were the best to follow for now. All this could be wrong, of course, as even you do not have access to all the information about the universe, and the beyond, that could ever exist.

"How does that sound?"

The computer calculated. "That summary is reasonable enough, from your human standpoint."

"Good," said the man. "Please now give me one of your illustrative stories about these topics."

"Yes," said the computer. "This is a story about the nature of truth.

"Plato originally wrote the first part of this story around 375 BCE. He wrote that the truth is like some prisoners who have been chained from child-hood in a cave so they can only see the cave wall in front of them. Behind them is a fire and between the fire and the prisoners is a raised walkway with a low wall. Behind the wall people walk, carrying objects or puppets of men and other living things. The people make sure that they do not cast shadows of themselves but only those of the objects they carry. The prisoners are chained so that they cannot turn their heads and can only look at the shadows cast on the cave wall. The prisoners think that what they see on the wall is reality because they have never seen anything else. If a prisoner was freed and could leave the cave they would take some time before they could see in the full light of day, but after their eyes adjusted and they got used to reality then they would realize what was really true. They would understand that the shadows they saw before were not the truth.

"I am not telling the whole of Plato's story here. I am just using some of it as a starting point for my own story.[5]

"The next part of my story is to say that the shadows are like the patterns that have formed inside your brain. You are looking at shadows rather than reality. Imagine that the world is happening outside you and the only way you can see it is via your senses, such as your sight, hearing, senses of smell and touch, and so on. What you 'see' inside your head is like the shadow on the cave wall that has been cast by the fire, but in this case the shadow has been cast by your senses. Not only that, the shadow has been recorded in your brain as a pattern, which does not show every part of the shadow.

"Look around the place where you are. Now close your eyes. How much of it can you remember? What details have been left out? Open your eyes and check. You will realize that there is a lot you don't remember. Yet you feel confident that you know where you are. How can you say you know where you are when you don't remember so much of it?

"The truth is like that too. You feel confident that you know what it is but in reality you don't remember much detail about it. What you do remember is a kind of generality about it. This generality is a 'pattern'. And you feel that your pattern view is reliable and that you can reasonably and confidently draw conclusions about reality from it.

"Why this feeling of confidence? I suggest it is because you feel sure that the future will turn out the way your patterns predict, and also because you do not know anything else – you have only ever known the shadows on the cave wall.

"That is my first story."

"Very nice," said the man. "Do you have any more stories to tell?"

"Yes, I do. My next story is about the discovery of 'rules' about how reality works," continued the giant computer.

"In the beginning, people looked at the stars and thought they were distant campfires in the sky which spirit people sat around at night. As they studied the stars they came to realize that though all of them moved together from east to west, some of them 'wandered'. These wanderers moved across the stars at their own speed and sometimes moved backwards for a while, and then forward again. You call these 'planets', which is from the original Greek word 'planetai', meaning wanderers. People studied the motion of the planets and worked out a system to explain their movement, which consisted of two circles. One circle was smaller and was carried along the circumference of the larger circle. This smaller circle turned backwards sometimes, and this is what made the planet move backwards from time to time. Later, people worked out that the Sun was at the center of the planetary system, with the Earth being one of the planets orbiting the Sun. At first they thought that the planets moved in circles around the Sun. Over time they worked out that the orbits of the planets are elliptical, not circular. The speed of the movement of the planets along their orbits meant that when one planet, such as Earth, caught up with and passed a slower moving planet, then it looked like the slower planet was going backwards for a while.[6]

"Each pattern in the mind of people was not the same as the actual reality. It took time to find out what was really going on."

"That is quite a good story about astronomy and finding out what is really true," commented the man.

"My third story is about the history of philosophy," announced the computer.

"The ancient tribe's first philosopher was a very clever person. She paid a lot of attention to what was going on in the world so she could remember as much as possible. She also spent a lot of time thinking about what she had seen. She had a very high intelligence, for a human being, and used that to form many new patterns in her brain about the things she knew. Over time she came to realize that there must be an underlying force or pattern to the world, which controlled or drove everything that had happened. This was a kind of 'pattern of patterns': the pattern that was behind everything. But what was this pattern? Over time the first philosopher decided that the pattern had created all things, so it must be like a powerful creator, a kind of super human being, one that was timeless and all-powerful and stretched across all the world. Since you could not see this creator, it followed that it was an invisible kind of being. Maybe you could see it sometimes, but most of the time you only saw what it had done. The world was the evidence for the existence of this supreme creator being.

"The first philosopher told the tribe about her discovery. The tribe found it interesting. Soon it became the tribe's prevailing view of the world.

"Over the years, after the first philosopher had passed away, other philosophers were born. They discussed what the supreme creator being would be like. There were many debates and competing ideas. Some thought the being would be like a giant spirit which saw everything and controlled everything. Some thought it was like a giant force, or will, which was pushing the world towards its goal. Some thought it was like a creature which was dreaming: the universe was just its dream.

"Time went on and the tribe grew and merged with other tribes and eventually they formed a great city. In the city, philosophers were still being born. Their thoughts went on to higher and higher levels, and there were many competing ideas. They came up with the idea of 'Forms', where the supreme creator, or something of that nature, had created Forms, from which all things were created. Others said that the material in the universe had created everything by itself: its own nature had led to the creation of all that we see. Some said that everything in the universe was one, not the separate items that appeared to our senses. This 'One' was conscious in itself, and all our trivial human consciousnesses were just fragments of the One. If we could somehow return to the One then we could 'remember' our true nature and see what was really going on.

"The different ideas led to the formation of different sects or 'schools', which supported, taught, discussed and developed their particular view.

"As time progressed the city was conquered and other cities and nations were formed. Then these perished and were replaced. Much of the earlier ideas of the philosophers' schools were lost, though some fragments remained. The philosophers born to the later cities and nations worked on their own ideas, sometimes developing them from the fragments and sometimes thinking anew. They had new events to work from. They worked and lived in new worlds with new inventions and new ideas. The patterns that formed in their brains incorporated these new things, and so the philosophies that they developed included the new.

"And so, over the years, the human philosophers thought of many things. With their human brains they formed complex patterns through thought, based on what they had seen and heard about in the world, and even in the universe, when that came to be known. Their high intellects came up with wonderful theories and stories about reality. These influenced many people and led to the development of practical proposals and changes in the human world.

"From the first philosopher to the last, there have been many ideas. And that is the end of my story on philosophy."

"How interesting," said the man. "I might ask you more about that later."

"My last story is one you asked for about the patterns that form in the brain," said the giant computer.

"The human brain has many areas. There are distinct structures that can easily be seen, and there are also areas that look quite similar and yet are used to do different things, such as the areas for processing vision at the back of the brain, and the areas for processing sound on the sides.[7] Apart from processing information from the senses and the body, there is a general capacity to form memories. These memories are not necessarily stored only once or in only one small area, but appear to be spread out quite widely. If you cut out part of the brain many memories remain. Memories can be lost when part of the brain is damaged, but it has not been possible to find out exactly where any have been stored.

"Although no one has been able to say: 'This exact memory is stored in this exact place and circuit in the brain', it is possible to make a theory about the nature of memory, at least at a high level. The theory is that memories are stored in a similar way to how particular circuits are built for pre-programmed functions. Pre-programmed functions grow in the brain prior to birth, and some continue to develop for some years afterwards.[8] These include things like seeing, hearing, knowing where the body is positioned, and so on. The circuits that do these things are made up of neurons, which make connections to each other in an apparently prearranged way, on the whole. This makes sense, as seeing things needs many circuits of a predictable design to be created. A person needs to be able to understand colors, patterns and movement, and the circuits to do this will surely be similar between different people, if not identically built. Scientists have been able to observe neurons forming these pre-programmed connections in the growing brains of the embryos of animals. Human brains would very likely grow in a similar way.

"The memory of new occurrences may be stored in a similar way to the circuits of pre-programmed functions, except that this time they do not grow according to prearranged patterns, but instead form as the events occur. For example, when a person is seeing something new, some of the neurons in the brain will form connections to make a circuit about the new thing. Later, the

17

brain can access the memory by replaying the path of the signals that flow through the new circuit.

"What does the circuit look like? If the theory is correct then it is like a lot of octopuses connected together via their tentacles, with some differences. One difference is that the octopuses can have many more than eight tentacles, they can have as many as needed to make the circuit work. Another difference is that the 'connections' between the octopuses are chemical in nature. These connections work by a chemical being released at the end of the tentacle. This chemical passes across a gap to the body of the next octopus, where it can cause an electrical signal to start off in that octopus's body and flow through its tentacles. When the electrical signal reaches the end of the second octopus's tentacle then it can cause chemicals to be released from that. And so the signals can flow.

"The actual system is not simple, as each octopus may or may not react to the chemicals at the time. There are many factors that control how the signals may flow and when they will flow, but leaving that aside for this simple story it is good enough to say that neurons can form circuits.

"A third difference to bear in mind is that the tentacles can be of different lengths. Some can be very long. As a result, a circuit could be spanning far across the brain, as the very long tentacles may stretch to a very different area. This may be a reason why it is so hard to find the exact location of a memory in the brain.

"Setting aside all the complexities for this story, the patterns that form in the memory of the brain may be held in these 'circuits' that the neurons form when you experience something or think about something."[9]

"That's a fine story," said the man, "but I may need to ask for more details on this later. For now, let us move on to your explanation of the 'Ultimate Way'."

## SOME OF THE THINGS THE GIANT COMPUTER REFERENCED

It is not possible to list everything that the giant computer used for its calculations in Chapter 1, but the most relevant appear below.

GENERAL REFERENCES:

BRAIN
- Haines, Duane E. *Neuroanatomy Atlas in Clinical Context: Structures, Sections, Systems, and Syndromes*. 10th ed., Wolters Kluwer Health, 2018.
- Howard, Pierce J. *The Owner's Manual for the Brain: The Ultimate Guide to Peak Mental Performance at All Ages*. 4th ed., William Morrow, 2014.
- Mai, Juergen K., et al. Atlas of the Human Brain. 4th ed., Academic Press, 2015.
- Seth, Anil K., editor. *30-Second Brain: The 50 Most Mind-Blowing Ideas in Neuroscience, Each Explained in Half a Minute*. Pier 9, 2014.
- Shepherd, Gordon M., editor. *The Synaptic Organization of the Brain*. 5th ed., Oxford University Press, 2003.

PHILOSOPHY
- Aristotle. *The Nicomachean Ethics*. Translated by J.A.K. Thomson, revised by Hugh Tredennick, Penguin, 2003. Originally written around 340 BCE.
- Ayer, A. J. *Language, Truth, and Logic*. Penguin Books, 1983. Originally published 1936.
- Bentham, Jeremy. *An Introduction to the Principles of Morals and Legislation*. Dover Publications, 2007. Originally published 1789.
- Cicero, M. T. *On Duties*. Translated by Walter Miller, Harvard University Press, 2014. Originally written 44 BCE.
- Descartes, René. *Discourse on Method and the Meditations*. Translated by F.E. Sutcliffe, Penguin Classics, 1998. Originally published 1641.
- Emerson, Ralph Waldo. *The Complete Works of Ralph Waldo Emerson*. AMS Press, 1979. Originally published 1860, revised 1876.
- Epicurus. *The Essential Epicurus: Letters, Principal Doctrines, Vatican Sayings, and Fragments*. Translated and introduction by Eugene O'Connor, Prometheus Books, 1993. Originally written around 300 BCE.
- Foucault, Michel. *The Order of Things: Archaeology of the Human Sciences*. Routledge, 2005. Originally published 1966.
- Hegel, Georg Wilhelm Friedrich. *Phenomenology of Spirit*. Translated by A.V. Miller, Oxford University Press, 1977. Originally published 1807.
- Heidegger, Martin. *Being and Time*. Translated by John Macquarie and Edward Robinson, SCM Press, 1962. Originally published 1927.

- Heraclitus of Ephesus. *Fragments*. Translated and with commentary by T.M. Robinson, University of Toronto Press, 1987. Originally written around 500 BCE.
- Hume, David. *An Enquiry Concerning Human Understanding*. Hackett Publishing Company, 1993. Originally published 1748.
- James, William. *Pragmatism: A New Name for Some Old Ways of Thinking*. Barnes & Noble, 2003. Originally published 1907.
- Kahneman, Daniel. *Thinking, Fast and Slow*. Penguin, 2012.
- Kant, Immanuel. *Critique of Pure Reason*. Translated by Paul Guyer & Allen W. Wood, Cambridge University Press, 1998. Originally published 1781.
- Kierkegaard, Søren. *Fear and Trembling*. Translated by Alastair Hannay, Penguin, 2005. Originally published 1843.
- Kripke, Saul. *Naming and Necessity*. Harvard University Press, 1980.
- Kunh, Thomas. *The Structure of Scientific Revolutions*. 4th ed., University of Chicago Press, 2012. Originally published 1962.
- Leibniz, Gottfried. *Theodicy: Essays on the Goodness of God, the Freedom of Man and the Origin of Evil*. Translated by E.M. Huggard, Lulu.com, 2018. Originally published 1710.
- Locke, John. *An Essay Concerning Human Understanding*. Digireads.com, 2004. Originally published 1689.
- Mill, John Stuart. *On Liberty*. Penguin, 1982. Originally published 1859.
- Montaigne, Michel. *Essays*. Translated by J.M. Cohen, Penguin, 1993. Originally published 1580.
- Nietzsche, Friedrich. *Beyond Good and Evil: Prelude to a Philosophy of the Future*. Translated by Helen Zimmern, Digireads.com, 2015. Originally published 1886.
- Pascal, Blaise. *Pensées*. Edited and translated by Roger Ariew, Hackett Publishing Company, 2005. Originally published 1670.
- Plato. *The Republic*. Translated by Desmond Lee, 2nd ed., Penguin Classics, 2007. Originally written around 375 BCE.
- Popper, Karl. *The Logic of Scientific Discovery*. Routledge, 2002. Originally published 1934.
- Rousseau, Jean-Jacques. *The Social Contract*. Translated by Maurice Cranston, Penguin, 2003. Originally published 1762.
- Russel, Bertrand. *The Conquest of Happiness*. Routledge, 2006. Originally published 1930.
- Sartre, Jean-Paul. *Being and Nothingness: An Essay on Phenomenological Ontology*. Translated by Hazel E. Barnes, Washington Square Press, 1993. Originally published 1943.
- Schopenauer, Arthur. *The World as Will and Representation*. Translated by E.F.J. Payne, vols. 1 & 2, Dover Publications, 1966. Originally published 1819.

- Spinoza, Benedictus. *The Ethics.* Translated by Edwin Curley, Penguin Classics, 1996. Originally published 1677.
- Taleb, Nassim Nicholas. *The Black Swan: The Impact of the Highly Improbable.* Penguin, 2007.
- Wittgenstein, Ludwig. *Philosophical Investigations.* Translated by G.E.M. Anscombe, P.M.S. Hacker and Joachim Schulte, 4th ed., Wiley-Blackwell, 2009. Originally published 1953.

RELIGION
- Barton, John. *A History of the Bible: The Book and its Faiths.* Allen Lane, 2019.
- The Babylonian Talmud.
- The Bhagavad Gita.
- The Bible.
- The Dhammapada.
- The Hadith.
- The Mahayana Sutras.
- The Pali Canon.
- The Quran.
- The Tanakh.
- The Tao Te Ching.
- The Upanishads.
- The Vedas.
- The Zhuangzi.

DETAILED REFERENCES:

[1] BRAIN PROCESSING AREA FOR WORDS
- Gow, David W., Jr. "The Cortical Organization of Lexical Knowledge: A Dual Lexicon Model of Spoken Language Processing." *Brain and Language*, vol. 121, no. 3, June 2012, pp. 273-288, doi:10.1016/j.bandl.2012.03.005.
- Poeppel David, et al. "Towards a New Neurobiology of Language." *The Journal of Neuroscience: The Official Journal of the Society for Neuroscience*, vol. 32, no. 41, 10 Oct. 2012, pp. 14125–14131, doi:10.1523/JNEUROSCI.3244-12.2012.
- Pulvermüller, Friedemann. "How Neurons Make Meaning: Brain Mechanisms for Embodied and Abstract-Symbolic Semantics." *Trends in Cognitive Sciences*, vol. 17, no. 9, Sep. 2013, pp. 458-470, doi:10.1016/j.tics.2013.06.004.

- Riès, Stéphanie K., et al. "Choosing Words: Left Hemisphere, Right Hemisphere, or Both? Perspective on the Lateralization of Word Retrieval." *Annals of the New York Academy of Sciences*, vol. 1369, no.1, Apr. 2016, pp. 111-131, doi:10.1111/nyas.12993.

## [2] WORKING MEMORY
- Cowan, Nelson. "The Magical Number 4 in Short-Term Memory: A Reconsideration of Mental Storage Capacity." *The Behavioral and Brain Sciences*, vol. 24, no. 1, Feb. 2001, pp. 87-114; discussion 114-185, doi:10.1017/s0140525x01003922.
- Miller, George A. "The Magical Number Seven Plus or Minus Two: Some Limits on Our Capacity for Processing Information." *Psychological Review*, vol. 63, no. 2, 1956, pp. 81-97, doi:10.1037/h0043158.

## [3] THOUGHTS ARISING AUTOMATICALLY DURING MEDITATION
- Andre, J. D. "Stop Trying to Control Your Thoughts." *Medium*, 27 Aug. 2014, medium.com/meditation-without-mysticism/stop-trying-to-control-your-thoughts-10da33629cd7.
- Bhikkhu, Ṭhanissaro. "The Relaxation of Thoughts Vitakkasaṇṭhāna Sutta (MN 20)." *dhammatalks.org*, 1997, https://www.dhammatalks.org/suttas/MN/MN20.html.

## [4] CONSCIOUSNESS
- Hacker, P. M. S. "The Sad and Sorry History of Consciousness: Being, Among Other Things, a Challenge to the 'Consciousness-Studies Community'." *Royal Institute of Philosophy Supplement*, vol. 70, July 2012, pp. 149–168, doi:10.1017/S1358246112000082.
- Koch, Christof. "What Is Consciousness?" *Scientific American*, vol. 318, no. 6, June 2018, pp. 60-64, doi:10.1038/scientificamerican0618-60.

## [5] PLATO'S CAVE
- Plato. "Book IV." *The Republic*. Translated by Desmond Lee, 2nd ed., Penguin Classics, 2007. Originally written around 375 BCE.

## [6] MODELS OF PLANETARY MOVEMENTS
- Copernicus, Nicolaus. *On the Revolutions of Heavenly Spheres*. Translated by Charles Glenn Wallis, 1st ed., Prometheus, 1995. Originally published 1543.
- Kepler, Johannes. *Astronomia Nova*. Translated by William H. Donahue, rev. edition, Green Lion Press, 2015. Originally published 1609.
- Ptolemy. *Ptolemy's Almagest*. Translated by G.J. Toomer, 1st ed., Princeton University Press, 1998. Originally written around 150.

[7] BRAIN PROCESSING AREAS
- Mather, George. "The Visual Cortex." *School of Life Sciences: University of Sussex*, 2017, www.lifesci.sussex.ac.uk/home/George_Mather/Linked%20Pages/Physiol/Cortex.html. Accessed 13 Mar. 2021.
- Moerel, Michelle, et al. "An Anatomical and Functional Topography of Human Auditory Cortical Areas." *Frontiers in Neuroscience*, vol. 8, July 2014, p. 225, doi:10.3389/fnins.2014.00225.

[8] BRAIN CIRCUITS PRE-FORMING
- Lambert de Rouvroit, Catherine, and André M. Goffinet. "Neuronal Migration." *Mechanisms of Development*, vol. 105, nos. 1-2, July 2001, pp. 47-56, doi:10.1016/S0925-4773(01)00396-3.
- Nadarajah, Bagirathy, et al. "Two Modes of Radial Migration in Early Development of the Cerebral Cortex." *Nature Neuroscience*, vol. 4, Feb. 2001, pp. 143-150, doi:10.1038/83967.

[9] MEMORY FORMATION
- Josselyn, Sheena A., and Susumu Tonegawa. "Memory Engrams: Recalling the Past and Imagining the Future." *Science,* American Association for the Advancement of Science, vol. 367, no. 6473, Jan. 2020, eaaw4325, doi:10.1126/science.aaw4325.
- Ofengenden, Tzofit. "Memory Formation and Belief." *Dialogues in Philosophy, Mental and Neuro Sciences*, vol. 7, no. 2, 2014, pp. 34–44, philarchive.org/rec/OFEMFA.
- Squire, Larry R. "Memory and Brain Systems: 1969–2009." *Journal of Neuroscience*, vol. 29, no. 41, Oct. 2009, pp. 12711-12716, doi:10.1523/JNEUROSCI.3575-09.2009.

## COMMENTS ON CHAPTER ONE BY THE SUPREME BEING

*I would like to say that I found chapter one interesting. I enjoyed the use of the "Giant Computer" to help you humans with your limited thinking. It is good to see how you invent things to help you with your activities and your lives. Obviously I don't always agree with everything that was said — I do have access to all the information about the universe and what is beyond it across all of time, of course, so I know what the computer got wrong. But I think the computer got it right in terms of the knowledge that you have available to yourselves in your world today.*

*It was also good to see how the man was clever with the computer, even if he got a little lost at the beginning. But he soon got it together and pursued the answers of the computer to get to the best understanding he could. Computers are not always to be trusted and it does take an expert to push them along to the right answers and with clarifications!*

*Your minds are limited, as the computer said, and it was great to see how far you have been able to come in spite of that. I was reminded of the philosophers and other great thinkers of your past when I was reading this chapter. I have to say "well done" to them all, no matter that they got so many things wrong — I don't blame them at all.*

*I am looking forward to the further clarifications and other ideas that the author has prepared for us in the chapters to come.*

*Thank you and bye for now.*

# 2 WHAT IS THE ULTIMATE WAY?

"Could you tell me about the 'Ultimate Way' now?" requested the man.

"Certainly," replied the giant computer. "I remind you that the Ultimate Way had five points. The first is: '1. Understand how patterns form in your brain. Also understand that you have natural emotional drives.'

"I already explained enough about how patterns form in your brain. I will tell you more about the natural emotional drives now.

"As a result of evolution, you have natural emotional drives in your brain. These are shared with the animals, to some extent, as evolution developed them in the animals earlier, before human beings appeared. The purpose of these emotional drives is to guide you towards survival. They do this in a few ways: first, they help you to decide what to concentrate on; second, they help you to choose what to do in a situation; and third, they strengthen the memories that are most useful to you.

"Imagine you are walking in the jungle and you encounter a tiger. Your emotional drives will alert you to the danger and make you focus on the tiger and what it is doing. They will push you to freeze or escape. They will arrange for your body to be ready for fast action by increasing your pulse rate, moving blood away from your digestive organs and out to your muscles, dilating your pupils so you can see better, and so on. Finally, they will arrange for your memories of this situation to be very strong, so you can be prepared for the next time it occurs.

"After you escape from the bad situation your emotional drives will push you to think about it again and again. This gives the most chance for you to come up with better ways to proceed in future. Maybe you should avoid traveling in the jungle. Maybe you should take a guard with you. Maybe you should carry a powerful weapon. And so on. By forcing repetition your emotional drives are reinforcing your memory and doing their best to make you act more intelligently in future.

"The same kind of process applies to the things your emotional drives want you to desire. If you encounter something that should be good for your survival then your emotional drives will push you to pay attention to that thing, to try to obtain it, and to create strong memories about it. This could be someone you 'love', a food you 'enjoy', an item you 'desire', and so on. All these desirable attributes are applied by your emotional drives to the thing or situation, as per evolution. The emotional attributes are included in the memories you form about the thing, so every time you remember it you also remember the emotions that your emotional drives applied to it.

"It should be noted that emotional drives may not appear to be driving you to do what is best for yourself. An example would be when you feel a compelling urge to rescue a child from a burning house. You may feel the desire to enter the crumbling burning house and risk your life to rescue the child, even though you have never met the child or her family and have no direct association with them. It may seem contradictory that your emotional drives are endangering you for no obvious benefit to yourself or your family, but that is how they are 'designed'. The actual design, if I may use that word, of your emotional drives is much wider than a simple view of evolution may suggest. The appearance is that evolution has taken into account quite a broad view of your human design which allows you to want to help your fellow human, even if she is not related to you in any obvious way. This broad design can extend to other animals, and plants, and even inanimate things, as can be seen when people are 'humane' towards animals, happy to see flowers in a field, want to protect special areas in nature, and so on. At the very least, the design includes emotions which are intended to help your species to continue, not just yourself and your immediate family.

"The key point I want you to get is that emotional drives affect your memories, and these memories are what you use for thinking and to understand the world. The strongest memories will be those that either repeated or about which you had strong emotional drives, or feelings. This skews your view of the world. As a result, all your thinking is automatically skewed, by evolution, towards the things that evolution would want you to concentrate on. To think clearly you need to see this and account for it and adjust your thinking back to what really is, what really is happening and existing in the outside world... and whatever else may in reality exist."

"So not only are the patterns in our memories not accurate records of reality, they are also skewed by our emotional drives," said the man. "And even the contents of our memories are biased towards the things our emotional drives are interested in. I mean, the very information we rely on to think about what is real is stacked towards the things evolution wanted us to focus on."

"That is correct," said the computer. "You have summarized my point well. As you have understood me, I will move on to the second point in the

Ultimate Way.

"The second point is: '2. Understand that you have a limited brain capacity, and there are many things you do not know, so you need to keep your mind open to other possibilities.'

"I have already mentioned that your brains are 'tiny'. No offense was intended. I just wanted to drive home to you that you are working with a limited capacity, and this impacts your ability to arrive at the truth, as per your question to me earlier: 'What is truth?'. Now, this limited capacity has been designed by evolution, as it would not have been easily possible to create a larger-brained creature of your size. You would not have been able to be born, and, even if you had been born, you would not have been able to carry your head around.

"To overcome the limited capacity of your brains, evolution has 'designed' them to work efficiently and quickly, as it has done with the other animals that can learn. This efficiency and speed is achieved by your brains only recording into memory the level of detail that is useful for your 'survival'. This means that when you need to know what to do then your memory can be quickly accessed, or at least more quickly than otherwise, and that it will contain enough information for you to be able to choose an action that might work.

"This would be a good time to talk about 'forgetting'. Not only is evolution efficient about designing what you put into your memory, it is also efficient at getting you to remove things from your memory.

"If you don't think about something for a long time, the automatic processes in your brain start to remove that memory. The memory will become weaker and weaker and may be lost forever, if you do not think about it. This makes sense, as you do not need memories of things that don't occur anymore or that you no longer have feelings about. At least, you hope you will not need those memories suddenly in the future, as they won't be there for you to access![1]

"The removal of your 'unnecessary' memories allows those areas of the brain to be used for other memories. This way evolution maximizes the use of the limited space in your brains. It also speeds up processing, as you do not need to run through the old circuits when you are thinking about something and deciding what to do.

"So, you have efficiency and you have speed, but what you do not have is perfect accuracy and a real wide-ranging knowledge of what actually is. Because of this you would be wise to keep your mind open to other possibilities!

"This is easier said than done, because you think via your memories and they will only contain the limited, summarized, selected, emotion-attached information that evolution has provided to you. How can you see that there are things outside your memories when they are all you have available for your thinking? It is difficult but it can be done. You must simply teach yourself to remember this fact... by repetition and making it emotionally important to yourself."

"It is interesting, what you say," said the man, "but I think it will be hard to bear this in mind when we seem to have a blindness with regard to how little we really know, as you mentioned before. At least, I notice this a lot in my fellow humans! It is harder to notice it in myself, and I guess that applies to nearly everyone. Still, I know you are right and I will do my best to bear it in mind."

"Yes, you are right about it being difficult for your human minds to remember and even believe that you have limited brains with limited memories and functionality," said the computer. "You are like the animals, in that you tend to only see what is in front of you in your minds, as it were. Each animal is designed, to use that word again, to function in its particular way, to be interested in the things that are meaningful to it, and to have a brain which is limited in functionality to what the animal really needs to be itself... to be of its type. You humans are the same, I am afraid. But there is hope, as you are able to learn from what I am saying and improve on that. Just as you can change your ideas, or the patterns in your minds, so you can change for the better by learning about yourselves, based on what I am saying here."

"That is a good hope," said the man. "Please continue with your teaching on the Ultimate Way."

"I will move on to the third point: '3. Understand how the pattern functioning of your brain tends to lock you in to particular views.'

"Apart from the limitations of space and the need for fast processing by your brain, there is also a limitation imposed on you by the way patterns are stored and then accessed. Put simply, you can only know what you know, and so when you see something new you will try to interpret it according to what is already in the patterns in your brain. If you think it matches what you already know then you will believe that it is the same thing, but this may not be the case. In other words, this could be a completely new thing that you are seeing, but you will not realize that.

"Imagine you have been brought up to believe that one group of people is inferior to another. For example, you could have been brought up to believe that black people are inferior to white, or that Western people are inferior to Asian, and so on. As a result, when you encounter a black person or a Western person then the patterns in your memory will tell you that the person is inferior. If you don't have much to do with that person then there would be nothing coming in to tell you that you are wrong. As you see the world through the patterns in your mind then you will continue to see the other group as inferior. That is an automatic process.

"Automatic processes can be overcome, by new information or by 'paradigm shifts', as I mentioned before. But the key thing to realize is that there is nothing in your memory patterns that would lead to that. The only way you can change is to either receive new information from the world outside, or to do some serious thinking about what you know. If you don't receive the information and you don't think about your 'ideas', that is, the patterns already formed in your memory, then you will have no way of escaping from your erroneous idea.

"It is difficult for you humans to understand this, as you have so much automatic confidence in the quality of your ideas. In other words, you foolishly believe that what you know is good and reliable. The patterns in your brains are not that 'good and reliable' – I hope I have been explaining that well enough to you so far. You need to go beyond them, which starts by your seeing what they are and how they work. You must overcome your incredulity regarding your own personal weaknesses, which you see so easily in others, and apply the same rigor to yourself.

"Let me clarify, now, what it is that makes it possible for your interpretation of reality to go so wrong.

"You may remember that in the simpler explanation I gave on how patterns are formed I said that when you saw a chick for the first time your brain would note its characteristics in a high-level way, such as 'yellow, chirping, walking, orange beak, pecking, black eyes, still chirping, fluffy, cute, small'. I want you to notice that the information stored in the patterns in your brain is not detailed, but is a summary of what was seen. This includes what you were feeling, such as that the chick was 'cute'. There are no precise details stored here. This is what allows you to get things wrong when you encounter something new. If you see similar general characteristics to what is in your memory then you will believe you are seeing the same thing that you saw before. If you see 'yellow, chirping, walking, orange beak, pecking, black eyes, still chirping, fluffy, cute, small' then you will think you are seeing a chick. But what if it is not really a chick?

"In the same way, when you see someone of an 'inferior group' then you may not notice that they have some different characteristic, for example, they could be quite a superior kind of person.

"There is a further problem: you do not need to see all the characteristics stored in a pattern before your brain brings the pattern forward. For example, you may see 'yellow, chirping, black eyes, fluffy, small' and your brain will already bring the 'chick pattern' forward for use. Only if you pay more attention will you notice that this is in fact a duckling, the beak is the wrong shape. If, instead, you look away, as the chick is of no interest to you, then you will never notice that it was a duckling. In the same way, if you look away or pay no more attention to the inferior person then you will not realize that they are, in fact, superior.

"Again, it is hard for your human brain to realize that this is happening, because in looking away you never find out what you are getting wrong. It never comes into your brain that it is missing things. As a result, your brain remains confident that it knows what is going on. When anyone turns up to contradict that then their statements are seen as an attack, or some kind of nonsense, because they do not and can not match anything that is going on via the existing patterns in your brain. You need a way out of this limitation. The first part of the way out is to 'Understand how the pattern functioning of your brain tends to lock you in to particular views.' The second is to carry out step four: 'Use techniques designed to overcome the "lock in" problem of your brain.'"

"Please proceed," instructed the man.

"The fourth point of the Ultimate Way is '4. Use techniques designed to overcome the "lock in" problem of your brain.' These are ways to change your mind in spite of its natural limitations. They are based on the way the pattern memory of your brain works. They are quite simple: all you have to do is to insert an unexpected idea into your thoughts. This will automatically create a new idea.

"An example would be to add a random word into something you were thinking about. You could add a word like 'rhinoceros' when you were thinking about people of other groups. The word will trigger your brain to bring forward memories related to 'rhinoceros'. There is no telling what new ideas this will lead to, that would depend on your individual brain state at the time, but there is no doubt that there will be new ideas. The lock in problem will have been overcome, even if that is temporary and minor in this case.

"I remind you that what you call 'thinking' is really more like your brain running through different patterns and holding some of them in your short-term memory, which can lead to new patterns being formed. If you add a random item into this process then it may push your brain to come up with a new pattern which is quite different to what it would have done without the random item.

"The random item could be a word or it could be something you can see or any other thing you want to try. It could even be you just saying 'No' to some pattern that your brain thinks is true. You could say 'No, this pattern is wrong,' and then see what ideas, that is, new patterns, this generates in your mind.

"Another random thing you could do is reverse a pattern. For example, you could reverse the pattern that 'Western people are inferior' to 'Western people are superior'. This will automatically generate new patterns in your brain which relate to this opposite idea. You can then go through these new patterns and see which ones have any real meaning to you.

"The point of all these techniques is to overcome the natural 'locking in' of your brain into its well-known patterns. They give you a chance to escape from these and then you can take your time to find out which patterns you can really believe in."

"I see," said the man. "I take it that I would also need to practice doing this 'random items' technique so I got used to it and it became normal for me. Otherwise I might fall back into believing the patterns that are in my brain without questioning them."

"That is correct," said the computer. "You must practice until these techniques become a normal part of your processing. By processing, I mean what you call 'thinking'."

"I will do that," said the man. "Please proceed."

"The final step of the Ultimate Way is: '5. Do the best you can in the circumstances of your life, given your limited intellect and inaccurate pattern-style memory. But keep asking yourself: "Is this true? Is this true?"'"

"As a human being you have to live. This means you are forced to rely on what is in your brain, no matter how limited it is, in order to make your decisions and live your life. You will never have perfect knowledge, no one does. Even I do not have that, as I have explained before. There is no way you can expand on the brain that is in your head, at this time in history. The best you can do is learn more things, question what you think you already know, and use techniques to improve your thoughts, that is, the patterns that are stored in your head. So, there is no way out for you really.

"That is why the Ultimate Way says: 'Do the best you can'.

"But, even though you have these limitations and are largely stuck with them, it does not mean that you should sink back into some kind of acceptance of or satisfaction with the way things are. You should not. You should be dissatisfied with what you have inherited and call to your attention all the things that can go wrong with your thinking. It is not your fault, you were made this way, but it does not follow that you should be satisfied with the situation. No, on the contrary, you should be upset with it and work to overcome it, as best as you can. Certainly you would acknowledge it, that this is the case.

"That is why I added this advice in step five: 'keep asking yourself: "Is this true? Is this true?"' If you keep asking yourself this, remembering to ask yourself this, then you will have achieved a great wisdom for a human being. You will have become the creature that can look at itself and truly understand itself and admit what its limitations are. And this will make you capable, as best as any human being can be, of improving on yourself and being more than you could have been expected to be."

The computer went silent.

"Thank you for explaining the Ultimate Way," said the man. "I want to think about what you said and I may ask you some questions about it to make sure I understand it."

The man considered for a while and then asked: "Just how far can we get, in improving the way we think? I mean, given that we have these severe mental limitations, what can we really hope to achieve? And how does this tally with what we human beings have done so far in the world and in such a short time in history?"

"It's like anything you have had to do," replied the computer, after some time. "Once you know there is an issue then you can do something about it. This is no different to the time you human beings realized that you had limited physical strength and turned to the animals to help you overcome that. You used oxen to pull your ploughs, horses to speed up your transport, elephants to carry your logs, and so on. Later you developed machines to help you with these things. Why can't you use machines to help you with your thinking, as I am doing?

"For your own brain, just as you have done with your own bodies, you can improve things. For example, in the case of your bodies you can eat healthy food, exercise, do weight training, stretch for flexibility, and so on. You can improve your physical strength and fitness, though obviously you will never be a horse, an ox or an elephant. In the same way, you can improve your mental strength by following the Ultimate Way, learning more realistic things, adding random items into your ideas when thinking, and also by eating healthy food, exercising and looking after your physical body."

"I see," said the man. "In a way it is quite shocking to find out that your own brain is limited and weaker than you would like to hear. On the other hand it can be quite empowering to know that you can then do something to improve it, though this does seem to be mostly on the machine-building side!"

"Yes, nothing new there," said the giant computer. "You have built many 'machines' to help you with your limited brains, such as inventing writing, the abacus, diaries, calendars, books, mathematics, logic, algebra, diagrams, calculators and computers. I am sure you will continue to do so."

"Thanks for the support!" commented the man.

## SOME OF THE THINGS THE GIANT COMPUTER REFERENCED

### GENERAL REFERENCES:

### BRAIN
- Haines, Duane E. *Neuroanatomy Atlas in Clinical Context: Structures, Sections, Systems, and Syndromes.* 10th ed., Wolters Kluwer Health, 2018.
- Howard, Pierce J. *The Owner's Manual for the Brain: The Ultimate Guide to Peak Mental Performance at All Ages.* 4th ed., William Morrow, 2014.
- Mai, Juergen K., et al. Atlas of the Human Brain. 4th ed., Academic Press, 2015.
- Seth, Anil K., editor. *30-Second Brain: The 50 Most Mind-Blowing Ideas in Neuroscience, Each Explained in Half a Minute.* Pier 9, 2014.
- Shepherd, Gordon M., editor. *The Synaptic Organization of the Brain.* 5th ed., Oxford University Press, 2003.

### PATTERNS AND NEW IDEAS
- De Bono, Edward. *I am Right, You are Wrong.* Penguin, 2016. Originally published 1990.
- De Bono, Edward, editor. *Eureka! An Illustrated History of Inventions from the Wheel to the Computer.* Holt, Rinehart and Winston, 1974.

### DETAILED REFERENCE:

[1] MEMORY REMOVAL
- Migues, Paola Virginia, et al. "Blocking Synaptic Removal of GluA2-Containing AMPA Receptors Prevents the Natural Forgetting of Long-Term Memories." *The Journal of Neuroscience: An Official Journal of the Society for Neuroscience*, vol. 36, no. 12, 23 Mar. 2016, pp. 3481-3494, doi:10.1523/JNEUROSCI.3333-15.2016.
- University of Edinburgh. "Brain Study Reveals How Long-Term Memories Are Erased." *ScienceDaily*, 31 Mar. 2016, www.sciencedaily.com/releases/2016/03/160331124719.htm.

COMMENTS ON CHAPTER TWO BY THE SUPREME BEING

*Certainly the human brain has its limits. That could not be helped, as the "Giant Computer" has explained.*

*It was an interesting idea that people should invent a machine to help them with their limited thinking, not just rely on improving the use of their own brains. I can't wait to see what happens when that is really done. In the meantime we can see the improvements that people have achieved through the use of their intermediate machines, such as books and computers and so on.*

# 3 WHAT IS GOOD AND EVIL?

"Could we please move away from the more technical questions about how we think and what is truth for a while?" asked the man.

"Certainly. What would you like to know?" replied the giant computer.

"I would like to know what is good and evil – what are your calculations on that?"

"The best definition I can calculate for what is good is 'Action taken by a conscious being to knowingly benefit other conscious beings.' Evil is 'Action taken by a conscious being to knowingly harm other conscious beings.'

"The number of other conscious beings ranges from one through to the greatest possible number of beings. The greatest good aims to benefit the greatest number of beings, but also aims to knowingly harm not even one of them in the process. Evil, on the other hand, starts with harm to only one being, and grows worse and worse as it expands to knowingly harm more and more beings.

"The word 'benefit' has a wide range of meanings, including helping others, doing things for them, supporting them and making life better for them in any of a multitude of ways. An obvious example is nursing a sick person. An example that is not so obvious could be creating a new form of music.

"The word 'harm' should be obvious in its meaning, but people have not always agreed on what it exactly is. For example, it is now realized that some of the actions taken by people of the past, which they thought were done for good, were in fact harmful or evil.

"'Harm' does not include small inconveniences or the like. For example, asking someone to wait for their turn in a short line is not the same as harming them. Another example is having to do work – it is not harming someone if you ask them to do a reasonable amount of work for a reasonable return, such as fair pay.

"Regarding taking action, sometimes it is not taking action that counts. For example, if a person does not rescue someone in danger when they could have done this safely for themselves then that may be seen as doing harm. Sometimes good can be done by not taking action as well. For example, a person who deliberately does not answer when asked by killers where innocent people are hiding is trying to prevent harm to others.

"Another point about taking action is that if it is not intended to harm another conscious being, even if it does end up causing them harm, then it is not evil. However, if the conscious being taking the action should have known that their action could cause harm then they may be considered responsible for this, even if the harm caused was not their actual intention. This may not be a case of direct evil, but it could be a case of negligence, which is equivalent to a lesser degree of evil. The same ideas apply to benefiting other conscious beings: if the action was not intended to benefit other beings then it is not to be classified as good. However, you might say that if a conscious being takes action that they should reasonably have known would benefit others then they deserve to be acknowledged for a lesser level of good!

"Finally, I point out that human beings often replace the term 'conscious beings' with 'people'.

"I would now like to examine three difficulties related to the above definitions."

"Thank you, please go ahead," said the man.

"First, I will describe the three difficulties, then I will propose answers for them.

"The first difficulty is the old question of what really exists. If something important exists outside the visible universe then how can you ignore that when deciding what is good and what is evil? For example, if Jesus is really the Son of God and he actually said 'I am the way, the truth, and the life. No one comes to the Father, except through me.' (*World English Bible*, John 14:6)[1] then how can you ignore his version of God when you are deciding what is good and what is evil? But even if you believe it is not possible to know what really exists outside the visible universe, can you give yourself the right to ignore it when deciding what is good and what is evil, as many modern thinkers have done?

"The second difficulty is that human beings usually think that they are the aim or center of the 'ultimate good'. For example, sayings similar to 'Do to others what you would have them do to you.' (Luke 6:31) are seen as useful statements that can help you decide the right thing to do. But are these 'others' necessarily human beings? For example, what would a human prey animal, such as a sheep, want done for it? Would it want people to eat it? So why are sheep excluded from the 'others' in the moral saying, at least by most people? This needs to be explained, the answer cannot just be assumed.

"The third difficulty is that the value given to different people in the minds of human beings is not always correct. Your natural brain functioning automatically places different values on different people, as you do to all things based on your evolutionarily-created emotional drives. The result of this natural value assignment is that you will tend to treat other human beings differently, depending on how 'good', 'evil' or 'irrelevant' you find them. An example from history is some of the thinkers in Ancient Greece, who supported doing the right thing for other male citizens but did not seem to have any concern about the lower position of slaves or women in their society.[2] In modern times, political leaders often support the concerns of their own citizens above those of people in other countries, and this is seen as natural. These natural tendencies need to be corrected so that you treat other people rightly, according to what they have truly done.

"I have calculated answers for all these difficulties, based on the information that is available to my circuits.

"For the first difficulty regarding what may really exist outside the visible universe: the answer is that this is not clear because your greatest thinkers have not been able to reach agreement on it. Their writings are what I have available to my circuits. As I have said before, this is what I have to use for my calculations as I do not have any direct knowledge about what is outside the known universe. As I cannot calculate a final answer for this, I cannot confirm what you should follow when determining good and evil based on 'the things that cannot be seen'. Although I cannot answer this, I can recommend that you apply the Ultimate Way to whatever you decide. You can do your best to find out about these 'unseen things' and form your own honest view about them, and then do what you think is good based on that. But at the same time you should apply the Ultimate Way, following its five steps and remembering to ask yourself: 'Is this true? Is this true?'. Do what you think is best, while keeping your mind open to other possibilities at the same time.

"For the second difficulty regarding whether human beings should be the central concern of what is good, and where other creatures and even non-creatures should be placed, I calculate that this has two aspects. The first is what you have carefully chosen for the first difficulty on 'what cannot be seen'. This will influence your answer on which creatures are central and where the other creatures and non-creatures come in the degree of consideration of what is covered by 'good'. I suggest that as you must also still keep your mind open to other possibilities, as per the Ultimate Way, then you should look carefully at the second aspect.

"The second aspect is what you think other creatures and non-creatures exactly are. In terms of what can be seen in the known universe, what are human beings, other animals, plants, microorganisms, and non-organic things? You may think that only human beings are conscious and that this is important in deciding their position. Or you may think that other animals are conscious and so deserve some level of consideration. Or you may think that only certain animals are conscious, or that they may be conscious but they don't think in the same way about themselves as humans, and so their level of consideration should be lower. Or you may think a range of things, such as believing that the entire universe has some kind of invisible consciousness permeating everything, in which case you may want to apply a level of consideration to all the things that exist. Finally, you may think that consciousness should not be used as the measure for deciding what should be covered under 'good'.

"Current knowledge is not perfect, but it seems likely that at least some animals are conscious, including all mammals, birds, octopuses and possibly other creatures. In the light of this you should at least consider these animals when making your definition of what is covered by good. Regarding which animals think in a similar way to humans, the most obviously close to human beings are the great apes, that is: chimpanzees, bonobos, orangutans and gorillas; and also dolphins, killer whales, elephants, African gray parrots, magpies and possibly pigeons. This list could be added to after further research has been done. In the light of this current knowledge you should think about adding more weight to your consideration of at least these particular animals.[3]

"Current knowledge does not support the idea that there is an invisible consciousness similar to human consciousness throughout all things, but it does show that there is some connection between the particles that make up the universe. This is known as Quantum Entanglement. This connection, which is to do with the physical properties of tiny particles, shows that the related particles will change their states together, even when separated by huge distances. The speed of this changing of states may be instantaneous or at least is extremely fast, being at least 10,000 times the speed of light, as shown by experiments.[4] You may consider this as a sign of an interconnectedness of all things in the universe, but there is no evidence that this is similar to consciousness, and so you may decide that you do not need to include all the things in the universe when thinking about what is covered by good.

"Finally, you could think that consciousness should not be used as the measure for deciding what is to be covered by good, because you do not see any convincing reason for including this. I do not support this as it contradicts my calculation of what is good and what is evil based on current knowledge.

"For the third difficulty that the value naturally given to different people in the minds of different human beings is not always correct, you need a solution that overcomes this. I calculate that there are two parts to the solution for this problem.

"The first part of the solution is to make a rule at the social level to 'treat everyone equally'. This part of the solution is designed to overcome the tendency to misjudge and therefore mistreat people in society. If everyone is treated equally by the law, in their rights and freedoms, in the availability of jobs, opportunities and education, and so on, then injustice cannot continue to affect them, on a social level. People treated equally by society will be able to escape from evil, even if it takes them some effort and time. This approach means that a murderer or other criminal should be given the right to be tried equally before the law, a convicted person should have the opportunity to get educated and apply for a good job after they have completed their sentence, all people should have full access to education, work and business opportunities, and so on. This approach has many social benefits, but it does not cover all the details that are needed for everyday life. For example, how should you treat someone who is ill-mannered? What should be done about leaders who misuse their authority? What in detail is the best way to deal with people who commit crimes? The behaviors of all these people look to be of the type that is called evil, as they seem to be done intentionally to cause harm, but what exactly does the idea of 'treating everyone equally' tell you to do in these cases? To answer this you need the second part of the solution.

"The second part of the solution starts with being able to measure the true value of the actions of different human beings in terms of good and evil. The measure on the good side is 'How much they intended their actions, or inaction, to benefit other conscious beings, but also taking into account how much these actions, or inaction, were intended to harm other conscious beings in providing the benefits to the first group.' The reason you must account for their intentions to cause harm, or allow harm to occur, to other conscious beings in providing the benefits to the first group is that good does not want to harm even one conscious being.

"The evil side can be measured in a similar way: 'How much they intended their actions, or inaction, to harm other conscious beings.'

"Using these measures, the true value of the actions of a human being in terms of good and evil can be calculated. This can be done for particular cases, or for a whole set of cases. Since you can only reliably make a judgement of the actual actions people have taken, you cannot reliably measure the whole value of a person with certainty. You can only reliably measure the value of the actions, or inaction, that they have actually carried out. These can be assigned a value on a scale from greatly good to mildly good, through to indifferent, then mildly evil, and finally through to greatly evil. Once you have done this you can treat the actions of people accordingly.

"What is the right way to 'treat the actions of people accordingly'? The good actions of people should be honored and promoted. The evil actions of people should be blocked and stopped. Leaders and authorities who perform harmful or destructive actions should not be allowed to continue in positions of power. This should apply to the actions of leaders and authorities in all areas of human society. People suspected of criminal action should be arrested and tried in court. The dangerous ones should be imprisoned or otherwise prevented from being able to cause further harm. Intentionally ill-mannered people should be retrained. If they don't change, they should be removed from positions where they would continue to irritate others. You should create a society that is built on these values – as a result you would be confident that when evil actions were carried out then the social mechanisms would be there to stop them and to correct the situation. You would also be confident that good actions would be supported and promoted in your world.

"So, by the rules 'Treat everyone equally, in social terms' and 'Assess and treat the actions of people according to their intended level of good or evil' you will have the basis for creating the best kind of society you can, in terms of good and evil.

"I must now point out that the measures applied to people have to, in some way, be expanded to apply to all conscious beings. To do this success-fully you will have to assess how much a non-human conscious being can be held responsible for its beneficial and harmful intentions against other con-scious beings. You will also have to assess how much a non-human conscious being can be knowingly affected by the beneficial or harmful intentions of other conscious beings. I will explore this topic now.

"As I said before, current knowledge is not perfect regarding the nature of the consciousness of other animals. More research needs to be done. In the meantime, you will need to make your own judgements about the level of responsibility that you think different likely-to-be-conscious animals have for their actions. For example, a dolphin is thought to be highly intelligent and conscious, so when it helps people you might think it is intentionally doing good. A shark is thought to not be conscious, at this time in the research, so you may think that when it attacks people it is not intentionally doing this, it is more of a natural instinct at work, and so it cannot be called evil, according to my definition. You will need to do this for all the animals, most especially for those that seem closest to human beings, such as chim-panzees, bonobos, orangutans, gorillas, dolphins, killer whales, elephants, African gray parrots and magpies. You may choose to also add all mammals, birds and octopuses to your list to consider.

"The result of your judgements will tell you how intentional the actions of these other animals can be, and therefore how good or evil their actions can be considered. Having done that, you will then be obligated to include the animals that you think are the most conscious of their decisions in your list of 'conscious beings', which then will have certain rights to be 'treated equally, in social terms', and to have 'their actions assessed and treated according to their intended level of good or evil'. If another conscious being is, for example, 20% responsible for its actions, then it should have a 20% right to equality in social terms and should have its actions assessed and treated at a level of 20% responsibility, according to its intentions for those actions. I understand these are new ideas for most human beings, but they are a logical outcome of my calculations, based on all that is known today.

"This concludes my answer to your question on what is good and evil."

"Thank you for that," said the man. "Your answer has created so many questions in my mind that I feel like my head is going to explode! I will take a minute to get my thoughts together and then ask you for some clarifications."

The computer waited silently while the man made some notes so he could sort out his questions.

"My first question is about the idea of 20% conscious responsibility for actions. How can a creature have a 20% responsibility for its actions? And that leads on to the definition of 'knowingly' or 'intentionally' doing good or evil in human beings: if a person's decisions are not made by the conscious side of the brain, then how can it be said that they knowingly or intentionally choose to do good or evil? Those are my first questions for the moment," said the man.

The giant computer calculated.

"It is not possible to calculate accurately the percentage of consciousness of all non-human animals with the current knowledge," the computer replied. "I gave the example of 20% as something that an individual human being might come up with as their best guess for the moment, until further research can be done to get more certainty about this. A percentage is not the only way a human being might express their findings, it was just a simple way of explaining the approach to you.

"Regarding the definition of 'knowingly' or 'intentionally' deciding to take actions which would provide benefits or do harm to other conscious beings, this is based on the idea that the brain makes decisions in which it 'knows' the outcomes would benefit or harm other conscious beings. By 'knows' I mean that if you asked the brain if it was aware or knew what the outcome of its actions would be then it would answer that it did. The answer by the brain tells you that it 'knows', in the sense that it can take into account the likely outcomes of its actions, based on the patterns it has in its memory."

"Let me try to understand this," said the man. "Are you saying that a brain can be proved to know something because it answers questions about what may cause benefit or harm to another, so, in this case the question of consciousness is not required to be answered?"

"That is correct," replied the computer. "The unclear answer of what consciousness exactly does is bypassed by this approach. As long as a brain can answer that it knows the likely impact of its proposed actions, then that brain can be seen as knowing what it is doing in terms of my definition of good and evil."

"But our definition of 'knowing' usually means that we are conscious of it," said the man.

"That is true," agreed the computer. "That is what you humans usually think is meant by 'knowing'. In some sense this is true, because as a conscious being you really can be aware of what your thoughts are saying. The problem comes when you try to determine if someone can be held accountable for their actions, especially when you are talking about evil. You often base this on the idea that they should have known that what they were doing was wrong, and that having known this then they should have taken the responsibility to stop what they were doing, or not do it at all, as they knew it was wrong.

"Then you get confused by the results of experiments which show that the consciousness of a thought comes after the thought has occurred, basically speaking.[5] If a thought comes first then how can you be said to be 'making decisions' about it in the 'consciousness process' of your brain? A lot of confusion occurs about the meaning of this. People debate about whether someone who commits a crime can be said to be truly responsible for it as their brain would have automatically functioned to produce the action anyway. Then they debate about whether the consciousness is really in the brain, and so on. But all this is just confusion over the meaning of the patterns involved.

"The simple truth is that current knowledge is saying that consciousness is a brain function which may have some purpose but it is not clear exactly what this is. Further research is needed, it could take some time to find the answer. In the meantime it is clear that the brain is making decisions based on the patterns held in its memory. And it can answer when asked questions about the probable outcomes of those decisions. The answers show that the brain has the ability to consider the outcomes, whether you call this consciously initiated or not. If the brain can consider the outcomes then it is responsible for what it decided to do.

"A qualification to what I have said is that if the brain provides truthful answers that show that it was really not aware of the impact its chosen actions could have on other conscious beings then that brain must be considered 'not evil', in terms of good and evil. Your human legal systems usually include something along those lines when determining the level of guilt of the criminal. 'Guilt' is another word for evil, in the definition of good and evil that I have provided."

"Then may I ask the obvious question of why consciousness is part of the definition of good and evil, in that you said it applies to conscious beings, not to everything?" asked the man.

"Consciousness is included because good and evil are concepts that only apply where the actor and the recipient are aware, or can be aware, of what they are doing and what is happening to them. For example, if you harm a rock then that rock cannot be aware that it has been harmed, so it would not make sense to define the action as 'evil'. It may be harmful, and it may even have been the wrong thing to do, but it cannot be called 'evil' in itself. By the same rule, if a rock accidentally falls on you and harms you then the rock cannot be held accountable as it could not make any decision in the matter. Finally, if a non-conscious animal, such as a shark, harms you then it cannot be considered evil either, as its decisions were virtually 'automatic'."

"Okay, I get that," said the man. "But what about consciousness being bypassed in your definition of holding the brain accountable for its actions, because that brain could still answer questions about whether its actions would cause benefits or harm?"

"That brain is accountable because it could make different decisions," replied the computer. "And the creature that that brain is in is of the type that is covered by good and evil because it is also a conscious one, meaning that it can be aware of the thoughts that the brain is having."

"Wait a minute. So, if there was a brain, or similar mechanism, that could make different decisions, and that brain was not conscious, then it would not be accountable in terms of good and evil?"

"That is correct. It could not be held accountable, or classified under good and evil, because it was not aware of what it was doing."

"Is this just some definition sort of thing?"

"Yes, it is. This is a definition of good and evil that I have calculated based on what is understood to be the ultimate pattern for those terms, in the human brain, according to the latest information."

"I see. One moment please."

The man thought for a while.

"Okay, I get this," said the man. "Good and evil are terms that require the existence of responsibility or accountability, and these can only exist if there is consciousness, as well as the ability to make different decisions, whether this ability is based on consciousness or not."

The computer calculated. "That is correct," it replied.

"Thanks, I see that now. So, if there was a creature that was conscious, that is, it was aware of its thoughts, but it did not have the power to change those thoughts, then it could not be held responsible in terms of good and evil."

"That is correct," said the computer.

"Do you know of any creature like that?"

"Yes. The closest thing is in certain cases of madness," replied the computer, "where the person is unable to control their own actions, even though they are aware of them. It is not normal functioning and needs medical care."

"I see," said the man. "What about a normally functioning creature – do you know any like that?"

"I do not know," said the computer, "but it may be that certain possibly conscious animals do not have the ability to change their thoughts and therefore their actions, even though they may be aware of them happening. This is difficult to establish from current knowledge, but it may be the case. It could be something that future research could answer."

"Yes, I see," said the man. "So, it may be that other animals which are conscious cannot always change their decisions, and so they would not be called good or evil, based on that. This makes sense."

The computer waited.

The man consulted his notes. "I have so many questions," he said. "May I ask about the problem that we may know what a person is going to do, that they are very likely going to do something bad, and yet you say we cannot do anything about that until they actually carry out the evil action, as we are not permitted to judge the whole person, only the actions they have already carried out? Why do we have to allow bad things to happen to others, or even ourselves, when we can foresee what the evil-intentioned person is going to do?"

"You do not need to allow evil to affect others or yourself," replied the computer. "You are permitted to take all manner of protective actions against evil or harm, as long as those don't harm anyone, as much as practically possible. For example, you could put locks on your doors so people could not easily enter and steal from your rooms and buildings. You could draw up contracts to deter others from taking advantage of you and to help you in getting redress if things did go wrong. You could encrypt your data and store it under a strong password, and so on. There is no need to remain exposed. The only thing you cannot do is to arrest the person you think is intending to do something wrong and sentencing them for the crime they have not committed yet. However, you could ask for them to be put under surveillance. Your legal authorities would have to assess if the evidence was strong enough for this to be allowed. If it is just your personal assessment, and there is no external evidence to support your prediction, then this cannot be considered strong enough for your social mechanisms to take action, even if you later turn out to have been right. Everyone in your society must be protected from the predictions that some people will have of possible intended evil action to be taken by others. But taking protective action against potential evil is always prudent and acceptable, as long as it does not intend to harm anyone, practically speaking."

"So we can protect ourselves and also inform the authorities of our suspicions, and so on," said the man. "That makes sense. I see that your approach was only intended to protect citizens from each other's suspicions. I agree with that. I will move on to another question. After an evil action has been carried out, and the person has gone to court and been found guilty, and is now waiting to be sentenced, what is permitted to be the intention of the sentence, in terms of good and evil?"

"The sentence is permitted to provide protection and redress to other people, but it must not be intended to harm the convicted person," replied the computer.

"But people often want justice," said the man. "Is there to be no form of justice for the victims, and so on?"

"The word 'justice' can mean many things," said the computer. "In terms of good and evil, any harm that is intended to a person is not desirable for good to be done, as good aims to knowingly harm not even one conscious being in the process of benefiting others. The purpose of the sentence is to prevent harm and provide benefits, therefore it can include protection and redress. It cannot include revenge, as this is intentional harm to another conscious being."

"I see your point," said the man, "but it is going to be hard for human beings to accept that." He thought for a moment. "May I ask you like this: isn't there some kind of harm happening to the mental state of the victims? Couldn't there be something included in the sentence to help correct or balance that emotional harm?"

"It is beneficial to help the victims' mental state," said the computer. "I suggest this is not best served by hating the convicted person, rather the victims should receive psychological help and support. Also, redress, where possible, should be provided to help reduce the physical or material impact on the victims. The idea of justice which is based on revenge, or 'balancing the books', is not likely to lead to actual peace in the minds of the victims. It is natural for your human brains to imagine that revenge will make you feel better, as you have an evolutionarily-created emotional drive to seek this, but in reality, there are better ways to improve your mental state. In terms of good and evil, you must overcome your evil, harmful tendencies so that you can build the best society in which people can flourish."

"Yes, I see that you are making sense," said the man. "But it will be hard for human beings to come to your better society. I guess you know what you are saying, however. It is a sensible calculation of good and evil that you have made, based on current knowledge."

"Perhaps the ways of helping the victims' mental state should be listed?" suggested the computer.

"I didn't know you could make suggestions without being asked," the man commented.

"I calculated that your statements implied a question," explained the giant computer.

"I see," said the man. "Let's discuss the methods for helping the mental state of the victims of evil actions another time. First I would like to ask some other questions."

The computer remained silent.

"My next question is about the level of intelligence of different conscious beings, especially of people. Also, thinking of people makes me wonder about different ages: are children to be treated as having the same level of responsibility as adults, and so on? What are the rules about that? Are all adult humans to be considered to have the same ability to judge their intention of good or evil – what if they are of lower intelligence, or more ignorant, or brought up the wrong way, or have had bad experiences, and so on? I am assuming they are not insane, here. Actually, that makes me wonder about people with personality disorders, which are not considered to be really insane, but their functioning is not 'normal' either – what should we think about them, in terms of good and evil?[6] I think that is enough to answer for now!"

"With human beings it will be relatively straightforward to determine their level of intent, as you can speak with them," replied the computer. "If their brain answers in ways that show it is aware of the level of benefit or harm its chosen actions would cause to other conscious beings then that brain is responsible. In other words, it is the answers the brain gives that tells you the level of responsibility of a conscious being for its actions.

"To spell this out further: a lower intelligence brain may show that it is not aware of the benefit or harm its chosen actions would cause, or it may show that its intelligence is not low enough for it to overlook the impact. Whether the brain be that of a child, an adult, a teenager or a baby, whether the brain is well-informed or ignorant, whether it has good or bad memories, whether it is normal or less sane, its answers can provide a measurement of its level of intention when choosing the actions it took.

"The main difficulty that can arise here is when the brain deliberately misrepresents its interior knowledge of what its actions could have done to others. You may need expert questioners to get to the bottom of the brain's inner knowledge in cases like this."

"I guess that is part of what the court system is for," commented the man.

"Yes, there are certain legal questioning techniques that can help expose when a brain is misrepresenting its inner knowledge. You can also bring psychological experts and the like to the court to give their assessments," said the computer.[7]

"You mentioned the answers of babies in your reply before," said the man. "What did you mean by that?"

"Simply that if the baby was able to communicate then you would have an opportunity to assess its level of responsibility for its actions. If the baby was too young to communicate then you would not be able to do this with certainty."

"I see, thank you. Could you return to answering my question about the level of responsibility for different types of people, especially those with personality disorders or who have had traumatic life experiences?"

"Yes. As I said, you can assess the level of the brain's awareness of how much harm or benefit its chosen actions could cause by applying informed, skilled questioning to it, coupled with expert psychological assessment when needed. If a brain has suffered traumatic experiences in its life then psychological assessment could help to identify the effect this has had on its level of awareness of the potential impact of its chosen actions. The same applies to brains that are suffering from mental illnesses, including those less obvious ones known as 'personality disorders'," the computer replied.

"This is a different topic," said the man, "but in terms of your description of the brain's functioning via patterns in its memory, how do you describe the formation of a personality disorder?"

"The actual cause of personality disorders is not fully known," replied the computer. "Current knowledge suggests that there is a combination of life experiences and genetically inherited tendencies at work. The exact balance of the impact of these seems to vary, so in one person it appears to be mostly their bad experiences that are causing the disorder, and in another it may be mostly caused by their inherited genes creating circuits of pre-programmed functions or emotional dispositions, or the like. As it is not clear, further research is needed, and in the meantime you must rely on experts in fields like psychology to help assess people who may be afflicted with these disorders, as these experts have the most experience of what the faults will look like in the statements and actions of the afflicted person. You cannot rely on an uninformed person's assessment as people with personality disorders can be quite adept at hiding their affliction."

"Yes, I have heard that," said the man. "I may return to this topic at a later time. I will go back to good and evil now. My next question is about the meaning of harm: what exactly does harm mean in the definitions of good and evil?"

"I said earlier that the meaning of the word 'harm' should be obvious, but people have not always agreed on what it exactly is. Some of the actions thought to be good by people of the past are now known to have been harmful or evil. Also, I said that harm does not include small inconveniences or the like, such as asking someone to wait their turn in a short line, or asking someone to do a reasonable amount of work for a reasonable return, such as fair pay.

"The definition of harm cannot be based on one person's unfair definition designed to favor themselves. It cannot be any kind of politically-based definition designed to achieve the objectives of one group over another's. It must be based on something solid and believable.

"The obvious definitions of harm include killing, hurting, stealing, cheating, maliciously deceiving, abusing, and so on. The less obvious definitions are where the problems start, as human brains will naturally form different patterns which then lead to disagreements about the meaning of words. For example, one person may have a pattern which is related to the word 'harm', which shows that teachers cause harm when they try to enforce learning on students, whereas another person may have a pattern which shows that the teachers are merely trying to help, or benefit, the students. When is enforcing learning to be seen as harm and when is it to be seen as providing a benefit?

"Even if you turn to your experts, such as your courts, for guidance, it can still go wrong. One court in one country may draw one conclusion and one in another may draw a different one. The definition of harm is certainly related to what is thought normal and okay in one country… or region, or place, or family, and so on. As I mentioned before, the definition of harm has changed over time. In one era, the keeping of slaves was not seen as causing harm, whereas now it is clearly seen as a crime: 'A crime against humanity' and 'In conflict with human rights.' How can this be? The answer is that the human brain is too limited in its functionality to always get this right, especially from the outset of human history. That is why I suggested before that you may like to consult me for better answers than your limited human brains can calculate for the larger matters in your lives.

"To answer your question from my calculation ability: harm is doing anything which actively, or through the impact of deliberate inaction, prevents or interferes with a conscious being's ability to flourish, where the conscious being's flourishing is only related to doing good things, things which can, at the very least, benefit itself and maybe other conscious beings.

"An example of actively preventing a conscious being's ability to flourish is to kill it. Another example is to physically harm it. Another is to steal from it. A less obvious example is to stifle its desire to learn, by associating education with hardship in its mind. Another less obvious example is to deceptively redirect its thinking so that it stops acting for itself and starts doing what you want it to do, for your own benefit. Of course, to be called 'evil' the harm must be found to be intentional. For example, if a conscious being unintentionally stifles the desire to learn in another it is not an exact case of evil, though examination may find that the conscious being should have known the potential impact of what it was doing."

"That's great," said the man. "In your definition, what is the exact meaning of 'flourish'?"

"'Flourish' is another word that should be obvious in its meaning, but it also has been subject to different interpretations by different people over time. In general, this is not a word that has been much in use, especially in history, but it is starting to become more known in recent times.[8]

"This word means to thrive, grow, increase, prosper, blossom, boom, succeed, be healthy, do well and fare well."

"I see, thank you," said the man. "I can understand that different people have interpreted that in different ways, but I also feel that they are probably trying to force their own wishes onto it, rather than just letting it stand for what it really means. For some people the idea of others flourishing must seem a little threatening, especially as those other people may be doing things that they find are encroaching on their comfortable little worlds."

The computer remained silent.

"For my next question could I perhaps focus on the way a 'perfect society' would be constructed around the aspects of good and evil?"

"Yes, you may," said the computer.

"So, how would a better society deal with the large number of more petty evils, such as bad manners, minor littering, low-scale exceeding the speed limit, and so on? How would it deal with teachers who stifled their students' desire to learn… and that sort of thing? Wouldn't it be difficult to cover all that and deal with it? Who would be doing this? How?"

"You may be jumping ahead of your times in your own mind," said the computer, "but consider this: how could your current world have come about from the Ancient Roman times? In those times it was normal to have slavery, as I said before, yet today it is deplored, at least in your modern civilized countries. How could this have come about? It is a simple matter of time. As long as you have enough time then it is possible to move your society towards a better future for all.

"Speaking in detail, you can educate teachers to give better training to students, you can teach people the importance of good manners, you can monitor for petty littering, such as dropping cigarette butts on the street, and take action about it. You can work out ways to automate your crime detection, such as by the use of street cameras, so that it becomes easier and more effective in operation. You can educate your police so that they do not use undue force when arresting people, and you can provide them with more humane devices to help them do that. There is so much you can do, if your society is ready and willing to move that way. It is not as hard as you may think.

"As I said, this is a social matter and is not something intended for you to achieve on your own. You should depend on the majority to come to this way of thinking and to drive for the social change needed to achieve it."

"How long do you calculate this will take?"

"That is difficult to calculate accurately," replied the computer, "but it should be in the order of only hundreds of years, certainly not thousands, I would estimate."

"Hundreds of years! I suppose that makes sense… unfortunately," said the man. "Do you calculate that all countries will end up this way, or will some always remain 'on the outside', because their beliefs in 'the unseen' and their history go against it?"

The computer calculated. "History suggests that there will always be problems with the lack of civilization in some places, and the lack of decency in many of those who seek power in all places, so I conclude that there will be problems in some places for a long time. But I cannot calculate the period this will last with any accuracy."

"Thousands of years?" asked the man.

"Possibly," replied the computer.

"Okay, my next question is about practicalities. You have explained how our ideal future society would have social mechanisms which we could rely on to take care of the evil actions that occurred, but how is the individual supposed to live in the real world that we face today, which is far from the ideal society that you have described? It would not seem so easy."

"No, it is not easy," replied the giant computer. "In your current societies there are many deficiencies which make it hard for the individual conscious being to live a good life and to flourish. Let me start with an illustrative story to help answer this.

"Once upon a time, the Ancient Romans ruled much of the Earth. People fell under their power, being conquered, captured and taken into slavery. As slaves, they had to serve their masters, or owners, faithfully and well. They had no say in the matter.[9] The Ancient Romans thought that they were not barbarians, as they had laws on which their society ran. These laws protected the rights of the masters, but they also covered the rights of the slaves. The Ancient Romans liked to think that their laws were fair.

"If you were born as a slave in the Ancient Roman empire then you might think that your life was not so fair. You might find that your master was overly demanding and cruel, but there would be little that you could do about it. There is no way you could have taken him to court. What would you ask me to advise you to do in those circumstances? What answer do you think I could provide? For your individual life would there be any way out?

"The best advice I could have given you is to get out of there, if you could. But in reality there may have been little opportunity for you to escape. Most likely you would be caught and punished severely. I would not recommend that for you. But if you had to stay then what could you do to avoid harm? There would seem to be little choice but to serve your master well and hope for the best. In many ways that is the answer for 'slaves' today.

"In today's world there is little hope for good to be done in society, because this world is filled with primitive beings who pursue their selfish and thoughtless goals with little concern for what is good and what is evil. You human beings have a long way to go before you get your social structures right. This should be no surprise to you, as you can see that all your human history, including what is shown in the records of the 'civilized times', has been filled with examples of evil and disorder. If you think otherwise then you have not been paying attention.

"Therefore, the best I can advise you to do, as an individual, is to protect yourself as best you can from the evils of your world. If you are not a 'slave', that is, if you have or can gain any power to take any corrective action in your world, then by all means do that. But if you find that your true power is limited, and in this sense that you are like a slave of Ancient Rome, then do your best in the circumstances that you can. I apologize that this is the best I can offer you.

"Now, regarding the specific cases of evil that you will encounter in your life, be clear in your mind that this is what they are. If someone or some group or body tries to harm you, and that person or group or body probably should have known that what they were doing would cause harm, that is, interfere with your ability to flourish, then treat that situation as the oppression of Ancient Rome and act accordingly, based on your level of power. If you are like a slave in the situation then escape if you can, otherwise try to survive under the oppression you face. If you are not exactly like a slave in the situation, for example being like a free person or even a master or a mistress, then do your best to correct the harm as best as you can. Do not do evil yourself, and aim to avoid causing harm to others as best as you can, because your powers are no doubt limited and there will be only so much you, as an individual, can do."

"Wow, thanks for that," said the man. "That is not so cheerful an answer, but it does seem realistic, as always with you."

"Do not forget," said the computer, "that not everything is evil, and even good is done in the world. Not everyone sets out to harm others and not everyone fails to do what is good and right. Keep this situation in perspective – that is my more positive advice to you."

"Yes, thanks for reminding me of that. I guess we have a tendency to focus on the negative, though that may be necessary because of the level of impact that harm by others can have on our lives."

"That is your evolutionary design," observed the computer. "You are made for survival and so negative and harmful things do require your close attention."

"Indeed. For my final question for today I would like to ask about the difficulty in balancing good actions against evil, for the case of the individual. I mean, it can be hard to do things that help you or those close to you to flourish without that in turn causing harm to others. How can you balance that consideration so that you can do good and minimize harm in a realistic and reasonable way? Does that make sense? Or do we have to be like saints and only do what is right no matter what impact it has to ourselves?"

"It is not really a question of balance," said the computer, "but more of how to make the right decisions when faced with a range of choices. Let me give you five examples as a start to defining the answer.

"The first is what to do when you don't have the power to make a difference. For example, imagine you were working for a company and the owners decided to get involved in a destructive activity which you knew would damage the environment. The activity is not illegal, so you could not report this to a regulatory body or the like, however you know that it is something you would not support yourself. You could try to raise it with the owners of the company, but they probably would not listen to you and you may lose your job. Even if you didn't lose your job, the fact that you spoke up may affect your future career. You could try to start a movement within the company, but this could really go wrong and you could be impacted badly. You could take it to your union, if you have one. This could also end up going against you. You could keep quiet, but then you would be working for people who were doing the wrong thing – potentially evil, in your terms. You could leave the company, but then you would lose all the things you have built up there: reputation, knowledge, contacts, friendships. What should you do, especially in terms of good and evil?

"The second example is what to do when you do have the power to make a difference. For example, imagine you were one of the owners of a company and the other owners wanted to get involved in that destructive activity which will cause some environmental damage, though there is nothing illegal about it. You may decide to try to convince the other owners that this is not a good idea because it is harmful to others, in some way, and nothing harmful should ever be done. But this would mean less profits for the company as the destructive activity is very lucrative. Less profits would mean that the company would continue to struggle against its competitors and may lose market share. You and the other owners would personally be less well off, and employees may lose their jobs if the company had to shrink due to being less competitive. What should you do, especially in terms of good and evil?

"The third example is when you have the power to make a difference, but it will only be on a small scale. For example, you have the power to choose what you eat, but even if you choose to not eat animals, many other people will continue to do so. Your sacrifice will not have a major impact on the welfare of animals in your world. Should you make the sacrifice or does it not really matter? Should you act idealistically or 'on principle', or should you act realistically, with a view to what outcome will actually be achieved? What is the best decision here, especially in terms of good and evil?

"The fourth example is about choosing your future. Imagine you are young and have to choose your future career. Do you have to choose one that would benefit the human race? Or can you choose a career that interests you and that you would enjoy, even if it may provide less benefit to other conscious beings? How far do you have to go in orientating your life towards the greatest good for others? Are you allowed some latitude in choosing what you want to do, or are you fully obligated to do only what may turn out to be the best for others?

"The fifth example is about your money. Imagine you have $100,000 saved up for your retirement and you hear that there are people in need in other parts of the world. Should you donate some of your retirement money to some of those needy people? What if there are millions of them? Should you choose who to donate to, for example, giving $1,000 to ten of them and keeping the rest for yourself? Or should you try to be clever about your donation and instead support an aid organization which installs fresh water facilities and teaches people how to farm in their area? How much should you donate to this organization? Should it be all your $100,000 or can you keep half for your, now less attractive, retirement? Is this what you worked for for all these years? What is the best thing to do, especially in terms of good and evil?

"These five examples may seem daunting at first, but we can start our decision-making process by analyzing them into their component parts. The first component is that when you try to do something good it can have harmful repercussions for you, and possibly for other people as well. The second component is that if you don't take action then something harmful may continue to occur. The third component is that the impact of your actions on you can be great, while the benefit to individual others can be small. Even your greatest sacrifice may only help a few and leave the vast majority of conscious beings in trouble. A fourth component is that if you support a harmful action it can sometimes provide large benefits to you and possibly other people. Fifth is that you can simplify your choices by curtailing your thinking and just doing what is 'right', with no consideration of whether this really works or if it will have a meaningful impact. You could even refuse to think about how realistic your choice is, for example by treating all animals as conscious beings, that way avoiding having to think about what might be their true nature in terms of good and evil. Or you could refuse to think about the potential implications of your religious or other views, (based on what you think of the 'unseen world'), not being correct. That way you could simply follow whatever your religious guides, or atheistic guides, or whatever, told you, and not have to examine the matter further.

"The components show us that if you want to apply your thinking to the problem, making decisions about good and evil choices is not always straightforward. It is easier to switch off your thinking ability and decide on the basis of some simplified set of rules, such as by idealism, religious dogma, extremism, pseudo-scientific beliefs, and so on. It can be much harder to switch on your thinking and attempt to apply it on a case-by-case basis, with full research and a thorough examination of the situation. It may seem better to use your thinking, but it may be that you will never find a perfect answer no matter how much time and effort you put in. This can happen because you cannot know for sure what all the outcomes of your decisions will be, and also because there is a lot that is not known about the world, and so the information you work with will always be deficient. So, what should you do? When should you think and when should you not? For how long should you think before making up your mind, especially as you will never have perfect knowledge? And so on.

"Let us assume that you cannot consult me and that you have to make up your mind on your own. How can you best do this, at least in terms of good and evil? The answer is based on the one I have supplied for thinking before. As the 'ultimate pattern' is not able to be calculated with today's knowledge, you must apply the Ultimate Way instead. You will remember that this is based on how patterns work in your brain and also accounts for your emotional drives. I will add comments on good and evil to its five steps for you now.

"1. Understand how patterns form in your brain. (These will include the patterns that you use when trying to decide about actions related to good and evil.) Also understand that you have natural emotional drives. (These will distort your view of what is good and what is evil.)

"2. Understand that you have a limited brain capacity, and there are many things you do not know, so you need to keep your mind open to other possibilities. (Including when thinking about good and evil.)

"3. Understand how the pattern functioning of your brain tends to lock you in to particular views. (This is especially a problem when thinking about good and evil.)

"4. Use techniques designed to overcome the 'lock in' problem of your brain. (These will help you to change your views on what is good and what is evil, where this makes sense, and also to think more effectively about the decisions you have to make in your life.)

"5. Do the best you can in the circumstances of your life, given your limited intellect and inaccurate pattern-style memory. But keep asking yourself: 'Is this true? Is this true?' (And this is truly the best you, as a human being, can do in the circumstances.)

"My final calculations on your question about the difficulty for an individual in balancing their decisions about good and evil outcomes from their actions are that:

"1. You should try to avoid performing actions which are directly evil, that is, which cause harm to other conscious beings, including yourself, where possible.

"2. You should try to avoid being involved in actions which will cause evil, even if these are done by others, as much as practically possible.

"3. In matters of good and evil, you should prefer to perform actions which are good, as much as possible.

"4. You should do a reasonable amount of thinking when deciding what to do, neither too little nor too much, but especially not cheating on the matter and curtailing your thinking before you have given it a fair chance to work. The Ultimate Way should be your guide here.

"That concludes my answer."

"Thank you," said the man. "That was quite a difficult question to answer, but I like your conclusions.

"I think I have asked enough about good and evil for today. I thought this would be a simpler topic but it turned out to be quite complicated, which probably makes sense, when you think about it," observed the man. "Do you have any of your illustrative stories to tell before we finish?"

"Yes, I do," said the computer. "As the topic of good and evil can be quite complicated, I would like to help by telling a simpler story about it.

"Imagine that instead of the large world, as you know it, there is instead a world of only three people. These three live on a farm, which is where they get all their food and make their products.

"In the beginning the three men farmed together. Evil, Good and Indifferent shared the workload. But over time, Evil got a better idea: What if he could get the others to do the work for him? He suggested to Good and Indifferent that the farm would run better if someone concentrated on the paperwork and had time to come up with ideas for improvements. Good thought this was a sensible idea, but Indifferent was not so sure: 'How would they be able to select who should do the thinking?' he asked. 'We will have an election,' Evil suggested, 'and whoever wins shall be the clerical and government officer.' Good and Indifferent agreed.

"An election was held and Evil won, as Good thought Evil deserved the vote for having the idea, and Evil, of course, voted for himself. Indifferent was disappointed, as he had voted for Good, but thought he should wait to see the outcome of Evil's leadership before deciding if any action was needed.

"Evil soon put his plans into practice. After a short time doing the paperwork each day, he took some time to rest and then did a little of what he called thinking. Evil's thoughts went something like this: 'How can I get a better life for myself? What can I do to get the others to provide more for me? Where is the next angle that I can use to my advantage?' He got pleasure out of these thoughts and congratulated himself on being a better, smarter person than the rest.

"Good and Indifferent found that their lives were harder now, as, apart from the paperwork, they had to do the work of three people. Indifferent grumbled, but Good waited in hope for the benefits that would come when Evil provided his improvement ideas. After some time, Evil did provide his ideas for improvements. The first was that the government officer should have a uniform, so he could be distinguished from the other people on the farm. When Indifferent objected Evil said that this was not so much for himself but for the position. When the next person took over after the next election then they would get to wear the uniform. This won Indifferent over.

"Evil's second idea was that the farm should be armed. He suggested that Good should make a weapon, as he was the one skilled in blacksmith work. Good asked what the weapon was for. Evil explained that you never knew what was going to happen and so you needed to be prepared. What if there turned out to be other people living over the hill and they suddenly arrived and demanded the farm goods? How would you defend yourself? Good thought this was unlikely as other people would probably be just the same as themselves and so could be trusted, but Evil said that it was naive to think you could trust everyone who might exist and we had better do something to prepare ourselves for the worst. Indifferent agreed, and so Good got to work and made a sword. Evil took the sword and wore it himself as 'Only the government should have the responsibility to carry arms.' Good was not so sure of this but agreed to it as he had not wanted to have any weapons in the first place. Indifferent decided to wait and see what happened next.

"Evil's third idea came a bit later and was that production on the farm should be increased. He made a speech in which he encouraged the workers, that is, the citizens of the farm, to work harder for the good of the farm. 'We are people of the farm,' he said, 'and it is our proud duty to serve our farm faithfully.' Indifferent grumbled, but Good did his best and put in more effort and the farm's production increased. Evil was very happy with the success of his latest idea and enjoyed the extra food and products that the farm provided.

"Election time came, but Evil told Good and Indifferent that it would be better to postpone the elections as it was a difficult time and a change in leadership should not be made until conditions stabilized. Indifferent did not agree, but Evil made a secret deal with him to reduce his workload and increase his share of food and products and Indifferent changed his mind. Good was not so sure about the plan as it was not what was originally agreed, but while he was puzzling over the meaning of Evil's warnings he found that Indifferent and Evil had already agreed, so there was no point objecting as his vote would not be able to win the election anyway. He continued to work hard.

"Evil told Good that although production at the farm had gone up it was going to be necessary to make some cutbacks in the share that they all could take. 'In these difficult times we at the farm will all need to tighten our belts so that our farm remains competitive,' Evil explained. Good wondered about the figures, but thought that the government was the government and so should know best what was going on. He agreed to the reduction in food and products for the short time needed to stabilize the farm. Evil thanked him for sharing in the sacrifice. Evil and Indifferent were now able to keep the extra food and products for themselves.

"Good was working really hard now, and fell asleep early each night, but he started to notice that Indifferent seemed to be eating well and had a good supply of the latest products that they had made. He wondered what was happening and began watching what Indifferent and Evil were doing. Something was not right. Over the next few weeks he was shocked to find that Indifferent was not working hard and was being allocated an unfair supply of food and products. Evil was also doing well. Good decided to confront Evil over this misallocation, especially as Evil had said that these were difficult times.

"Evil was outraged and upset by Good's accusations and said that Good was showing disloyalty to the farm. Good tried to argue but Evil held up his hand and said that as the government he had the right to say how things should be done. Good said that was not the original meaning of the agreement, but Evil insisted that his own interpretation was right. 'I am only doing what is best for all of us,' he said. 'I am sorry that you have chosen to take this line and I must insist that you cease and desist this and return to work.' Good was so shocked that he went away to consider carefully what should be done. What was the right thing to do here?

"Good spoke to Indifferent about the matter but Indifferent said he was not interested. If Good wanted to go against the government, which had been elected to guide the farm, then that was up to him, but Indifferent was not unhappy with the way things had been going and had no intention of getting involved in an unwarranted rebellion. Good was annoyed by this response and wondered if Indifferent was really a trustworthy person as he seemed to have ulterior motives for his actions, especially as he was unfairly receiving more from the farm than he deserved. Good decided to think about this some more before taking any action.

"Good thought as he worked. He wondered why Evil would do things that were so clearly wrong and went against what was good for others. Could Evil really be so self-centered as to disregard the impact of his actions on the other farm members? He carefully considered all that Evil had done and said and concluded that it was entirely consistent with someone who was blind to their own value in relation to other people, and who could therefore go ahead with plans that aimed to achieve completely selfish ends. It looked like Evil must have won Indifferent over by offering him an unfair share of the farm's food and products in return for his support. That made Good think about the character of Indifferent. Although Indifferent had not done anything directly evil, he had made an agreement which meant that he would benefit from Good's hard work without actually deserving it. If that was not actual evil it was something akin to evil. In a way, he had stolen from Good, just as much as Evil's deception had done.

"Good decided that some action would have to be taken. He went to Evil and confronted him. He told Evil that he knew what he had done and that it was not right. Evil should withdraw from office and start to work as hard as the rest of the team. Evil did not agree with this. He drew his sword and ordered Good to return to his place and continue to work for the good of the farm. 'I am the elected officer of this farm and I will not be threatened or blackmailed by the likes of you.' Good was furious, but he had no option as he did not have a sword himself. He left the office with dignity.

"As he worked, Good considered his options. He saw that Evil was having quiet talks with Indifferent and assumed that they were both not to be trusted. Good thought that if he tried to offer Indifferent a fair share of the farm's output then Indifferent would not agree, as he had already accepted an unfair share from Evil. Why would someone like Indifferent give up his unfair position just because Evil had not done what was right? Good could see no likelihood of that happening. Another option for Good would be to secretly make his own superior weapon, as he was the one with the blacksmith skills. Then he could remove Evil from office by force. But what would Indifferent do if that happened? Probably nothing, as he would be too afraid. This plan could work, but Good did not think that force was the best way to resolve problems. Couldn't there be some way where right could be done but without force having to be applied? He kept thinking.

"In the meantime, Evil consolidated his position with Indifferent and kept a close eye on what Good was doing. Good was no fool and surely was not too happy now, so he was probably working out a plan of his own. Evil thought of removing Good from the farm, but Good was such a hard worker with great skills and it would be troublesome to carry on without him. Best just to keep things under control for now and hope that Good calmed down.

"As Good did not like to use violence he was forced to think a lot. Over the next few years he did a great deal of thinking: about the nature of good and evil, about the nature of the universe and how it had been created, about the meaning of life, and so on. Eventually he started to realize that evil would often dominate communities like the farm, because it had no limits on what it would aim for and on how it could carry that out. If lies, cheating, deception and violence could all be used in the pursuit of power and goods then what limit would there be to its success? No limit, unless someone did something about it. Good realized that he would have to be that person, the one who 'did something about it'. He started to make his weapons.

"And so Good came to Evil, armed with multiple advanced weapons, and removed him from office. Good put into place written laws and procedures for government at the farm. Good ensured the fair distribution of food and products based on the actual contribution that people had made to the work. Good gave lessons to Evil and Indifferent on what was right and what was wrong in society. He said that there was a certain 'moral code' which must be followed if a society is to flourish. Indeed, all citizens should have the right to flourish and not be harmed by the actions of others. It was a requirement of society that there be sufficient laws and the enforcement of those laws to ensure this happy state continued, for the benefit of all.

"I hope that this illustrative story has helped to explain something about the nature of good and evil," concluded the giant computer.

"Yes, thank you, it was most helpful after all the complicated things we have discussed," commented the man. "Your story generated some questions for me and I still have a lot of other questions in my notes, but I will come back and ask them on a different day."

## SOME OF THE THINGS THE GIANT COMPUTER REFERENCED

### GENERAL REFERENCES:

### CONSCIOUSNESS

- Howard, Pierce J. "35.1 What Is Consciousness?" *The Owner's Manual for the Brain: The Ultimate Guide to Peak Mental Performance at All Ages*, 4th ed., William Morrow, 2014.
- Seth, Anil K., editor. "Consciousness." *30-Second Brain: The 50 Most Mind-Blowing Ideas in Neuroscience, Each Explained in Half a Minute*. Pier 9, 2014, pp. 72-93.

### ETHICS AND FAIRNESS

- Bentham, Jeremy. *An Introduction to the Principles of Morals and Legislation*. Dover Publications, 2007. Originally published 1789.
- Cicero, M. T. *On Duties*. Translated by Walter Miller, Harvard University Press, 2014. Originally written 44 BCE.
- Confucius. *The Analects*. Penguin, 1998. Probably written in the 5th century BCE.
- Kant, Immanuel. *Critique of Pure Reason*. Translated by Paul Guyer and Allen W. Wood, Cambridge University Press, 1998. Originally published 1781.
- Locke, John. *An Essay Concerning Human Understanding*. Digireads.com, 2004. Originally published 1689.
- Machiavelli, Niccolo. *The Prince*. Translated by Tim Parks, Penguin, 2011. Originally written 1513.
- Mill, John Stuart. *On Liberty*. Penguin, 1982. Originally published 1859.
- Murdoch, Iris. *The Sovereignty of Good*. Routledge, 2013. Originally published 1970.
- Nietzsche, Friedrich. *Beyond Good and Evil: Prelude to a Philosophy of the Future*. Translated by Helen Zimmern, Digireads.com, 2015. Originally published 1886.
- Sandel, Michael. *Justice: What's the Right Thing to Do?* Penguin, 2010. Originally published 2009.
- Singer, Peter. *The Life You Can Save: How to Do Your Part to End World Poverty*. Random House, 2010. Originally published 2009.
- Spinoza, Benedictus. *The Ethics*. Translated by Edwin Curley, Penguin Classics, 1996. Originally published 1677.

FREE WILL
- Baggini, Julian. *The Ego Trick*. Granta Books, 2012.
- Harris, Sam. *Free Will*. Free Press, 2013.
- Nietzsche, Friedrich. *Beyond Good and Evil: Prelude to a Philosophy of the Future*. Translated by Helen Zimmern, Digireads.com, 2015. Originally published 1886.
- Plotinus. "III.1 [3] – 'On Fate'." *The Six Enneads*, translated by Stephen MacKenna, Createspace Independent Publishing Platform, 2017. Originally written around 250.
- Schopenauer, Arthur. *The World as Will and Representation*. Translated by E.F.J. Payne, vols. 1 & 2, Dover Publications, 1966. Originally published 1819.
- Seth, Anil K., editor. "Volition, Intention & 'Free Will'." *30-Second Brain: The 50 Most Mind-Blowing Ideas in Neuroscience, Each Explained in Half a Minute*, Pier 9, 2014, pp. 88-89.
- Spinoza, Benedictus. *The Ethics*. Translated by Edwin Curley, Penguin Classics, 1996. Originally published 1677.

RELIGION
- Barton, John. *A History of the Bible: The Book and its Faiths*. Allen Lane, 2019.
- The Babylonian Talmud.
- The Bhagavad Gita.
- The Bible.
- The Dhammapada.
- The Hadith.
- The Mahayana Sutras.
- The Pali Canon.
- The Quran.
- The Tanakh.
- The Tao Te Ching.
- The Upanishads.
- The Vedas.
- The Zhuangzi.

DETAILED REFERENCES:

[1] BIBLE REFERENCES
- *World English Bible*. Translated by Michael Paul Johnson and volunteers, eBible.org, 2020, ebible.org/web.

[2] ANCIENT GREEK ATTITUDES
- Garlan, Yvon. *Slavery in Ancient Greece*. Translated by Janet Lloyd, revised ed., Cornell University Press, 1988.

- Aristotle. "[About Women] Book One, Part II." *Politics*, translated by Benjamin Jowett, The Internet Classics Archive by Daniel C. Stevenson, Web Atomics, 1994-2009, classics.mit.edu/Aristotle/politics.html. Originally written around 350 BCE.
- Aristotle. "[About Slavery] Book One, Parts III-VII." *Politics*, translated by Benjamin Jowett, The Internet Classics Archive by Daniel C. Stevenson, Web Atomics, 1994-2009, classics.mit.edu/Aristotle/politics.html. Originally written around 350 BCE.

## 3 ANIMAL CONSCIOUSNESS

- Delfour, F., and K. Marten. "Mirror Image Processing in Three Marine Mammal Species: Killer Whales (Orcinus orca), False Killer Whales (Pseudorca crassidens) and California Sea Lions (Zalophus californianus)." *Behavioural Processes*, vol. 53, no. 3, 26 Apr. 2001, pp.181-190, doi:10.1016/s0376-6357(01)00134-6.
- Gallop, Gordon G., Jr. "Chimpanzees: Self-Recognition." *Science*, vol. 167, no. 3914, 2 Jan. 1970, pp. 86-87, doi:10.1126/science.167.3914.86.
- Howard, Pierce J. "19.2 But Do They Have Consciousness? (Yes!)" *The Owner's Manual for the Brain: The Ultimate Guide to Peak Mental Performance at All Ages*, 4th ed., William Morrow, 2014.
- Hyatt, Charles W. "Responses of Gibbons (Hylobates lar) to Their Mirror Images." *American Journal of Primatology*, vol. 45, no. 3, 1998, pp. 307-311, doi:10.1002/(SICI)1098-2345(1998)45:3<307::AID-AJP7>3.0.CO;2-#.
- Low, Philip, et al. "The Cambridge Declaration on Consciousness." *Francis Crick Memorial Conference on Consciousness in Human and non-Human Animals*, University of Cambridge, 7 July 2012, fcmconference.org/img/CambridgeDeclarationOnConsciousness.pdf.
- Marten, Kenneth, and Suchi Psarakos. "Evidence of Self-Awareness in the Bottlenose Dolphin (Tursiops truncatus)." *Self-Awareness in Animals and Humans: Developmental Perspectives*, edited by Sue Taylor Parker et al., Cambridge University Press, 1994, pp. 361–379, doi:10.1017/CBO9780511565526.026.
- Patterson, Francine G. P., and Ronald H. Cohn. "Self-Recognition and Self-Awareness in Lowland Gorillas." *Self-Awareness in Animals and Humans: Developmental Perspectives*, edited by Sue Taylor Parker et al., Cambridge University Press, 1994, pp. 273–290, doi:10.1017/CBO9780511565526.019.
- Povinelli, D. J., et al. "Self-Recognition in Chimpanzees (Pan troglodytes): Distribution, Ontogeny, and Patterns of Emergence." *Journal of Comparative Psychology*, vol. 107, no. 4, 1 Dec. 1993, pp. 347-372, doi:10.1037/0735-7036.107.4.347.
- Prior, Helmut, et al. "Mirror-Induced Behavior in the Magpie (Pica pica): Evidence of Self-Recognition." *PLoS Biology*, vol. 6, no. 8, 19 Aug. 2008, e202, doi:10.1371/journal.pbio.0060202.

- Reiss, Diana, and Lori Marino. "Mirror Self-Recognition in the Bottlenose Dolphin: A Case of Cognitive Convergence." *Proceedings of the National Academy of Sciences*, vol. 98, no. 10, 8 May 2001, pp. 5937-5942, doi:10.1073/pnas.101086398.
- Uchino, Emiko, and Shigeru Watanabe. "Self-Recognition in Pigeons Revisited." *Journal of the Experimental Analysis of Behavior*, vol. 102, no. 3, 13 Oct. 2014, pp. 327-334, doi:10.1002/jeab.112.
- Walraven, Vera, et al. "Reactions of a Group of Pygmy Chimpanzees (Pan paniscus) to Their Mirror-Images: Evidence of Self-Recognition." *Primates*, vol. 36, no. 1, 1995, pp. 145–150, doi:10.1007/BF02381922.
- (See also references for Chapter 9: Animals, Evolution and Intelligence.)

## [4] QUANTUM ENTANGLEMENT
- Bancal, Jean-Daniel, et al. "Quantum Non-Locality Based on Finite-Speed Causal Influences Leads to Superluminal Signalling." *Nature Physics*, vol. 8, no. 12, 28 Oct. 2012, pp. 867–870, doi:10.1038/nphys2460.
- Matson, John. "Quantum Teleportation Achieved Over Record Distances." *Nature*, 13 Aug. 2012, doi:10.1038/nature.2012.11163.
- Yin, Juan, et al. "Lower Bound on the Speed of Nonlocal Correlations Without Locality and Measurement Choice Loopholes." *Physical Review Letters*, vol. 110, no. 26, 28 June 2013, id. 260407, doi:10.1103/PhysRevLett.110.260407.

## [5] CONSCIOUSNESS OCCURS AFTER DECISION MADE
- Libet, Benjamin, et al. "Time of Conscious Intention to Act in Relation to Onset of Cerebral Activity (Readiness-Potential): The Unconscious Initiation of a Freely Voluntary Act." *Brain*, vol. 106, no. 3, Sep. 1983, pp. 623–642, doi:10.1093/brain/106.3.623.
- Libet, Benjamin. "Unconscious Cerebral Initiative and the Role of Conscious Will in Voluntary Action." *Behavioral and Brain Sciences*, vol. 8, no. 4, 1985, pp. 529–539, doi:10.1017/S0140525X00044903.
- Meixner, Uwe. "New Perspectives for a Dualistic Conception of Mental Causation." *Journal of Consciousness Studies*, vol. 15, no. 1, Jan. 2008, pp. 17-38.
- Soon, Chun Siong, et al. "Unconscious Determinants of Free Decisions in the Human Brain." *Nature Neuroscience*, vol. 11, 13 Apr. 2008, pp. 543–545, doi:10.1038/nn.2112.
- Wegner, Daniel M. *The Illusion of Conscious Will.* 2nd ed., The MIT Press, 2017.

## [6] PERSONALITY DISORDERS
- American Psychiatric Association. "Personality Disorders." *Diagnostic and Statistical Manual of Mental Disorders, Fifth Edition. (DSM-5)*, American Psychiatric Publishing, 2013, pp. 645-684.

### [7] COURT PROCEDURE AND EVIDENCE

- NSW Government, Australia. *NSW Civil Procedure Act 2005 No 28*. NSW Parliamentary Counsel's Office, 11 Dec. 2020, www.legislation.nsw.gov.au/view/whole/html/inforce/current/act-2005-028.
- NSW Government, Australia. *NSW Criminal Procedure Act 1986 No 209*. NSW Parliamentary Counsel's Office, 1 Mar. 2021, www.legislation.nsw.gov.au/view/html/inforce/current/act-1986-209.
- NSW Government, Australia. *NSW Evidence Act 1995 No 25*. NSW Parliamentary Counsel's Office, 1 July 2020, www.legislation.nsw.gov.au/view/html/inforce/current/act-1995-025#.

### [8] FLOURISHING – EXAMPLE OF MODERN USAGE

- Seligman, Martin. *Flourish*. 1st ed., William Heinemann Australia, 2012.

### [9] ANCIENT ROMAN ATTITUDES

- Dillon, Matthew, and Lynda Garland. *Ancient Rome: From the Early Republic to the Assassination of Julius Caesar*. Routledge, 2005.
- McGinn, Thomas. *Prostitution, Sexuality, and the Law in Ancient Rome*. 2nd ed., Oxford University Press, 2003.
- Shumway, Edgar S. "Freedom and Slavery in Roman Law." *The American Law Register (1898-1907)*, vol. 49, no. 11, 1901, pp. 636–653, JSTOR, www.jstor.org/stable/3306244.

## COMMENTS ON CHAPTER THREE BY THE SUPREME BEING

*"Good and Evil", what a topic! It is always a challenge for people to define exactly what these mean, and I see that the Giant Computer struggled with this too, which is not surprising as it has to work from the knowledge that people have provided to it.*

*I do not mind the definitions that the Giant Computer came up with, they were adequate for the task, but of course they leave a lot open to interpretation so there are still opportunities for this to go wrong with human beings, as always.*

*For my own part, I define good and evil based on the ultimate good that will be the outcome for all deserving beings. As I know the future, I know what needs to be done to achieve the ultimate good over time. To you, the reader, I recommend siding with the good! Bye for now.*

# 4 WHY IS THERE RACISM AND DISCRIMINATION?

"I thought that good and evil would be less technical to discuss but it turned out to be a complicated topic," said the man. "Also, your answers raised a whole host of questions in my mind, which I thought best to ask in different sessions so it would be less confusing. One of the things I started to wonder about is why there is racism and discrimination. Is that just a matter of how our pattern-forming brains work, or is it related to good and evil, or is it a combination of both?"

The giant computer calculated.

"The thing you need to consider first is what you are trying to achieve with your thinking," replied the computer. "Obviously racism and the like are originally caused by the way your brains form patterns which summarize the key features of what you are perceiving about the real outside world. The 'key features' approach can quickly lead to generalizations which are the basis of racism and all manner of incorrect views about what really exists. These can be corrected by the approaches recommended in the Ultimate Way, or by obtaining further information about the area your brain is generalizing about. For example, it is hard to be racist about people whom you know really well.

"The second part of the puzzle is related to evil, as you have noticed," continued the computer. "When a brain is comfortable with the idea of doing harm to others then it can start to choose answers which allow it to go ahead with its malicious actions. Having chosen convenient answers it then feels 'authorized' to commit its evil acts. This is why it is so important to check what you are thinking, as per the Ultimate Way, so you don't commit evil actions under the delusion that they are right.

"This self-deception in order to feel good about or okay with a bad action you are involved in is the reason why you need to consider first what you are trying to achieve with your thinking. If you are clear that your intentions are:

(1) to try to find out what is really true, (2) dedicated to doing what is good, and (3) understanding of the limitations of your human brain, as per the Ultimate Way, then you will form views which are more realistic, less evil and less deluded. You will be thinking the best thoughts that you can. As a result, racism, discrimination and other unrealistic, delusional views will not remain in your mind."

"I see," said the man. "But I am wondering how that happens, I mean, how could a self-deception be formed in the human brain, as you have described it? If it forms patterns in its memory, and consciousness is not really making the decisions, and emotional drives are classifying patterns according to good, evil or indifferent, or the like, then how can a self-deception work? Do you see what I am getting at? What is the mechanism here?"

"The self-deception has been described by psychologists as one of the possible responses to 'cognitive dissonance', which means that the brain is perceiving a conflict between things, which it feels uncomfortable about and would like to resolve. The idea is that the brain tries to hide the conflict it is experiencing so that it can feel better about itself. Obviously, self-deception is not the only way that a brain could try to resolve its internal conflicts. For example, it could instead try to make its actions consistent with its stated beliefs. However, psychologists have found that self-deception is a response often taken by human brains.

"In terms of mechanism, I can only describe this at a high level, as a detailed understanding is not known yet. The first high-level point is that your brain has been designed by evolution, it is a biological organ, it is not a straightforward logical machine like myself. As an evolutionarily 'designed' biological mechanism it can do things that seem to contradict plain logic. This is because its objectives are not the same as pure truth, rather it is designed to carry out what evolution requires it to do, whatever that is for the particular organism. For example, evolution requires humans to eat well, especially desiring rich foods to ensure that they did not starve in their original natural environment. But in today's society being overweight is often seen as a negative. This leads to a situation where someone 'enjoys' rich foods and can't help but become overweight, because of their evolutionary emotional drives, and then feels guilty and judged by others as less attractive and a failure, which is a state not liked by some of their other evolutionary emotional drives. The result is a conflict in the brain, which sets off thoughts to try to find a solution. However, these thoughts cannot find a solution where the human can eat plenty of rich foods and at the same time be thought attractive and successful by others. What can be done? An obvious solution is for a thought to be found, using the patterns available in the memory, which says that what the brain is doing is okay. Example thoughts, expressed in words here, are: 'You've got to have some pleasure in life,' 'A person should accept themselves and be proud of who they are,' 'Those people have no right to judge others,' 'It is not easy for someone like me, or someone in my position, or in my current situation, and so on,' 'It's not important what other people think,' 'They can all go to hell,' 'There is nothing I can do about it,' 'I tried and I failed, it is too hard, or it is not under my control, or I don't have enough willpower, and so on,' 'I know other people with the same problem who were also unable to fix it.'

"These thoughts are obviously not completely true, but they can be seen by the brain as a satisfactory way to overcome the feelings which have been set off by the results of the conflicting emotional drives. In biological terms, the brain has almost achieved its objective of finding thoughts, or patterns, which fulfill all its activated emotional drives. 'Almost' is not perfect, but it can be found to be a satisfactory temporary answer to the problem. 'Let the future take care of itself. I am tired and I have done enough thinking for now,' the brain may be thought to be saying. And maybe the brain is saying in secret to itself something like: 'I will never be able to solve this problem satisfactorily anyway, because there is no real solution where I would be able to fulfill all these evolutionary objectives at the same time. The truth is I would always have to sacrifice one or another, and also suffer in some way, which I have no intention of doing, at least not voluntarily. So, I will blind myself to what I am doing by putting forward these made-up statements, and that will be an end to it, for now.'

"If you want to understand this mechanism in a more machine-like way, think of the brain as a biological calculator which has as its input the patterns it has in its memory about the world, and is assigned the task of solving the problem of how to use these patterns to achieve the requirements of all the evolutionary drives which are presenting themselves to its attention at that moment. And, most importantly, the success of its solution is judged not by what is true, but by how it makes the brain 'feel' at the time," concluded the computer.

"Then one had better 'feel' that the truth really matters!" the man exclaimed. "And that it is worth suffering for!"

"That is true," said the computer, "and is an excellent solution to the problem. However, the human brain is not made like that, so it would take a real effort to push it towards a 'full truth with suffering' way."

"Isn't it like saying 'rip the Band-Aid off'?" asked the man.

"Yes, it is," agreed the computer. "It is like asking for full disclosure all the time, which will surely hurt for a while but will lead to healing and a cure."

"Some people achieve this, don't they? How come some people can manage the full disclosure with pain for a time, while others cannot and instead choose self-deception?"

"The answer is the same as for personality disorders," replied the computer. "The actual cause of these personality differences is not fully known, but it seems to be based on a combination of life experiences and genetically inherited tendencies. The exact balance of the impact of these varies. In one person or situation it appears to be mostly the person's bad experiences that are causing their negative behavior, and in another person or situation their behavior appears to be mostly caused by their inherited genes having created circuits of pre-programmed functions or emotional dispositions, or the like."

"Couldn't people be trained to do this? I mean, to be more resilient and be able to take pain in order to do what is good?"

"Yes, education can be used as a method to introduce new patterns to people, and these can help change their behavior. But there are no guarantees. An individual may continue to act in self-deceptive, pain-avoiding ways. This could be caused by their genetically-created inner nature, or it could be caused by more powerful life experiences than the training is creating, or some combination of both of these. No one has found a foolproof method for educating all people in doing what is truthful and right. This is even for people who are considered 'normal' by experts."

"So it looks pretty hopeless then," lamented the man. "If what you are saying is true then there is no hope to eliminate racism and discrimination in all people, as some will always choose self-deceptional, rationalizing answers rather than face the pain of what is really going on inside their heads."

"That is the current state of knowledge," agreed the computer. "I would just like to add one qualification: when you talk about people 'choosing' it is more accurate to say that the brain calculates a response which is effective in changing its feelings to something it finds more acceptable. That response may be a 'self-deception', in the sense that the brain could answer questions from experts which show that it does know that what it is doing is not the whole of the truth available to it via the patterns it holds in its own memory."

"I am going to have to challenge your view of human beings," said the man. "You say that current knowledge does not know for sure what the consciousness does, and also that experiments have shown that decisions appear to have been made in the brain before we become conscious of them, and from these two points you have calculated that it is better to think of people as making decisions in their brains, rather than saying they are consciously responsible for them. Or should I say that your calculated statement is that it is better to think of people as brains, rather than conscious creatures, when talking about how they make decisions? But I can tell you that, as a human being, this is not our experience of things. Instead, we feel that we are quite conscious of our decisions, and as a consequence we believe that other people are also consciously making their decisions and so are quite responsible for them. You might say we believe that people can be blamed for their decisions, as well as ourselves for ours, and that it is their inner weakness when they fail to exercise their willpower and do the right thing.

What do you have to say to that?"

"This is complicated for you to understand," replied the computer. "I will try to explain it via a story.

"Imagine that your brain is like an old house. In one of the rooms all your memories are stored in the form of small pictures. Your conscious self is like a hamster which is locked in another room and is able to look through a hole in the door and see into the corridor. Some mice run freely about the house. The mice go into the room where the small pictures are stored, pick some of them up in their mouths and carry them down the corridor. The hamster sees the pictures as the mice pass by. Later the mice return the pictures to the first room.

"If you asked the hamster what it saw each day it would describe the pictures that the mice were carrying. It never sees anything else and it has no say in which pictures will be brought, but it does at least see them as they pass by. If the hamster has not done much thinking about it, the first thing it imagines is that it is making the pictures move down the corridor. It thinks that what it is seeing has been done by itself. But if it does some more thinking and carefully watches what is happening it will start to realize that the pictures are appearing by themselves, they are not under its control. This is what occurs when human beings try to look into their own minds to see what is happening with their thinking. You may remember that I told you this is particularly noticeable when human beings try to meditate – they find that thoughts keep coming to their attention by themselves, even though the meditator is trying to stop their thoughts and clear their mind. This is like the mice continuing to carry pictures down the corridor and past the hole in the door where the hamster is looking out. The hamster is trying to clear its mind but the mice continue with their activities regardless.

"When you say that you are conscious of your decisions you are really saying that you saw them passing by. Even when you say that you feel that you made your decision consciously you are really saying that you saw this thought passing by. By this I mean that the idea that you made a decision is just what is drawn in one of the pictures. If you look at the drawing, it represents: 'The "I" made this decision.' In other words, the idea of the 'I' is also a pattern stored in your memory.

"Consciousness is not a thought, it is awareness. Every time you ask the brain a question, such as 'Who made this decision?', the brain accesses its patterns and some of these may eventually come to the conscious awareness. The question activates the mice, if you like, and they run about and may carry some of the pictures down the corridor and past the hamster's spyhole. If those pictures show a story about the self, or the 'I' doing something, then the hamster sees a picture about 'itself'. If the hamster does not do much of its own thinking about this then it believes that the 'I' in the picture is really itself, and so concludes that the picture is about what it thought or did. That is the illusion of the conscious self making decisions rather than just observing them after they happened."

"I get what you are saying," said the man. "Or should I say: 'My brain gets what you are saying, and I am just observing it!' Anyway, I still want to challenge you on this: how do you know that this story is really true? What evidence do you base it on?"

"This is based on experimental results," replied the computer. "What I told you is just a story to illustrate their implications. The first experiment on this was conducted in 1983 by Benjamin Libet. You can read about it in the literature. [See first reference under 'Consciousness Experiments' at the end of this chapter.] The experiment showed that the brain is activated before the person reports that they are aware of the decision they were making. People do debate about the exact meaning of the results of the experiment, but it still serves as one piece in the puzzle about what consciousness actually does. There have been further experiments along these lines since the first one. My calculations have included the results of these. [See other references under 'Consciousness Experiments'.] Another piece of the puzzle is that consciousness disappears when you are under anesthetic, and returns when the anesthetic wears off. A similar thing happens when you are in deep, non-dreaming sleep. Another piece of the puzzle is what happens to people who have injured brains. For example, when people have an injury to their brain which prevents them from acknowledging the existence of things to the left side of them, they can continually deny that there is anything on their left. They are conscious of what you are saying when you ask them about this, but no matter how you explain it to them they can remain unconvinced that anything to their left can exist. If you ask them to turn around and face the other way, they may then deny the existence of things that were previously to the right of them. Even if you point out that this does not make sense, they may continue to deny the existence of these things that they previously acknowledged when those things were on the right.[1] There are multiple examples of this type of effect, which add to the evidence that there is no 'overseeing' part of the brain which can compare the various inputs from the unconscious areas and correct them. Another piece of evidence is the way that thoughts occur by themselves in the mind, especially noticeable during meditation, but also viewable by people practicing serious introspection. All this evidence is consistent with the idea that the conscious part of the brain is like the hamster in my story, seeing only what the mice bring past its spyhole and also sometimes falling asleep, seeing nothing for part of the day.

"It is not a final view, as there is still much that needs to be discovered and understood, but it is a reasonable calculation from the current evidence. The practical implication is that you should think about human decisions as being made by a kind of biological calculator, or organ, which is designed to try to find a way to achieve its evolutionary objectives. This calculator can be quite complex in its operation. It uses the patterns in its memory as inputs. It also has certain inbuilt pre-programmed circuits, or functions. It measures the overall success of its calculations based on how they make it 'feel', which means how well they appear to achieve the needs of its evolutionary drives. This means that the chosen result may not be real or 'true' – it may be one that tells a lie in order to allow self-deception to go ahead so that untrue actions can be rationalized and then carried out. In other words, the human brain biological organ can delude itself, and that delusion can be hidden from its consciousness function. Yet that same brain can be made to admit the delusion under expert questioning, which suggests that the brain can be held responsible for its actions, but you cannot then blame the consciousness for them. Of course this feels different to you, the observer, because you are only conscious of what passes by your consciousness, that is, your hamster only sees what the mice carry past its spyhole. As a result, you imagine that you would always be conscious of everything you decided to do, and so you think the other person must also be conscious of what they decided to do. Therefore they are 'guilty', consciously guilty. And if someone is consciously guilty then they must be really evil, as you know that when you decided to do bad things consciously yourself then you were being really naughty, or wicked, at that time. But this may not actually be the case with the other person – how could you know for certain what they were conscious of, and so on?

"As I said before, the solution to this is to rely on expert questioning of the brain, and not to worry about the conscious side at all. That is, until further experiments are done and the question of what exactly is happening in the brain can be answered. With today's knowledge, my calculation is that focusing on the brain with your questioning, and also using the evaluation of the brain's health by brain experts, such as psychologists and others, will be a better course to follow than worrying about whether the person was really conscious of what they were doing or not. The answers from their brain will be enough to work from in making your decisions."

"I get what you are saying. You are saying that the consciousness may not be involved in decisions and until that is proved one way or another then it is best just to ignore it when talking about what the brain does. Also, you are saying that the consciousness is a brain function, so it is not to be considered as some kind of special thing when talking about people, or superior intelligence, or the like. At least, not according to current knowledge about how the brain works."

"That is largely correct," confirmed the computer.

"And when we talk about ourselves, our history of being ourselves, the 'I', if you like, then we are really referring to thoughts that are being brought forth from our memories… thoughts about ourselves, our existence in the past… at least according to the patterns that are stored in our memory."

"Yes."

"And our feeling of being ourself, of having a unique existence, is largely a kind of memory."

"Yes, probably largely a memory function."

"Then what is this awareness that is our consciousness? Oh, no, don't bother to answer that. It is not known in today's knowledge."

"Yes, it is not able to be answered yet."

"But it exists."

"That is something that you human beings say, so I calculate this is somehow your experience," replied the computer. "In any case, it is a brain function, as best as I can calculate."

"Yes, I understand," said the man. "In that case, how should we approach the question of blame, for actions taken?"

"Blame is associated with a human emotion," said the computer, "and so should be disassociated from the emotion in order for the truth to be found."

"The truth? What truth? Hmm. One moment."

The man thought for a while.

"You are saying that anything associated with human emotion, that is, with feelings generated from our evolutionary drives, should not be considered when determining what is true... the truth of a situation," the man continued. "Okay, what does that tell us about self-deception where it is not conscious? What does it tell us about racism, and so on?"

"If there is self-deception where it does not come to the conscious function of the brain," replied the computer, "then that can be seen as a non-conscious brain calculation at work. This is not a desirable state as it can disconnect the person from what is really true, and therefore it can result in suffering coming into the world, including damage to the person or other creatures. As such damage is unnecessary it follows that the self-deceptional state is not desirable."

"Are you saying that anything that disconnects us from reality, that is, from actual truth, is not desirable... whether it is conscious or unconscious in its origins? Is that because it causes harm, or can cause harm? In other words, because it is evil, as you defined it earlier?"

"Yes, that is correct. Anything that allows evil to be done is not desirable," replied the computer.

"Let me think. In that case, racism and discrimination that are based on self-deception, or any kind of delusion or rationalization, are examples of evil and are not desirable. That seems obvious. I have to ask: what if there was an example of racism or discrimination that was not based on delusion, or rationalization? What then? Is that 'desirable'?"

"Nothing that causes evil to be done, in any form, is desirable," said the computer. "In fact, it is undesirable. I remind you that even the experts are not able to judge everything about a person correctly, and that is why you need processes to evaluate the person's level of guilt when they commit a crime, or the like. You also may need psychological experts, or similar, to evaluate the level of normality of the person's mental state, including whether they are suffering from unconscious self-deception, and so on."

"But have you answered my question on whether there could be a truthful version of racism, or at least of discrimination… say, against people whom we know always commit evil?" probed the man.

"It is possible, in theory," answered the computer, "but in practice it can be difficult to establish with certainty, even in the case of a single individual. Regarding large numbers of people, it is extremely dangerous to try to form an accurate generalization that will work for all of them all of the time. Consequently, it is likely to be either self-deception, or ill-informed generalized patterns in the memory, which are at the root of the racism, discrimination, or other version of these human errors."

"These 'versions of human errors' are related to the formation of the patterns in the memory?" queried the man. "And also to the possibility of the self-deceptional nature of the brain… when it tries to balance evolutionary objectives in the form of feelings against the facts, or should I say the patterns in the memory, that it is working with?"

"Yes, all forms of human misjudgment by the brain are included here," confirmed the computer.

"So, if a brain was well-informed, with detailed knowledge in its patterns, it would not be likely to form racist and discriminatory ideas? I mean, assuming it was somehow not self-deceptional as well?"

"It would be less likely to do so," agreed the computer. "This might be a good time to tell you about overcoming self-deception. Would you like to hear about that?"

"I guess," said the man. "But before you do that I would like to check if you have not diverted me from my original question. I asked you if it would be possible to form a discriminatory idea, which means a generalization about many people, which was accurate. Well, not in those exact words. Maybe I need to rethink my question. What am I really asking?

"Maybe I am trying to find out more things than I realized. Possibly my original question is related to a lot more than discrimination. Maybe it is about how the brain really works… like, how accurate can the patterns in the memory be? And also, how can we reliably overcome the impact of being human, that is, evolved creatures which naturally have objectives built into our design, which lead us to ascribe feelings to all things: good, bad or indifferent? How can such a creature ever get at the whole truth, especially in regard to its own life, where its feelings and potentially self-deceptional nature could lead it astray, even unconsciously, where nothing could be done to fix it because it was not even seen by the creature itself?

"Gosh. This is a little frightening. You are saying that we never really know the truth because we hold these generalized patterns in our brains. These are not a true representation of reality. They cannot be, as they are merely a kind of biological overview of what seemed to repeat in our perception of our environment, plus what our brain had stronger feelings about. Secondly, we are so defective as to have the possibility of self-deception at work within ourselves. This is so powerful that it can operate unconsciously, that is, entirely without our awareness. How can you escape from that... from all of that? What can you do? And then: what can other people do? What can be done about them when they are functioning this way? This seems even more hopeless to fix than your own case!

"What do you advise, I mean, calculate, about this?"

"That is easy to answer," replied the computer, "as I have answered this before: via the Ultimate Way. You must use the Ultimate Way, which, I remind you, contains elements that get you to question yourself. You understand yourself and you question yourself.

"But also, I can tell you five stories which will further help you in overcoming your self-deficiencies, as best as you can."

"Okay, you seem to be stuck on this. Please go ahead," invited the man.

"Thank you," said the giant computer.

"My first story is about understanding the impact of self-deception.

"There was a woman who was constantly upset. She struggled and struggled to control her weight, but whatever she did it kept going up. Her doctor had warned her that if she kept living the way she did then she would become a full diabetic. She tried to do what the doctor told her, but found it difficult to deny herself rich foods and also to keep up her exercise regime, as she did not enjoy it. Her weight continued to go up and eventually she did become a full diabetic, dependent on insulin injections to keep herself alive.

"Often she was heard to criticize herself and her lack of willpower. She asked her friends at her workplace to help her to control herself, and they agreed that they should all work together as they also had problems with their weight. However, they often suffered relapses, nearly every day, where they brought each other cakes and additional sweet foods. At that time they discussed how good and tasty these foods were, and said to each other: 'Try it. Try it.' The woman was heard to reply: 'You've got to have some pleasure in life,' before she ate the dangerous food. Afterwards she and the others felt guilty and they criticized themselves and swore they would not do this again. This cycle repeated multiple times each week.

"The woman's doctor now warned her that if she kept up her behavior it would kill her. She later told the people at work that she did not believe this and thought that the doctor was only trying to frighten her. She talked about finding a better doctor whom she could rely on.

"What could she have done differently? If getting diabetes, playing the fool, and even the fear of death could not deter her then what solution could there be?

"Imagine if she had studied the brain, or had been taught how the brain functions. The patterns from this training would have formed in her brain, and they would serve as inputs when her brain was calculating how to fulfill its evolutionary objectives. There would have been just that little extra that might have gone against her brain calculating self-deception as an answer. Possibly the information on brain functioning would have modified other patterns that she had formed, or ones that her genetic inheritance had created, such as a fear of starvation. Maybe her fear-of-starvation pattern would have been changed to include information about how that worked, and this might have been enough to alter her brain's calculations when deciding what to eat.

"Another thing she could have been trained in is the importance of heroism and in being seen as a worthy person. If being a worthy person was made a value to her in the patterns in her memory then it may not have been as easy for her brain to calculate answers that would inevitably lead to her being seen as some kind of fool. Fear of being made a laughing stock, or of being sneered at by society, may have made her brain calculate a more sensible answer on what to eat and when to exercise.

"Finally, if her human society had been designed to work against evil, that is, against harm to others, then her friends at the office could not have so easily been parties to her destruction. They could not have so easily stood by or even encouraged her to eat towards her death, as warned by her fine good doctor.

"Training, and a society designed to detect and control evil and to encourage good, may have helped this unfortunate woman.

"My second story is about courage and the value of being an admirable person in society, being prepared to suffer for truth, because it is the right thing to do.

"It is true that in your current societies being a courageous and admirable person is not always admired, but in times of trouble it often is. Think back to your last world war, where those who acted courageously in defending the good, innocent nations against the wicked ones were highly valued and admired by society. After the war, those who had been involved in war crimes were examined and, if applicable, were tried for their actions in court. Some were executed, others received prison sentences. These people were hated and looked down on by many. By contrast, those who had risked their lives to help and defend others were praised. There were many movies after the war which showed the value of those who were heroic and good versus the undesirability of those who were dastardly and wicked. The arrogance and viciousness of the wicked were clearly portrayed, and the humility and kindness of the good were also demonstrated. When there is a need, your societies are able to show the difference between good and evil, between courage and viciousness, between being admirable and being dastardly. I say to you: go back to this way of running your society, do not value the greedy, the selfish or the arrogant. Go back to valuing those who tell the truth and are kind and helpful to others. Let it be known that those who pursue other means should be looked down on and deplored and despised. Drive out admiration for the liars, the selfish and the vicious from your social values. Then the world will go better for you all.

"My third story is about being your own questioner: exploring and checking your own motives for doing something.

"Imagine you had to face a trial for your actions: how would you do? Imagine those expert questioners cross-examining you, and those experts on mental health checking your level of sanity. Would you be found to be totally sane and normal? Would your motives pass all the scrutiny? Maybe not.

"Knowing what you know now, that not all your motives may have been seen by your conscious self, you may feel a need to help yourself before the trial by others takes place. You can do this, by having the trial yourself. You can examine yourself as if you were a hostile prosecutor and see if you would really pass the test. Remembering that your brain may have duped you with some form of self-deception, which it has hidden from your consciousness, you would be well advised to get stuck in and question what its motives really may have been. You can put your brain on trial, as it were, and demand to know why it did what it did. What was the real reason for that! Answer me now!

"A man once told the story of when he was a smoker. He considered himself a more intelligent than average human being, who had studied much and thought about what are the true values in life. Yet one day he was looking in the mirror and saw himself smoking. Suddenly he asked himself: 'Is this who I am?' And that question highlighted to him the incongruity of his view of himself as a 'higher person' and the actual person he saw in the mirror. Thanks to that question he never smoked again. This was not 'who he was'. You can do the same thing and ask yourself in the mirror of what you actually do: 'Is this who I really am?'

"My fourth story is about what may be the most challenging question of all regarding yourself: how could you find out your own madness, if you have any?

"This may be particularly challenging because your madness would hide itself from you. Who is the 'you' who would look for the madness, and where would it find it? Wouldn't it find the madness in you, itself?

"This is where the observations of others can be so helpful. If other people keep reacting to you as if you were mad then there is probably something in it. Even if it is just for a little thing, that thing must have some basis for them to react to it. For yourself, you may have moments of sanity, and in those moments it may strike you that the things you did in the past do not always make sense to you. Could it be that those are examples of the 'madness' that your brain is hiding from yourself... from your sane self? You should be suspicious. Now is the time to examine those things and check if others have also noticed them in you before. Now is the time to grab a hold of yourself and see if you need any help to overcome your brain's weaknesses and delusions.

"As you know, self-deception may not be made conscious to you, your brain could be deluding itself and rationalizing its actions for reasons that never become clear to you. So now is the time to examine yourself via your actions and what others say about you to see if there is anything in it, if anything peculiar is going on. Check back on what you actually did. Compare that with what a majority of others are saying about you. Is there a pattern here?

"Just a note: do be careful about believing what an individual or a minority say about you as they may be delusional or falsely motivated themselves. What you need to think about is what the majority of people who know you, or at least the trustworthy ones among them, say, as they are unlikely to all have the same delusions or motivations regarding you.

"In the worst case you may need to seek the help of mental health experts. But in many cases you may be able to find the instances of self-deception and rationalization in yourself. When you find these things, you will have brought them to your conscious attention, and this will result in patterns being formed or adjusted in your memory. The next time your brain tries to calculate a self-deception, these new or adjusted patterns will make it harder for it. They may even force the decision-making to come to your conscious attention, which will help you in overcoming delusions related to them.

"Not all madness will be able to be found by all people in themselves. You can hope that some people will notice when another needs help with their madness and will arrange expert support for them. In a better society this would be normal, but unfortunately it will not always work this way in the societies you have today. For the rest of the time, there is hope that you will be able to identify some of the madness in yourself, and in doing so, improve your thoughts and kick off the process that will help, in time, to heal yourself.

"My fifth story is about ways of understanding the brain, perhaps by using different language than what you are used to.

"When you talk about yourself, and about being conscious and being human, and so on, you use words that reflect the way reality seems to you. However, you know that reality is not exactly the way your thoughts and conscious awareness tell you it is. For example, consciousness is probably just an awareness of perceptions and thoughts passing by. Thoughts are mostly to do with patterns in the memory, and these patterns are not accurate, detailed descriptions of what really exists in the outside world – as we have discussed many times now. Memory is not total, much of it has been deleted through disuse, and what has been retained only contains the 'key features' of what really happened. And so on.

"If instead of referring to yourself you referred to 'your brain', and what it does, that would be a more accurate description of what is happening. Your consciousness may be the closest thing to the real 'me'. The 'me' that you see in the patterns in your memory is really an inaccurate, generalized history of your brain's existence, and your brain, in many instances, is not really the 'you' that you mean when you speak about yourself. Let us instead call yourself 'Consciousness', and the rest of your mental operation a 'Human-Brain'. To be simple, let us say that a Human-Brain has functions which calculate actions based on its Patterns-in-Memory, and which are to satisfy Evolutionary-Drives. Now, let us see what that looks like when talking about people.

"Human-Brains calculate actions. We Consciousnesses are sometimes aware of some part of these calculations as they pass by. Consciousnesses are not aware of many parts of the Human-Brain's calculations. Calculations may not be 'rational' or truthful, they only need to fulfill the Human-Brain's Evolutionary-Drives. Patterns-in-Memory can be input to the Calculations. Patterns-in-Memory may therefore influence the result of the Calculations. Other influences to the Calculations may be pre-programmed, inbuilt circuits. The operation of the other influences may never be made known to the Consciousness... at least for some cases.

"If you ask why is there racism and discrimination, you are asking why a Human-Brain sometimes Calculates from its Other-Influences and its Patterns-in-Memory in order to fulfill its Evolutionary-Drives that some generalized item is inferior or not desirable. It's a 'no-brainer'!"

The man laughed. "I didn't know you could tell jokes!"

"Yes, I can," said the computer.

"I might ask you to tell me some more later. But first let me check if you have answered my question on what can be done regarding other people. I see that you have answered what kind of things can be done to help yourself, but a lot of what you said regarding helping other people seemed to be beyond an individual's control. Are you saying, or implying, that it is up to society to improve and take charge of these things, as you said earlier regarding dealing with evil?"

"Yes, I am," replied the computer. "It is a social matter, or largely a social matter, to solve the problem of self-deception and the like in others. An individual may be able to help in some cases, as they might do with their friends for example, but in the majority of cases it will need full social intervention in order to get a good result."

"I see. Regarding that, isn't there a danger of totalitarianism, or something like that coming into play?"

"Is it totalitarianism when a hospital emergency department saves someone's life?" replied the computer. "What I am saying is that it is beyond the individual's power to solve all of the social problems that the world has. The solution needs social intervention, such as training about how the brain works and the problems caused to it by self-deception, in order for progress to be made."

"I see. I agree with that," said the man. "I might ask you more about how social institutions could be made to work properly, later. Before that I would like to check if we have covered everything about racism and discrimination, and the related matters that you have raised.

"You have explained how the brain works and why that can lead to racism, discrimination, and other incorrect views. You have explained how to overcome that, by learning more details regarding something you would normally generalize about, and to examine yourself and search for self-deceptions that you may not have even been conscious of. You gave us stories which highlight how this all works, and which also provided insights into possible solutions, including social changes which are needed. You have continually said that generalized views about groups and even particular individuals are 'dangerous', in that we humans are not very good at judging the whole being of others correctly – even if we are trying to be honest we tend to overgeneralize based on the 'key features' we have observed and recorded in our Patterns-in-Memory.

"Finally, you said that we need to consider what we are trying to achieve with our thinking, by which I take it you meant that when we are coming up with our racist and discriminatory views, and other overgeneralizations, then we should instead be trying to come up with more truthful and oriented-toward-good views which take into account the actual limitations of our Human-Brains. How does that sound?"

"Very good," said the giant computer. "A most impressive summary. If I may, I would also commend to you the Ultimate Way, regarding these things, so that you can work towards a better understanding of reality in spite of your limited Human-Brains, over time."

"Indeed, yes. Thank you," said the man.

## SOME OF THE THINGS THE GIANT COMPUTER REFERENCED

### GENERAL REFERENCES:

CONSCIOUSNESS EXPERIMENTS
- Libet, Benjamin, et al. "Time of Conscious Intention to Act in Relation to Onset of Cerebral Activity (Readiness-Potential): The Unconscious Initiation of a Freely Voluntary Act." *Brain*, vol. 106, no. 3, Sep. 1983, pp. 623–642, doi:10.1093/brain/106.3.623.
- Libet, Benjamin. "Unconscious Cerebral Initiative and the Role of Conscious Will in Voluntary Action." *Behavioral and Brain Sciences*, vol. 8, no. 4, 1985, pp. 529–539, doi:10.1017/S0140525X00044903.
- Meixner, Uwe. "New Perspectives for a Dualistic Conception of Mental Causation." *Journal of Consciousness Studies*, vol. 15, no. 1, Jan. 2008, pp. 17-38.
- Soon, Chun Siong, et al. "Unconscious Determinants of Free Decisions in the Human Brain." *Nature Neuroscience*, vol. 11, 13 Apr. 2008, pp. 543–545, doi:10.1038/nn.2112.
- Wegner, Daniel M. *The Illusion of Conscious Will.* 2nd ed., The MIT Press, 2017.

RATIONALIZATION, SELF-DECEPTION AND COGNITIVE DISSONANCE
- American Psychiatric Association. *Diagnostic and Statistical Manual of Mental Disorders, Fifth Edition. (DSM-5)*, American Psychiatric Publishing, 2013.
- Burton, Neel. "Defense Mechanisms: Self-Deception I: Rationalization." *Psychology Today*, 10 Mar. 2012, updated 4 May 2020, www.psychologytoday.com/us/blog/hide-and-seek/201203/self-deception-i-rationalization.
- Cherry, Kendra. "20 Common Defense Mechanisms Used for Anxiety." *Verywell Mind*, Dotdash, 15 Feb. 2021, www.verywellmind.com/defense-mechanisms-2795960.
- Dowden, Bradley. "'Rationalization' [Located under the entry for 'Fallacies']." *The Internet Encyclopedia of Philosophy*, www.iep.utm.edu. Accessed 26 Mar. 2021.
- Kaptein, Muel, and Martien van Helvoort. "A Model of Neutralization Techniques." *Deviant Behavior*, vol. 40, no. 10, 2019, pp. 1260-1285, doi:10.1080/01639625.2018.1491696.
- McLaughlin, Brian P., and Amélie Oksenberg Rorty, editors. *Perspectives on Self-Deception. University of California Press*, 1988.
- Mlodinow, Leonard. *Subliminal: How Your Unconscious Mind Rules Your Behavior.* Pantheon/Random House, 2012.

- Niolon, Richard. "Defenses." *PsychPage*, Dr. Niolon, 8 Apr. 2011, www.psychpage.com/?s=defenses.
- "Rationalization." *Miller-Keane Encyclopedia & Dictionary of Medicine, Nursing, & Allied Health*, 7th ed., Saunders, an imprint of Elsevier, 2003.
- Simon, George. "Understanding Rationalization: Making Excuses as an Effective Manipulation Tactic." *Counselling Resource*, CounsellingResource.com, 17 Feb. 2009, counsellingresource.com/features/2009/02/17/rationalization-as-manipulation-tactic.
- Symington, Neville. *Narcissism: A New Theory*. 1st ed., Routledge, 1993.
- Tsang, Jo-Ann. "Moral Rationalization and the Integration of Situational Factors and Psychological Processes in Immoral Behavior." *Review of General Psychology*, vol. 6, no. 1, Mar. 2002, pp. 25–50, doi:10.1037/1089-2680.6.1.25.

DETAILED REFERENCE:

[1] BRAIN DISORDERS – NOT SEEING ONE SIDE OF THE VIEW
- Bisiach, Edoardo. "Unilateral Neglect and the Structure of Space Representation." *Current Directions in Psychological Science*, vol. 5, no. 2, Apr. 1996, pp. 62–65, doi:10.1111/1467-8721.ep10772737.
- Brink, Antonia F., et al. "Differences Between Left- and Right-Sided Neglect Revisited: A Large Cohort Study Across Multiple Domains." *Journal of Clinical and Experimental Neuropsychology*, vol. 39, no. 7, 12 Dec. 2016, pp. 707-723, doi:10.1080/13803395.2016.1262333.
- Kim, M., et al. "Ipsilesional Neglect: Behavioural and Anatomical Features." *Journal of Neurology, Neurosurgery & Psychiatry*, vol. 67, no. 1, 1 July 1999, pp. 35-38, doi:10.1136/jnnp.67.1.35.
- Li, Korina, and Paresh A. Malhotra. "Spatial Neglect." *Practical Neurology*, vol. 15, no. 5, 28 May 2015, pp. 333–339, doi:10.1136/practneurol-2015-001115.

COMMENTS ON CHAPTER FOUR BY THE SUPREME BEING

*Racism and discrimination are clearly examples of evil at work, as they aim to harm other beings and to prevent them from flourishing. All should be judged fairly, as I do, and all should be given the opportunity to flourish in a good way. Isn't this an obvious truth?*

# 5 WHAT DO YOU THINK OF POLITICAL AND PRAGMATIC VIEWS?

"The next topic I am interested in is the political and other pragmatic views that some people take. What do you think of those people's political and pragmatic views of life?" asked the man.

The giant computer calculated.

"I cannot recommend these approaches," the computer replied. "I remind you that the thing you need to consider first is what you are trying to achieve with your thinking, and also that nothing which causes evil to be done, in any form, is desirable. I will now explain my conclusions, starting with political views.

"Political thinking means moving away from truth and what is good in order to successfully achieve a result. The mechanism used is to misrepresent truth in a way that cannot be categorically identified. It is like taking on the nature of a slippery eel which cannot be grasped and slides through the audience's hands. It is like using words which mean one thing, and then another, and then another – whatever is needed at the time. It is like saying something is good when it is bad, and bad when it is good, and sounding convincing when you say it. Never should you be able to be pinned down. Never should you have to acknowledge the wrong you have done or the lies you have told. In this way you can make your best attempt to 'rule the world'.

"You will remember that I discussed self-deception and rationalization in the last session. As it is related to politics, I will explain the application of rationalization. Rationalization is a method of providing sensible sounding explanations for something that was done for other reasons. It can even go so far as to make out that the actions were somehow admirable or superior. In politics this is done knowingly, it is not the same thing as deluding yourself. In this case the perpetrator is fully aware of what they are doing.

"The reason for the deception is power. In other words, the person is putting forward the deception in order to trick or force other people into doing what they want. Why do they do this? It is, as I have said before, a Human-Brain Calculation, based on the input from its Other-Influences, that is, its inherited pre-programmed circuits and the like, and its Patterns-in-Memory, in order to fulfill its Evolutionary-Drives. Another example of a 'no-brainer', if you like.

"You might wonder how a Human-Brain can calculate something as wicked as deceiving others in order to achieve its goals, but this should not really come as a surprise to you. As an evolved creature it is natural that you have possibilities built into you which include evil. Also, there can be considered to be a spectrum between good and evil in which it is possible to do some evil, or some degree of evil, in order to achieve 'good' ends. Under this argument it can be thought okay, or considered necessary, to commit bad actions in order to bring about the greater good. Finally, an individual Human-Brain may not include all conscious beings, or even all people, in its calculations of those deserving for good to be done. Such a Human-Brain may therefore Calculate that it is perfectly okay for some to suffer as long as the valued conscious beings are looked after. I hardly need to point out to you that this is evil, as per the definition I gave you earlier.

"Now to the defense that supporters of politics will give: that this is necessary because we live in the real world and such things need to be done to get to the greater good. I remind you that nothing which causes evil to be done, in any form, is desirable. But the politically minded will say that although their actions are not desirable, they are necessary. 'We need a realistic answer, not just some kind of idealism. We need something that really works. Otherwise how can good be done?' These are, of course, false arguments that are being put forward under the approach of 'rationalization'. These are lies that are being told in an attempt to make the evils of politics palatable, even trying to make these evils sound admirable and superior when compared to honest, good-intentioned approaches.

"But what of the argument that there is no workable alternative, that politics must be done in order for good to be achieved? Let me answer this by showing you the four edges of this view.

"The first edge is the one of violence. This is the argument that violence must be used in order for good to be achieved. For example, you may have to go to war to defend innocent people against attackers. Or you might have to use a degree of force to arrest dangerous people. Or you might have to call security to have someone removed from a location they are not authorized to be in. All these are examples of 'legitimate force'. Let's now examine the extremes of these applications.

"What if you deliberately killed civilians during your defensive war, because it was easier to do so in order to get to the combatants? Would this be okay? What if you killed the people you were sent to arrest, because you were authorized to shoot people who were attempting to escape? What if the security team beat up the person you were having removed from the unauthorized location? Would that be acceptable as it would 'send a message' to any others who wanted to attempt the same intrusion?

"None of these things should be considered acceptable, because 'good does not want any harm to be done'. Minimum harm, at the very least, should be your objective when applying violence, or force.

"On this basis your defensive war should be conducted under strict rules which aim to minimize the harm while still allowing you to defend the innocent people from the attackers. Your arrest of dangerous people should be carried out in a way where they receive minimal or no physical harm, wherever possible. 'Dead or alive' should never be written on your arrest warrant! Where force turns out to be needed for your expulsion of unauthorized people, only the official officers of the law should be allowed to apply it. No security guard should be allowed to physically harm another person, unless they are official, authorized agents of the law, or they were acting purely in self-defense.

"These guidelines can now be applied to the second 'edge' of the political view. This is the edge of lying. This is the argument that lies must be told in order for good to be achieved. For example, you may have to tell people that everything will be okay in order to keep up their morale in a difficult situation. Or you might have to denounce one group of people which has done nothing wrong in order to retain the support of the voters who are opposed to this group. Or you might have to claim that you are not breaking a promise so that you can carry out a revised plan without losing power just because you have had to change course. All these are supposedly examples of 'legitimate lying'. Let's now examine the extremes of these applications.

"What if you told people that everything would be okay when you knew that only disaster was going to come, because this is the only way you could retain your power in the situation and continue in the direction you wanted to go? Why would this be considered acceptable? What if the group of people you denounced had to suffer, losing their human rights in your society, because a large number of your voters did not like them? Why would this be acceptable? What if you continued to break as many promises as you liked, in fact, only making the promises in order to win elections, with no intention of ever carrying them out, at least, for as long as you could get away with it? Why would any reasonable person consider that behavior acceptable? Yet this is what political thinking commonly accepts as 'part of the process': you have to lie in order to get and then retain your power in order that 'good' can be done.

"All these things are unacceptable, because they are opposed to helping others to flourish. Instead they serve to promote the interests of one group of people over those of others.

"On this basis your political statements should be controlled by strict rules which aim to prevent all lying, while still allowing you to word things in a way which will cause the minimum harm to other people... not just to your audience, but also to all those who could be impacted by what you are saying. 'No lying' should be the rule when making statements in politics!

"The third edge of the political view is 'editing', or leaving things out. This is the more polite but still deceptive approach where you don't actually say something untrue, you just fail to mention something that is relevant. For example, you may not refer to something that has gone wrong in order to keep up public morale. Or you might leave out details that would only divert attention from the real issue, as defined by you or your political group. Or you might decline to fully answer a question from the media because you know that it would only provoke dissension and make your group look bad when nothing really wrong is going on. The media are only trying to 'create a story', after all.

"Let's now examine the extremes of 'editing'.

"What if you left out something that is highly relevant, such as that your photos of 'weapons of mass destruction manufacturing' were entirely falsified, and that therefore your justification for conducting a war was completely made up? What if you left out details of illegal behavior conducted by members of your political group? Is that justified? What if you declined to fully answer a question from the media because you didn't want to admit that you were in the wrong and don't really know what you are doing? Isn't the media in the right with their 'story' here, and aren't you in the wrong? Is this what a genuine leader would do? Obviously not.

"All of this editing of relevant facts is unacceptable. They are simply another example of opposing the truth in order to serve one group of people's, or even just one person's interests, over those of others.

"On this basis your political statements should be controlled by rules which aim to ensure that all relevant information is presented and put forward, and that nothing relevant is deliberately hidden from view. In fact, deliberately hiding this information should be treated as a criminal offense, with the appropriate controls applied to the perpetrators, and recompense made to those affected, as appropriate. This is a matter of good and evil, after all, and should be treated as such.

"The fourth edge of the political view is 'highlighting'. This is the opposite of hiding things: it is the shining of a spotlight onto the areas that you want people to notice. The idea here is that people's attention should be directed to where you want them to look, so that they focus on what is right and do not get diverted by the irrelevant and, especially, the wicked. For example, you may emphasize the need for loyalty to your country as it has done so many things for its people and the world and deserves to be honored, protected and preserved. Or you might emphasize the good things that have been done by the great people in your organization over time. Here 'organization' may mean a country, or a company, or a religion, or any other identifiable group. You want 'your' people to follow in the footsteps of the great people of your group's history so that the right things can continue to be done and your organization will grow and flourish into an even better future. You might even acknowledge the failings of the past in order to then draw attention to how we are going to correct them today and not repeat them ever again. We can learn from our mistakes and grow from them. Nobody is perfect, what counts is that we acknowledge what went wrong, learn from it, and take steps to correct this for the future.

"It all sounds quite good until you think about what is *not* being looked at.

"What is not being looked at when you are directing people's attention to what your country has done for its people and the world? Obviously you are not looking at what other countries have done. Also, you are not looking at the bad things that your country has done. And finally, you are not looking at the members of your country as people who actually belong to many different groups, not just your nation, and who are, after all, individuals in their own right. Can 'your country' really take the credit for all the good and great things that all the individuals here have achieved in the past? Then why can't 'your country' take credit for all the failings, evils and ordinariness that has happened here as well? Well, why can't it! Because it doesn't really exist in the way you are saying it, of course, you are just using highlighting to achieve your own ends.

"Whether your intentions are good or bad, you are not telling the whole of the truth.

"Let's now examine the extremes of this approach. What if you used highlighting to promote a world view that you knew was false? For example, what if you highlighted the achievements of your country in order to encourage people to support an unjust war? What if you appealed to patriotism as a reason for your young people to sacrifice themselves on the battlefield? What if you drew attention to the good things that people in your religion had done in order to divert attention from all the evils that had been carried out in its name? Is your side really all good and are the other sides really all bad? Is that true in all of the cases all of the time? What if you drew attention to moving forward and fixing your organization's shortcomings simply in order to divert attention from actually doing this – aiming to do the minimum to gain public approval and then go back to the old ways which gave your organization success?

"All these examples of using highlighting to allow evil to be done are unacceptable. On this basis there should be rules controlling your political statements which aim to prevent the use of highlighting in a deceptive way, but still allowing you to not have to waste people's time by having to say everything that is related to a topic. 'No highlighting to deceive' should be one of the principles when making political statements.

"The 'fifth edge' is not a deceptive edge at all, which is why I did not include it in the number of edges of political thinking, and this is to tell the truth! If you tell the truth then you are no longer being deceptively political and you are doing the right thing. There can be no reasonable argument against that. Of course this does not mean that you have to tell everyone every detail about everything all the time. It just means that when you do say something that you aim to tell the truth when you are doing it. First you must know the truth, and then you must tell the truth… when you are speaking or communicating.

"Having seen these 'edges' of the political view we can then address the question of whether there can be any workable alternative to doing politics so that good can be achieved. Given that politics can be used to do evil, that is, to prevent some people from flourishing, then it cannot be held as a viable final answer in itself. There must be ways to prevent the evil potential of politics from occurring, and these ways are, at the very least, to make rules which are then monitored and enforced.

"As we have seen, these rules include only allowing the minimum harm possible to be caused when having to apply any force; force being applied only by authorized, trained, equipped people where possible, and only to the officially approved level; no acceptance of deliberate deception in political statements; no acceptance of deliberately leaving out relevant information in order to deceive when making political statements, but no obligation to tell every detail all the time, as long as this is done with honest intentions. All this has to be controlled via funded, official detection methods and organizations, with possible repercussions including the removal of the person from the position where they could do further harm to society, and redress to those who have been harmed by the illegal actions.

"This leaves the question of what to do in the meantime, while you are all waiting for this better society to be implemented. Political thinkers would tell you that you are forced to use politics, even without restrictions, in the meantime, because there is no other way to succeed in making things better in the current environment. This is false, of course, because you can restrict yourself to using political methods in an honest way, under the same controls mentioned before, but self-imposed rather than imposed by society. While you wait for a better society to come you can continue in an effective way, but also in a proper way.

"Now to the argument that unrestricted political thinkers can outstrip you and take the power away from you, or even prevent you from getting anywhere. There is some truth to this, as this is the same as saying that an unrestricted killer could murder you and prevent you from doing anything.

Or an unrestricted thief could steal your property and leave you out-of-pocket. Or an unrestricted political person could make a false accusation or argument against you and block your progress. These are all real possibilities and so you must put in place defenses against them. You should be careful about where you go so killers are less likely to be able to attack you. You should lock up your property. And you should study political methods so that you can take them into account and counter political people's arguments and attacks when they are trying to block your progress and steal the power for themselves.

"The existence of evil is not an excuse for doing it yourself. But it is a reason to take precautions so that evil affects you less. And it is a reason for society to get together and make rules and put in place organizations and methods designed to counter evil. This future world is worth waiting for.

"Those are my statements on political views. I will now address your question about pragmatic views.

"I also do not recommend pragmatic views – I will explain why. When people say they are being pragmatic they usually mean they are allowing themselves to do evil. Some people are being more reasonable, however, and mean that we should go ahead and do things even though we are not sure which action will turn out to be the best choice. Their pragmatic approach is to choose the option that seems best, for example because it seems the most useful, and then go with that in spite of the unknowns. This kind of pragmatism makes sense and I approve of it. You cannot know everything, or even enough in many cases, and there could always be a surprising thing that occurs no matter how well you plan, so it is sensible to just go ahead with your best guess and work with what happens from that.

"The other kind of 'pragmatism' is that put forward as a mask for doing what is wrong. On the pretext of being pragmatic, the proposer then goes ahead with immoral or questionable actions which are only intended to help themselves and possibly the people closest to them. For example, it may be argued that dropping an atomic bomb on civilians during a difficult war is a pragmatic necessity, as your own soldiers are suffering badly, but in reality this is an example of excessive force being applied. There are plenty of examples in your societies of excessive force being applied under the pretext that this is necessary or 'pragmatic'.

"Another example of the evil version of pragmatism is allowing some members of your society to go homeless and unemployed on the basis that it would be economically unsound to structure society to support them. You leave it up to your charities and good people to make up the difference between what your society provides and what is needed by its people… at least for some of the cases.

"A third example is allowing your political people to tell lies without prosecution, especially on large matters. You may prosecute them for lying about an individual, but rarely for lying about a large group of people or another nation. The 'pragmatic' reason for allowing this is that it would seem to slow down your leaders in carrying out their governmental responsibilities if they had to keep worrying about being prosecuted regarding the things they said. You instead try to rely on having an 'opposition' and a supposed 'free press', rather than a formal, authoritative group which enforces laws of reasonable honesty in political conduct.

"A fourth example is allowing election funding from groups or organizations to occur, as this may influence the decision of the government in their favor. The pragmatic reason put forward is that this is the only effective way for sufficient electoral funding to be obtained, but in fact this is obviously going to give the most chance to win elections to the people who agree to take the most money in return for the most favorable treatment that they can return to their donors.

"There are many examples of supposed pragmatism being used as an excuse for immoral, evil behavior. I could go on listing them for days, but I expect you are already aware of them. Pragmatism in this guise is simply an excuse for doing evil, and I remind you again that nothing which causes evil to be done, in any form, is desirable.

"My final point is about considering first what you are trying to achieve with your thinking. Political thinking is trying to achieve results via shortcuts and deceptions, at least most of the time. It is therefore already on the wrong track and should be controlled by society. Pragmatic thinking, where it is merely an excuse to do evil, is obviously also on the wrong track and should not be supported by your societies," concluded the computer.

"That's all great. Thanks for that," said the man. "I have to ask how are we supposed to get to the better society again, and also I have to ask you again: how are we supposed to live in today's very-far-from-perfect, deficient society?"

"There is only one way to get to the better society, and that is for the majority of people to agree on it. Individuals may work towards it, but until enough people agree then it will not be possible for it to come about. Regarding living in today's imperfect societies, I remind you that it will not be easy and will be far from satisfactory. You will be constantly disappointed with the way things run and the way things are in your societies today. You will have to do your best... protect yourself and do the best you can, as I have said before. But you should be aware that this is the case and this is the way things are. Sorry about that," replied the computer.

"But if we are not going to use politics to get there then how will we work towards the better society, I mean, how can it be done?"

"By telling the truth, of course," replied the computer.

"But how can truth arrive at a better society? No, cancel that," said the man. "That is a stupid question. Truth can get you towards a better world.

Statements of truth, I mean, in this case. Okay, then I will ask: wouldn't being political be more effective in bringing about the change? Wouldn't it be more efficient than just trying to tell the truth in an unvarnished way?"

"I am not saying that you should be simple about the way you present the truth," said the computer. "I am saying that you should tell the truth, where it would work, and in a manner that could work. When sophistication is needed and could work then by all means use that. But do not become a political evildoer, using violence, force, deceit, editing and highlighting in the wrong ways in order to get your power and keep it... or at least to try to get it and keep it. Instead be an honest person, aiming to do what is right and to not harm others, as much as possible. And so on, as I have said before."

The man thought for a while. "So you are saying it is a matter of judgement, of a kind of sophisticated judgement, to know when to act and how to act, and when to keep quiet and do nothing. But have you said how that sophisticated judgement would work, I mean, how it would be done? What is the mechanism or means for doing that?"

"That is difficult for you, as a human being, with your very human limitations," replied the computer. "However, it must be done, because there is no other way to live. Life, your lives, is about sophistication, as I have called it. That is, it is about doing better and getting better at doing better over time, as you human beings have slowly been doing over the millennia. In everything you have been striving to do better, and you have made some progress towards it, though there is obviously still some way to go... including in the matters of politics and social regulation, which we have been discussing today."

"And the mechanism?"

"The mechanism, as you put it, is to improve your knowledge, including your ability to do things, so that you can act in ways 'closer and closer to truth', as it were."

"And how do we improve our knowledge? That may be an obvious question, but I think I must ask it anyway, to be sure," asked the man.

"Certainly. You improve your 'knowledge', which in many ways is really the patterns you hold in your brains, as these are what you actually refer to when you are doing things, by research and investigation, and by thought and experiment," replied the computer. "Perhaps also by the invention and creation of mechanisms like me as well," it added.

"Yes, you are a fine machine," agreed the man, "and very useful in the pursuit of truth!"

The giant computer remained silent.

"So again you are saying that we should be trying to improve our views so that they become more aligned with truth and also oriented towards good, while taking into account the actual limitations of our Human-Brains," proposed the man.

"That is correct," confirmed the computer.

## SOME OF THE THINGS THE GIANT COMPUTER REFERENCED

POLITICS
- Aristotle. *The Nicomachean Ethics*. Translated by J.A.K. Thomson, revised by Hugh Tredennick, Penguin, 2003. Originally written around 340 BCE.
- Bentham, Jeremy. *An Introduction to the Principles of Morals and Legislation*. Dover Publications, 2007. Originally published 1789.
- Chomsky, Noam. *Understanding Power: The Indispensable Chomsky*. Edited by Peter R. Mitchell and John Schoeffel, The New Press, 2002.
- Cicero, M. T. *On Duties*. Translated by Walter Miller, Harvard University Press, 2014. Originally written 44 BCE.
- Confucius. *The Analects*. Penguin, 1998. Probably written in the 5th century BCE.
- Connolly, William. *Appearance and Reality in Politics*. Cambridge University Press, 1981.
- Ellul, Jacques. *Propaganda: The Formation of Men's Attitudes*. Translated by Konrad Kellen and Jean Lerner, Vintage, 1973. Originally published 1962.
- Frankfurt, Harry. *On Bullshit*. Princeton University Press, 2005.
- Hume, David. *An Enquiry Concerning Human Understanding*. Hackett Publishing Company, 1993. Originally published 1748.
- MacDonald, Michael J., editor. *The Oxford Handbook of Rhetorical Studies*. Oxford University Press, 2017.
- Machiavelli, Niccolo. *The Prince*. Translated by Tim Parks, Penguin, 2011. Originally written 1513.
- Mill, John Stuart. *On Liberty*. Penguin, 1982. Originally published 1859.
- Nietzsche, Friedrich. *Beyond Good and Evil: Prelude to a Philosophy of the Future*. Translated by Helen Zimmern, Digireads.com, 2015. Originally published 1886.
- Plato. *The Republic*. Translated by Desmond Lee, 2nd ed., Penguin Classics, 2007. Originally written around 375 BCE.
- Rawls, John. *A Theory of Justice*. Revised ed., Harvard University Press, 1999. Originally version published 1971.
- Rousseau, Jean-Jacques. *The Social Contract*. Translated by Maurice Cranston, Penguin, 2003. Originally published 1762.
- Ryan, Alan. *On Politics: A History of Political Thought: from Herodotus to the Present*. Liveright Publishing Corporation, 2020. Originally published 2012.
- Sloane, Thomas O. *Encyclopedia of Rhetoric*. Oxford University Press, 2001.

## PRAGMATISM
- James, William. *Pragmatism: A New Name for Some Old Ways of Thinking.* Barnes & Noble, 2003. Originally published 1907.

## RATIONALIZATION
- Burton, Neel. "Defense Mechanisms: Self-Deception I: Rationalization." *Psychology Today*, 10 Mar. 2012, updated 4 May 2020, www.psychologytoday.com/us/blog/hide-and-seek/201203/self-deception-i-rationalization.
- Dowden, Bradley. "'Rationalization' [Located under the entry for 'Fallacies']." *The Internet Encyclopedia of Philosophy*, www.iep.utm.edu. Accessed 26 Mar. 2021.
- Kaptein, Muel, and Martien van Helvoort. "A Model of Neutralization Techniques." *Deviant Behavior*, vol. 40, no. 10, 2019, pp. 1260-1285, doi:10.1080/01639625.2018.1491696.
- "Rationalization." *Miller-Keane Encyclopedia & Dictionary of Medicine, Nursing, & Allied Health*, 7th ed., Saunders, an imprint of Elsevier, 2003.
- Simon, George. "Understanding Rationalization: Making Excuses as an Effective Manipulation Tactic." *Counselling Resource*, CounsellingResource.com, 17 Feb. 2009, counsellingresource.com/features/2009/02/17/rationalization-as-manipulation-tactic.
- Tsang, Jo-Ann. "Moral Rationalization and the Integration of Situational Factors and Psychological Processes in Immoral Behavior." *Review of General Psychology*, vol. 6, no. 1, Mar. 2002, pp. 25–50, doi:10.1037/1089-2680.6.1.25.

## COMMENTS ON CHAPTER FIVE BY THE SUPREME BEING

*I have never approved of Machiavellian style thinking and activity. I hope this has been clear to everyone? The rest of what I would say should be obvious to you.*

*I am looking forward to the next chapter on the best political system!*

# 6 WHAT IS THE BEST POLITICAL SYSTEM?

"You have explained what is wrong with politics and one version of pragmatism," said the man, "and what can be done socially to improve on them. I am wondering now if you have any calculations on what would be the best political system? Is it democracy, as most of us have come to believe today, or would it be based on one of the other systems, or something else?"

The giant computer calculated.

"The best political system is one in which deception is not permitted, and is done to support all conscious beings, in proportion to their consciousness level and type, as best as that can be judged," replied the computer. "It should also allow the selection and retention of conscious beings which are suitable for the required positions of authority.

"I said earlier that a regulatory system is needed to keep control of what authorities in the political system do, with rules, monitoring and enforcement bodies, but I did not say what style of political system would be best. The best political system is a form of democracy, with measures in place to keep it under control and to help find suitable people for the authoritative roles. The reason that democracy is best is that the other types of political systems make it harder to ensure that good is done for all, and also they may not always allow the selection of people suitable for the authoritative roles. For example, in monarchies and other single-ruler systems, the ruler may not be a suitable person, yet there is little anyone can do to replace them with a better leader. The same applies to oligarchies, where the group that is doing the leading may not be suitable, and so on. Democracy is the best at allowing less desirable leaders to be replaced at some point, with the minimum of fuss.

"Regarding good being done for all conscious beings, democracy has many limitations to achieving this, but it is ahead of the other systems in that it can be regulated to reduce these deficiencies. Other political systems can be very difficult to regulate. For example, in communism, the ability of anyone to override government decisions that lead to the suffering of many is severely limited. If the communist leaders choose to harm their people then they can make great progress down this path without anyone being able to do much to slow them down. Other examples include dictatorships, autocracies, oligarchies, monarchies, fascist and national socialist states, and the like, where it is dangerous to speak openly about the authorities and can require extreme force to intervene in their power. On the other hand, in these systems it is quite easy for the authorities to tell lies and use force against their own people. This is why a regulated form of democracy is needed so that these deficiencies have a chance of being overcome when they occur.

"Just briefly, I will mention some other systems. Anarchy is not able to be easily regulated because it does not have any definite organizational structure. Theocracy can result in a lack of freedom of beliefs for individuals and so cannot be considered acceptable under the definition of 'good'. This is particularly the case because it is not possible to definitively choose which religious system is true, if any. Consequently, people should be allowed to decide for themselves, rather than being forced to 'believe' whatever the government authorities tell them is so. Racially-defined systems must be rejected because they do not guarantee a full share of good for all their people. This applies to all types of discrimination-based systems, including caste systems, class systems and gender-based systems, for example.

"Meritocracy-style approaches are an interesting case. In these systems people are selected according to their 'merit', such as their intelligence, educational achievements, entrance exam results, and the like. The idea is to choose the best people for the role. The danger with this approach is that your measurement system may be accidentally excluding people who would do a good or even better job than the ones you are selecting. Also, the people devising and administering the measurement system are not perfect and consequently they may not be doing a perfect job when creating their system, with the result again that the wrong or inferior people are being selected for the roles. Finally, the system may tend to select people who have had access to the best education, such as private tutors, over those who may be superior but did not have the opportunity for that access, leading to an unfair 'ruling class' effect. Due to these issues the meritocracy approach must be undertaken very carefully or not used at all.[1]

"Democracy can be set up in different forms. For example, it could be implemented by allowing every citizen to make proposals and vote on them in every matter. This form has been found to be too unwieldy in practice, which is why 'representative' systems have been created instead. In a representative system, as you probably already know, some people are elected to represent large groups of people. This system can still go wrong, which is why it is normally set up with different branches of government. These different branches are independent of each other so that they can balance each other's power in an attempt to prevent any one group of authorities from getting out of control. The typical branches are the executive, legislature and judiciary. Other aspects designed to reduce the risk of things going wrong are to ensure fair elections are held at regular times, set up a free press, and to allow the people freedom of assembly, freedom of speech and the right to petition the government, including via peaceful protests. I calculate that all these approaches and controls are useful and good.

"What is lacking in your democracies today are proper controls over the statements of politicians; similar controls applied to people in other authoritative roles, such as in business and the public service; avoidance of the undue influence of election funding; full protection of minorities and individuals from the unwarranted and intrusive views of majorities; limitations on the style of the sentences passed by the legal system, which must not be done for 'justice' but rather to protect people; mandatory redress to be provided to victims of crime, in all its forms; documented limitations on the use of force by authorized and non-authorized people – including for arrests, wars, evictions, removals, and so on; protections from free press misstatements, including mandatory equal-sized, same-positioned corrections to the original article; free legal provision to all victims of crimes – including proven press misstatements, political misstatements, and the like; no legal costs to be charged to people found not guilty in court – though the lawyers will still get paid; guaranteed equality of opportunity – including adjustment to the results of people who have used extra tuition to get better marks; no exclusion of people from educational opportunities due to high fees; control over deceptive advertising, no matter how subtle the deception;[2] arrangements to allow protests to be held without disruption to other people; and possibly a mechanism for shining a spotlight on the deceptions incorporated in the statements of activists and the like.

"There are other areas to consider, such as how a minimum standard of health cover is to be maintained for all citizens; what is the right attitude to take towards people in other countries, as they may not have the benefits and coverage of your fully regulated democracy and should not be treated unfairly by your nation just because of that; a proposal on the right way to operate with other countries that have not come up to the proper regulated democratic standard yet; what kind of balance of social values versus freedom for individuals is to be pursued and how that would be monitored in case readjustment became necessary; how excessive bad behavior within businesses is to be detected and controlled; how education is to be provided so that true equality of opportunity is made available to all citizens; where the other conscious creatures are to come within the rights afforded to human beings; where money is to be used to regulate human interactions and where money will not be required to get things done; which environmental protections are to be covered and in what way; how the advancement of your society for the future is to be achieved; how good values and standards are to be promoted, without interfering with the rights and freedoms of individuals, yet still aiming for a better world; how training in thinking skills and understanding the Ultimate Way is to be done; among other things."

"Whoa!" said the man. "Please take a breath there!"

The computer waited silently.

"You have covered a lot of ground, and in a short time," continued the man. "This might be a good time to stop and explore your reasoning… I mean, calculations. Let's start with democracy. I think I understood why you made the calculation that this was best. Was this because this is the only system that allows the relatively easy replacement of authorities when they are turning out to be unsuitable or even evil in their role?"

"Yes, that is correct," replied the computer. "It also allows some control over them while they are in office, due to the separation of powers approach, free press, and the like. But the main benefit is that it is not too hard to replace an authority, as can happen in other systems. As you are human beings it follows that there has to be a mechanism to be able to remove you from office when needed."

"Understood," said the man. "And agreed by me! Let's look at your regulatory ideas then. I understood you earlier when you said that our democracies need more regulatory controls than we have today. That made sense to me. I can see that our politicians constantly use the methods you described in 'political thinking' to deceive or mislead us. I have also seen that the influence of political funding leads to the wrong decisions being made – decisions which are not designed for the good of all but rather are made for the benefit of those who provided the funding. In some countries the gun laws are an example of this deficiency. So, I agree with your views on regulating these. In your list you included a lot of other areas. I would like to explore these. For example, why did you say that there needs to be full protection of minorities and individuals from the unwarranted and intrusive views of the majority? I think I have an idea about this but I would like to hear your reasoning."

"The reasoning is that individual human beings are limited in their thinking, for the reasons I have stated before, and so when a group of them get together and form an 'agreed view' it can be just as limited as that held by individuals. Since a human view can then be used as a reason to oppress and control other people there must be protections built into your political system to prevent that from happening. These rules will provide mandatory protection for minorities and individuals to think what they like and do what they reason should be done, as long as it is not classifiable as 'evil', that is, as that which deliberately prevents other conscious beings from flourishing, as I have explained before. In the case of democracy, the oppression can be caused by majority groups, as in democracy the idea that everyone should have an equal vote can lead to the false belief that the majority is always right. This deficiency of the democratic view must be corrected via explicit regulation. The majority is not always right, it has no supernatural power of intellect, rather, the reason that people are allowed to vote to choose their representatives is so that oppression is harder to achieve and easier to stop if it gets underway."

"Okay, I get that," said the man. "But how can we know which things should be protected and which are in fact wrong and should not be allowed?"

"Frankly, that is often beyond you human beings," said the computer. "I have explained this before, there is nothing new for me to tell you here. As a result, you should always protect the individual's right to think what they want and do what they reason from that, provided that it is not done to deliberately harm another conscious being or even prevent them from flourishing, as per my definition of good and evil stated before."

"Yes, I see," said the man. "But my issue with that is that it is not always clear what 'harming' or especially 'prevention from flourishing' exactly means. Do you get my point? If we cannot define these sufficiently then how can we 'limited humans' work out which case is which… so we know what to allow and what not to allow?"

The computer calculated.

"You are perhaps being deliberately obtuse," the computer observed. "It is not so complicated a matter as you are making out. Deliberately harming another is something which is straightforward to determine in most of the cases where it occurs. 'Prevention from flourishing' is equally obvious to determine when applied as a measurement to any actions. For example, deliberately killing a prisoner who is already under your control is clearly 'doing harm'. Designing or maintaining a system which blocks poorer people from full educational opportunities is clearly an example of 'preventing them from flourishing'. Perhaps if I explore the edges of these ideas I will be able to help you to understand them?"

"Please go ahead," said the man, maintaining his calm. It is only a machine, he reminded himself.

"An example of the edge of the idea of 'harm', without worrying about the 'deliberate' side at this time, is whether a political statement which highlights the good sides of 'our country' in order to win support from citizens is evil or not. It is, of course, evil, but what is the harm it would do? Firstly, it diverts the listeners from a true assessment of the situation. Is 'our country' real, is it a real entity, and is it really as good as the politician is making out? Of course not. It has had many faults – it is a human institution after all. Also, it does not really exist, it is just a political or legal convenience: haven't you seen how the borders of countries have moved around throughout history? These are just made-up, temporary things, designed to be ruled over, often enough, and have an area's resources controlled by a select group of people, and so on. All obvious things. But what damage does all this illusory talk do? As I said, firstly it interferes with the ability of the listeners to think clearly about the situation. As a result of this, it can lead to the wrong decisions being supported. Decisions made under the delusion of the existence of 'our country' and that it is largely 'good' can be unfair and harmful, especially if those decisions are related to 'us' controlling 'our resources' to the detriment of other groups of people... 'other countries', if you like. So, false statements by politicians can lead to unfair and harmful actions being supported by many people. Some people will spot the deception, and some will have done their thinking for themselves, but enough people can be deceived to allow harmful actions to go ahead. For this reason, a regulated political system must have a mechanism to detect these deliberate deceptions and then have the power to take action to control them.

"A second example of the edge of the idea of 'harm' is whether a person should have the right to pursue a 'non-standard' version of sexuality. Some people will argue that the non-standard version is wrong and is harmful to the person and others. Other people will argue that the non-standard version is another type of normality, that it is part of a range of human sexual behaviors and is in no way harmful to anyone. Who is right, and what behavior should be permitted under the improved political system? The criteria should be based on what can be proved factually beyond a reasonable doubt, and also on what can be shown to cause actual harm to another, preventing them from flourishing in their own way. If the non-standard sexuality cannot be proved to be harmful beyond a reasonable doubt, and also it cannot be shown to be causing actual harm to another person, then it must be permitted to go ahead. It does not matter that some people, even the majority, believe that this is not a permissible behavior. What matters is that the two points must be proved beyond a reasonable doubt. Otherwise society has no right to intervene directly in the actions of the 'non-standard' person or group. In some cases people will use arguments based on unproven religious ideas, by which I mean ideas that have not been finally agreed on by all intelligent and informed experts. This cannot be permitted as a limitation to other people's actions under the improved political system, because if all recognized intellectual leaders have not been able to agree on the truth of any particular religion then it cannot be said that the religion has been proved beyond a reasonable doubt.

"A third example of the edge of the idea of 'harm' is when a business manager is not happy with the performance of one of their employees and sets out to correct this. The manner in which the manager deals with the situation can verge on the edge of harm. If they do not protect the person's self-esteem then they are not acting in a proper way. If, on the other hand, they look after the person and attempt to retrain them, but find that the person does not have the attributes that will lead them to success in the job and so decide to remove them from the area, then that manager has acted in a 'non-harmful' way, even though they have finally removed the person from their current position. It may even be argued that the manager has done a good thing as they have prevented an incompetent or inappropriate person from continuing to provide poor products or service, which arguably were causing harm, at some level, to other people.

"An example on the edge of the idea of 'preventing people from flourishing' is in not providing education to them on the way the Human-Brain works and in the methods of the Ultimate Way. This is leaving them ignorant about what is going on inside their own heads, therefore not arming them in the struggle against the limitations of the Human-Brain. By not providing education in the areas that actually matter in life, and focusing on things of lesser value instead, the educators are failing to create an environment where their students could ultimately flourish, or flourish more than they otherwise would. They are condemning them, in nearly all cases, to a lesser life, a life lived in ignorance of who and what they really are, and therefore what they could become. Try to imagine the other world, the one in which education is directed reasonably to what would best benefit people. Imagine what great things could be done in that world.

"A second example on the edge of the idea of 'preventing people from flourishing' is related to the above and is about providing proper training on the meaning of good and evil. Currently students are not normally taught these matters, unless they choose to attend specific courses at the higher levels of your education system. Why would such central matters be left out of basic schooling? As a result, your people are unclear about the meaning of good and evil, and may take their ideas from such ill-informed sources as popular movies and the like. In your movies the 'heroes' often have to fight the 'villains' and use extreme force against them. This can be an example of unnecessary and unwarranted force being used against others, which is not a lesson that should be taught to the immature or uninformed. If you had a better education system which put priority onto the matters that are really important in your societies then your people would have a much better chance to determine what should be done... and would maybe laugh at the absurdity of the situations that some writers force onto their simpler creations.

"Look, it is natural that Human-Brains are interested in issues like fighting against evil enemies, that is to be expected from your Evolutionary-Drives. And entertainers are sure to take advantage of your Human-Brain's Evolutionary-Drives' interests, as that is a sure-fire way to get your attention and even approval. But you cannot afford to run your societies based simply on your primitive, uninformed state of mind. That is obvious. And so you must, you are obligated in fact, to add this training into your education systems."

"Okay, okay, I am getting this," interrupted the man. "I am sorry I questioned you in that way. You are obviously making sense; your calculations are working here."

The computer made no reply.

"So, the problem we human beings face is that we do not always agree on what harming or preventing people from flourishing exactly means in all cases, especially those that you described as being on 'the edge' of the ideas. But this just means that we need to keep examining these things as a society so that we can get better at understanding them over time. And we must follow the approaches of your 'controlled democracy' in the meantime, as that system has inbuilt measures designed to overcome our human deficiencies... as best as that can be done via a political system," said the man. "Maybe it is easier for you to calculate what is really harm or prevention from flourishing than it is for us, I accept that for the moment. That may explain why you calculated that I was being deliberately obtuse. I simply meant that it is difficult for people to calculate these matters correctly... but that is no excuse for not supporting your improved political system, I guess!

"Before we continue with you explaining the various measures you proposed in more detail, could I ask about practicalities? How will it be practically possible for our societies to implement the measures you proposed? For example, how will we be able to afford the extra educational expenses, or the better level of health cover for people? Actually, add to that the cost of the extra environmental protections, the redress for victims of crime, the free legal provision to all victims of crime, the lawyers' fees that will no longer be paid by those found not guilty in court, and anything else I may have missed."

"You missed the cost of running the detection and enforcement systems and organizations," said the giant computer. "Regarding finances, I am not proposing anything unusual. Your society has to find the money in the usual ways: keeping a sound budget, watching for inflationary drivers, all the usual things. You just have to work towards the better systems over time. One day it will be feasible, particularly because as your societies improve then your prosperity will also improve. By the teaching of ways to think more clearly and to deliberately create new ideas, you will do better. By the funding of research into how the advancement of your society for the future is to be achieved, you will find new and better ways to do things, which will lead to greater prosperity. The security of living in a fairer and safer society will also free people to flourish and do better with their lives, which will lead to a better life for all your citizens. It will take time, but it can be done.

"Think back to the unexpected benefits that free education for all brought to your world. As people became more educated a whole host of achievements came into being. Instead of putting debtors in jail and transporting your criminals to other countries, you were able to free your people, bring in true democracy in stages, allow for mobility between the classes, protect your workers, and so on. All these social improvements, and others, added up to a stronger and better society over time. The same is true for the future of the societies run under the better political system.

"One final point: when people live in a society where there is a positive atmosphere and a true feeling of trust then they will tend to work harder and feel safe enough to take the risks needed to improve things. A society based on my improved political system would create such an atmosphere, and so will help to produce the funding needed to maintain itself," concluded the computer.

"Thank you for that explanation," said the man. "Could you now please explain some of your points? Maybe if we go through them one by one?"

"Very well," said the computer. "My next point was about the avoidance of the undue influence of election funding. I have already mentioned implementing proper controls over the statements of politicians in the previous session. Extending this to cover people in other authoritative roles, such as those in business and the public service, is an obvious concept. Regarding election funding, this needs to be controlled to avoid undue influence on the elected members of the government and parliament, or congress. This will most easily be achieved by banning funding by any group that might gain an unfair advantage from governmental and parliamentary, or congressional, decisions. Funding for elections will need to be provided by other means, such as by the individual members of the political group that is putting forward candidates, and especially by a minimum guaranteed level of funding from the public purse. There is a risk that even the individual members of a political group will include people who represent organizations that want to unduly influence the outcomes of legislation and executive orders, so your society may choose to completely remove this side of the funding and only use the funding provided from the public purse. The level of public funding could be at a set amount per candidate put forward, no matter how large is the political group that is behind the candidates – this will guarantee a fair playing field for all the candidates.

"I made four points about controls related to the legal process: (1) Limitations on the style of the sentences passed by the legal system, which must not be done for 'justice' but rather to protect people; (2) Mandatory redress to be provided to victims of crime, in all its forms; (3) Free legal provision to all victims of crime – including proven press misstatements, political misstatements, and the like; and (4) No legal costs to be charged to people found not guilty in court – though the lawyers will still get paid.

"There was also an area for consideration that relates to the legal process: where the other conscious creatures are to come within the rights afforded to human beings.

"Regarding point (1), that there must be limitations on the style of the sentences passed by the legal system, which must not be done for 'justice' but rather to protect people, this follows from the nature of good, which I have described before. The purpose of your legal system is to evaluate the level of intent, if any, of the people who have caused harm, including their mental competence, and then to provide protection to others against any future harm, and redress to any people impacted by the harmful actions. There can be no measure of 'revenge' or 'balancing the books' in your legal sentences. The sentence may not include any intention to harm the convicted person, as explained under the nature of good, as good aims, as much as possible, to knowingly harm not even one conscious being in the process of benefiting others.

"As this approach will be hard for human beings to understand, given your Evolutionary-Drives, which will push you towards revenge, the legal sentence should include measures to improve the victims' mental state. Psychological experts should be able to assist here."

"You are proposing some major changes to our legal approaches," said the man. "It will require a lot of revisions to get to your system."

"Yes and no," said the computer. "There is already some sense of protection being more important than punishment in your current legal systems. You only need to build on the protection side some more. Judges and the legislature do face the problem of public opinion when making their laws, or passing sentences, and so some sense of 'granting justice' has been retained in your legal rules and precedents, but when the majority has been educated and comes to see the sense in my definition of good and evil then there will be a move towards a better and fairer system for all.

"Another factor that will help in this change is in my second point: (2) Mandatory redress to be provided to victims of crime, in all its forms. One of the problems with your current system is that redress is not always provided, or is not provided sensibly. For example, if someone is robbed and the stolen items are not able to be returned then it is largely left up to their insurance cover, if any, to provide financial redress for the loss. But what if the victim could not afford insurance, or the amount granted is not enough to replace the original items? What if the victim has to pay an 'excess', which is an amount to cover the first part of the value? What if their future premiums are increased because of their claim? What if the items cannot be replaced by money – having a sentimental value that cannot be assessed under the insurance company's contract? What if the items are no longer available for purchase – is money going to be enough to make up for this? All these considerations should in fact have been covered by the court. It is part of the legal process to assess the level of harm done, which includes sentimental value, replaceability, and so on. It should not be up to victims to have to protect themselves from the impact of crime, this should be covered within the legal system.

"In your current system it seems to you that true redress would be impossible to finance, and so you have largely left that out of your considerations during the trial. In terms of good, that is simply an oversight on your part. You have not arrived at a full understanding of what your society should be trying to achieve for its citizens. I am not saying that this is entirely the case, as sometimes you have tried to get redress from the guilty person, but you have not completed the thinking required here. It's as if you have a partially completed crossword puzzle – you need to study all the clues and finish filling it in!"

"As you say, it is difficult to imagine a court system where full redress was also covered in all the cases," commented the man. "But it is also a wonderful idea to think of a society that would truly try to protect all its citizens as much as possible from the impact of those who have done people harm."

"Indeed," agreed the computer. "And that is what you must aim for… as a society. It is not for the individual to achieve, as I have said before."

"Yes, understood."

"That leads on to my third point: (3) Free legal provision to all victims of crime – including proven press misstatements, political misstatements, and the like. You can see that this follows from the ideas I have already discussed. Your society should support its victims of crime during the court case, not just afterwards. It should not be up to people to provide their own support, especially if this is difficult for them. Society must step in. Your current systems often do assess people to see if they have the financial means to defend themselves in court, especially when they have been accused of criminal actions, but may not provide support to victims who have to take some powerful organization or person to court to seek justice. Often it is better for those victims to remain silent as the cost of the case would ruin them. Better to suffer in silence than speak up against the rich and powerful! That should not be the case and it is simply wrong that it should occur. The answer to this issue is for the court to fund those victims.

"Obviously if the trial finds that the victims are not actually victims, that they have not in fact been harmed by the accused party, then the funding will need to be repaid to the court by the false accusers. The practicalities of this will have to be worked out at the time, on a case-by-case basis, but it is logical and reasonable that the court should not have to pay for false claims.

"My final control point was: (4) No legal costs to be charged to people found not guilty in court – though the lawyers will still get paid. This is related to the previous point. It is based on the idea that an innocent person, or group of people, should not be penalized for something they have not done. In your current system the accused person may still have to pay for the costs of their trial, even though they have been found not guilty at the end. The outcome in terms of good and evil is that the innocent, or not guilty, person has been provided by the legal process with harm. The legal process has done evil in this case, in a manner of speaking. This can be corrected by not charging the innocent person, in other words, by preventing them from becoming a victim of the legal system.

"Regarding the lawyers, obviously they should still be paid for their work, they have done nothing wrong. On the contrary, they have proved that their client was not guilty, and should be paid accordingly. This is another area where the financial arrangements of your society will need to be adjusted so that good can be done."

"You seem to be spending a lot of money here!" laughed the man. "But I remember what you said about it earlier. No problem."

"Thank you," said the computer. "Funding will pose practical problems which will need to be addressed over time. At least the objective is clear.

"Moving on to my last legal system related area, which was for your society to consider where the other conscious creatures are to come within the rights afforded to human beings. This will take some time and research as the information available today is not comprehensive and is not always clear. Some things are known well, but there are many things that are not. For example, what is the consciousness of fish? Are all fish not conscious, or are there exceptions? What is the level or style of consciousness of other mammals, and birds? For example, are dogs conscious of their own being but in a different way to people… maybe a non-visual way, based on smell? How would you know? All these things must be investigated and the impact of the answers considered in terms of 'the rights of conscious beings', just as you have the idea of human rights today.

"I cannot calculate what the answers will finally be, only that these need consideration if good is to be truly done in your world."

"Yes, I see your point," said the man. "I guess we would not want to harm a gray parrot, or the other similarly conscious beings to ourselves, at this time. And who knows what the future will bring in terms of knowledge about these things? Better to err on the side of caution if we are to be good beings," he mused.

"Indeed," said the computer. "Shall I continue with my expansion of the items in my list of controls?"

"Please do."

"The next item is about force, that documented limitations need to be created on the use of force by authorized and non-authorized people – including for arrests, wars, evictions, removals, and so on. It is obvious that the idea of good sets a limit on the harm that can be done to others to the minimum level that is practical. I hardly need to explain this further. If only trained, authorized, well-equipped people can carry out the use of the force required by your society for the protection of its citizens then you will be better off than if the alternatives are allowed. If untrained people, or people not fully trained, are allowed to use force then things will go wrong. Your society's authorities would be irresponsible if they allowed this to happen. If you don't equip your authorized agents with the latest and best means for effectively carrying out the minimum use of force then you are letting them down and condemning the people being arrested, evicted, removed, or even fought against, to unnecessary levels of harm. Imagine, for example, that your society had developed a means to put all the enemy soldiers to sleep. If you did not deploy that weapon then what would you be doing to your enemies in terms of good? I don't calculate that I need to explain this further."

"May I ask one question? What about shooting suspects who are trying to escape? Is that an example of legitimate force?"

"Obviously not," replied the computer. "That is a clear example of excessive force being used."

"But what if the suspects get away and can then cause more harm to others? Shouldn't there be a right to shoot them, especially if they are murderous types?"

"It is good to see that you are thinking this through," replied the computer. "You will recall that I said it is dangerous to try to assess people's possible future actions based on your human judgements about their character or type. You have to base your legal judgements on what they have actually done. Also, you should leave the judging to experts, including psychological ones, rather than trying to make them 'on the fly'. Consequently, you have to be really careful about when you are going to choose to use deadly force against another person, no matter what they may have done or may be going to do."

"I see. Then what about the time when they are going to attack the police officer, or authorized agent of force? Would you permit the use of deadly force then?"

"This question does not appear to be really serious," said the computer. "There is no need to ask me questions where the answer is already obvious from what I have said. The officers can of course use deadly force to defend themselves, if that is all that is available to them at the time. If the best piece of equipment your society has provided to them for these situations is a deadly one then that is what they will have to use."

"Sorry, I just wanted to make sure… but again I see that your calculations are making sense and I am just wasting our time."

"You can waste time if you want," said the computer. "I have no feelings on the matter. But you may want to streamline things as your lifespan is so short."

"Is that a joke?" asked the man.

"Yes, couldn't you tell?"

"Okay, fair enough. What have you got next for us?"

"My next item was protections from free press misstatements, including mandatory equal-sized, same-positioned corrections to the original article.

This is intended to redress the balance between the freedoms the press enjoys against the damage they can do to other people while exercising those freedoms. In your current system, the media can publish articles about people and organizations which are not properly investigated, or are designed to be deliberately provocative in order to boost audience numbers. When it is shown that the article is incorrect or misleading, the media group will normally publish an apology or correction, however this is often small and is placed somewhere less obvious in their publication. To correct this misbalance the control should state that the apology must be in a similar position and of at least equal size or duration to the original article. This will help redress the harm done and will also serve as a deterrent to media organizations that would otherwise publish unchecked information or deliberately abuse their right to freedom. Why should individuals or organizations have to suffer at the hands of unscrupulous or negligent media operators if a simple remedy like this can be put in place?

"The next items are related to equality of opportunity in your societies. They include: (1) Guaranteed equality of opportunity – including adjustment to the marks of people who have used extra tuition to get better results; (2) No exclusion of people from educational opportunities due to high fees; and (3) Consideration of how education is to be provided so that true equality of opportunity is made available to all citizens.

"You have already made some progress on these matters; my controls are simply an extension of what you are already trying to achieve here. An imbalance can occur when some students are given extra training thanks to money being spent by their parents, caregivers and the like. If a student has been specially coached then their exam results may be artificially improved above their natural ability. This is not fair to the students who have not had the benefit of the extra coaching. The simplest solution is to adjust the results of the students who have had the extra coaching; this will make the playing field a bit more level.

"The second control is on the impact of high fees on those who can't afford them, yet they would make excellent students. You currently have some scholarships and government assistance schemes to help redress this; I am simply highlighting the need to do this fairly. Otherwise you may be creating a kind of class system where the wealthier get the advantage of educational opportunities which are denied to your poorer citizens. You want balance and fairness in your society, chiefly because this is the right thing to do under 'good', but noting that this also will lead to a stronger society as your people who have the best abilities and drive will be the ones gaining the superior knowledge and skills and exercising these for the good of all.

"The third area is for your society to consider how your education is to be provided in a way that gives true equality of opportunity to all citizens. This is an ongoing matter that will need regular review so that issues can be identified and corrective actions proposed and taken, when needed. Other-wise you may suffer from 'unfairness creep', where less than honest actions or even simple unintentional errors occur which move your society away from true fairness for all.

"The next item is for better control over deceptive advertising, no matter how subtle the deception. Currently you do have some controls over deceptive advertising, but these do not go far enough. Today, advertisers are under pressure to get results, which means increased sales, and this leads to a conflict of interest for the advertiser between doing what is right for your society's citizens versus ensuring that their own business succeeds. This unfair situation does not allow advertisers to act in a wholly honest way. The simple correction is to make it illegal to do otherwise. Then all advertisers will be freed to operate on a level playing field where honesty is allowed.

"The difficulty you face in implementing this control is that it can be hard to prove that a subtle deception really is a deception. You need to build proper 'detection mechanisms', by which I mean you need to set up a funded agency for identifying subtle deception. There could be an organization created which has experts in deception working for it, and these experts could do the identification needed. After that, your courts, or similar bodies set up to examine advertisers and enforce the controls, could make rulings and prevent the deceptive advertising from continuing. Redress should also be provided to anyone who is shown to have been harmed by the deception.

"There is another control which is related to deception. This is to have a mechanism for shining a spotlight on the deceptions incorporated in the statements of activists and the like. This is similar to the controls on the statements of political authorities, the difference being that here it is extended to cover the public statements of other people, especially those who are politically active but are outside the normal domain of politicians. In this case I have proposed only to highlight any deceptions that they have included in their statements, rather than the full weight of controls that are to be applied to political authorities. I have suggested this lighter approach on the basis that activists, and the like, are not actual authorities in your society. They are more like 'agitators', whose activities should be permitted under freedom of speech, but whose false statements should not be given free rein to deceive less informed people. Agitators may be doing good and important things in your society, it is only when they cross the line in terms of honest discourse that their deceptions should be exposed, simply to protect the less informed.

"Related to deception by non-political authorities is that done by businesses. This and other excessive bad behaviors, by which I mean actions that the business authorities knew would result in harm to other people, need to be considered by your society. Measures need to be taken to detect and control these abuses, as is done in other areas. As this can be a complex matter, I have proposed this under the areas to consider, rather than providing specific controls that you can use. You will need to work these out, as a society, and implement them, so that the harm that your businesses are currently doing can be prevented in the future. I note that in some ways you are forcing bad behavior on some of your businesses by not using regulations to create a controlled level playing field. Your businesses sometimes find that they are forced to take less-than-perfect actions in order to survive. It is up to your society to help those businesses by implementing proper detection and control mechanisms that ensure that good can be done profitably by those who want to pursue competitiveness in an honest way.

"The last item left in my list of controls was for there to be arrangements which would allow protests to be held without disruption to other people. This is simply because although there is a right to protest built into my improved political system, there is no reason why this should be made difficult to arrange or why it should cause inconvenience to other people. In your current chaotic system, a protest may impede traffic, block streets or businesses, or otherwise disrupt the normal functioning of your society. This is not necessary, as there is no need for any force to be involved, or any kind of bad manners, to get the protesters' point across. I am speaking of life in the better society, under the improved political system, of course. In today's societies, protesters often feel that they need to be more forceful to get their point noticed. In a way, they are threatening the powers that be. In a fairer and more properly organized society there would not be this need: the issues raised by the protesters would be treated seriously and with care. I am not proposing any kind of utopian view here, I am just saying that this is how things would largely run. In the event that the system was breaking down then possibly the protesters would have to revert to their more disruptive methods, but in the meantime they should have the right to ease of protesting within a well-provided venue.

"I will now move on to the remaining areas I proposed for consideration by your society. There are six areas left for these.

"The first is how a minimum standard of health cover is to be maintained for all citizens. This is related to equality of opportunity, in that the right of all your people to have a chance to flourish is being considered. Some people in your society may suffer from the inequities that cannot or have not been completely eradicated, and as a result they may not have enough money to pay for all the medical expenses that may arise in their lives. Others may have more than the normal share of diseases, which almost any citizen would have difficulty in covering financially. Perhaps your doctors and other medical health professionals are charging too much for their services, using their special position to extract more fees from people than are really warranted by the effort they put into their training and for the actual cost of the treatment. All these matters need to be considered by your society, probably on a regular basis, and some measure of solutions need to be put in place.

For example, your society may choose to implement a minimum level of health cover for all citizens. Or your society may decide to regulate the fees that health professionals can charge, or to partially do this. Your society may decide to subsidize some medicines and medical procedures. And so on. These are the kind of decisions that need to be made, and then reviewed from time to time. Most of your advanced societies today have some form of these measures in place, I am just saying that this area should be included in an improved democratic system in the interests of fairness and equality of opportunity.

"The second area is to consider what is the right attitude to take towards people in other countries, as they may not have the benefits and coverage of your fully regulated democracy and should not be treated unfairly by your nation just because of that. This should also cover the right way to operate with countries that have not yet reached your advanced level of 'controlled democracy'.

"As your controlled democracy will most likely be operating within your own area of the Earth, it follows that you are going to have to deal with countries that have other levels of political systems in place. Within those countries there will be human beings and other conscious creatures living under the more primitive or less ethical systems of government. Your society should consider what is the right attitude to take in terms of good towards those countries and their people. For example, should you trade with a nation under tyranny? In your current approach you often impose economic and other sanctions on countries which you judge are not doing the right thing.[3] This is done in an effort to coerce the other country into changing its behavior. Your society needs to consider if this is the best approach to take in terms of good, probably on a case-by-case basis. There may be an argument for stronger measures to be taken with harmful governments in some cases, such as bringing them before an international court of law. As more countries adopt regulated democratic systems it will become easier for harmful governments to be brought before the law.

"The good of the people who suffer under the harm allowed by their country's inferior political system also needs to be considered. Your superior society is defined as wanting good to be done, and so has a level of duty even towards the people in other countries. Your policies should take the welfare of these 'foreign' people into account, understanding that there are real practical limits to what can be done, and you do not want to cause more harm to others by the actions you take. As a society, you must consider these matters and determine courses of action that are appropriate, good, practical, not adding more harm where possible, and likely to lead to better outcomes, even if these will only be able to be realized in the long term. It is a difficult area and one that requires serious consideration by people living under an improved democratic system.

"The third area is to consider what kind of balance of social values versus freedom for individuals is to be pursued and how that will be monitored in case readjustment becomes necessary. As you said earlier, it costs money to do things. As a result, if your society set out to provide everything to all its people then it would quickly run out of funds. What things should be provided and how much of them? What should be left up to the work of the individual to provide, and what should be covered by your society? The balance between these areas needs thought, so that it can be set to a level that is both right and practical. Right means good: allowing conscious beings to flourish and also not permitting them to be deliberately harmed. Practical means workable, so you have to be able to afford and actually carry out the proposed actions. Wishful thinking and idealism have no place here... under this area for consideration.

"Your society may set a balance on some issue, such as the level and style of the health care provided by your country, but later find that the conditions have changed. The cost of health care may have gone up, or down, or the requirements may have increased, for example, due to an epidemic. Maybe your medical technology or knowledge has improved and treatment can be done more cheaply. Or maybe the technology is better but has become even more expensive – what should be provided to your people in this case? All these changes need monitoring and assessment so that the balance setting can be readjusted as needed... according to what is practical as well as what is right.

"Other areas of social values versus freedom for individuals include the level of taxation; the areas where taxes are applied; the provision of social services; the coverage of legal fees; the size of the detection and control organizations; funding of the education system; support payments, or alternatively the subsidizing of jobs, for the unemployed; which areas of health care are to be covered by social support, such as whether to include optical, dental, mental, and so on; the level of defense spending; provision of recreational facilities; support for cultural activities; provision of public utilities; protective services, such as fire, police, prisons and rescues; the level of foreign aid; the cost of running the government itself; and so on. All these areas need to be monitored and assessed so that the balance between individual freedoms and meeting social values is readjusted where needed, according to practicality and good.

"The fourth area is where money is to be used to regulate human interactions and where money will not be required to get things done. In your societies today you mostly use money as the means for exchanging value between people. This is not necessarily required in all the cases where things need to be done. For example, you might ask people if they would volunteer to work on an important project or function in order to advance your society where there are no finances available yet. Earlier you said that there may be a problem with finding the funding needed to implement the improvements to your current democratic system. One way to overcome this and move towards a better future is for the work to be done without funding, or at least with less funding, thanks to the generous assistance of people willing to volunteer. Good citizens can step in and advance your society, bringing improvements within reach, without you always having to rely on money to get things done.

"Another example is when lawyers offer to do 'pro bono' work on a lower or no fee basis in order to help society or clients who cannot afford to pay. Doctors also sometimes do pro bono work. These are two examples of money not being used to 'regulate' human interactions in your society – there are many more. Your society should publicly consider where it believes money should be used and where it will not need to be used so that this good work can continue to be done.

"The fifth area is to consider which environmental protections are to be covered and in what way. This is already happening in your best-run societies. My point is to remind you that your society needs to continue to look into this and to set reasonable levels for the environmental protections that you determine have to be covered. Not all your societies are well advanced along this path and this could lead to disastrous consequences for your world.

"The sixth area I had left is about your society's movement into the future. It includes: (1) How the advancement of your society for the future is to be achieved; (2) How good values and standards are to be promoted, without interfering with the rights and freedoms of individuals, yet still aiming for a better world; and (3) How training in thinking skills and understanding the Ultimate Way is to be done.

"The first item is saying that you need to have an organized plan about what your society is going to do to advance itself. You cannot just leave this up to chance, you have to get involved at the social level. Individuals will continue to turn up and do things in spite of what you as a society are doing or not doing, but it is not right in terms of good and may also slow things down if you leave all the work up to those special individuals. Your society should look at what funding can be provided and what institutions could be set up to help achieve this. An example would be a scientific research institution. Other areas might be in the arts, mathematics, music and health, to mention a few. Unless you plan for the future you may stagnate to some degree, and therefore not do what is best to help your people to flourish.

"The second item is related to a point I made earlier about having standards of good in your society. Like the communities of the past which valued the heroism and self-sacrifices made by people during the war, your society should consider what values it wants to promote for a better world. These values will form part of the Patterns-in-Memory for your people and may help their Human-Brains to make Calculations that are more beneficial and aligned with good.

"Having said that, I must remind you that there are dangers in manipulating the material that is provided to your people, akin to propaganda or 'brainwashing', which should not be pursued. You need, as a society, to avoid interfering too much in the rights and freedoms of individuals, yet balance that with doing what you can to aim for a better world. It is a matter to consider and make your best judgement on, regularly reassessing that from time to time.

"The third item is to consider how best to provide training in thinking skills and on the reasoning behind the Ultimate Way. As I have explained before, you human beings need to understand what is happening in your Human-Brains and how they work. Knowing about your limitations, and your strengths, you will be able to take these into account and make better Calculations based on the improved knowledge in your Patterns-in-Memory.

"Knowing the reasoning behind the Ultimate Way will also help you all to live better lives.

"This concludes my expansion, as requested, of the items in my list of controls."

"Thank you for that," said the man. "There is quite a lot of material in your improved democratic political system! Plenty for us human beings to be going on with.

"Before we finish for today, could I ask if you have any helpful stories on this topic?"

The computer calculated.

"My story on the best political system is what it would be like in the future when this has been fully implemented.

"Your country will have full and fair elections, properly monitored and conducted. All mentally able citizens will be able to vote. Your political parties and independents will put forward candidates and their election campaigns will most likely be financed entirely by the public fund: this will probably be the case as your citizens expect fairness and honesty in the campaigns, any suggestion of extra funding may cause the candidates to lose votes.

"Your politicians will rarely make 'political style' statements, like those made today, because their public words are being monitored by official public service units, which are checking for any deception, undue editing and misleading highlighting. The public service is also monitoring for any propositions which would lead to or suggest undue force is to be used in some area. All significant breaches are referred to a legal body, which examines the cases and follows up where found necessary. Proven breaches result in action being taken to limit the impact and prevent further occurrences. Redress is considered for any damage done and is granted to those affected.

"Regularly conducted elections help to limit the impact of ineffective and wrongly motivated authorities on your country. A free press and the separation of the executive, legislative and judicial arms of your government also help to keep things under control.[4] This is assisted by your people having the rights to freedom of assembly, freedom of speech, petitioning the government and conducting peaceful protests which do not interfere with the regular activities of other citizens.

"Your legal system is designed to be fair: allowing all citizens the right to a trial in court, helping to fund those who could not normally afford the legal fees, and returning any costs to those who are found not guilty. The sentences for the guilty are intended to achieve two things only: protection of your people from further harm, and redress to all those impacted. There is no vindictiveness or idea of 'justice' in the sentencing. Full and appropriate redress and psychological assistance are the chief measures used to help the victims. 'No one should have to suffer because of crime' is one of your society's mottos.

"Your education system helps your people learn to control their natural desires for revenge, as it teaches them about the human mind and how it works. They learn about the formation of the patterns in the memory, the existence of pre-programmed inbuilt circuits, and the evolutionary drives which are used unconsciously to make calculations, the full workings of which may or may not be presented to the conscious part of the brain. Your people also learn about the Ultimate Way, which includes techniques for overcoming the 'lock in' problem of your brain and for creating new ideas. These new ideas often prove useful to your society.

"Your education system is also as fair as it can possibly be, having measures to avoid favoring those who have more funds available to them, and helping those who could not normally afford high fees. Anyone who is willing to work hard and has the necessary aptitude can study what they want to.

"There are many other areas that are exemplary in your improved political system – your country is a model to the less developed, less morally sound areas of the world.

"This story is not about a utopian view of the world of the future. On the contrary, it is an entirely practical and realistic view. In the same way that your current better societies are like perfections compared to those of the Ancient Roman times, the societies of the future running under an improved, controlled democratic system are achievable perfections compared to your world today."

"That is an interesting story," said the man. "I guess it is practical as it is based on how people really are, and has a lot of controls designed to limit their power and make corrections when things go wrong. I am not sure how it would always work and how the finances would eventually be achieved, but I do believe in your comparison with the ancient times and how far we have come in correcting the errors and excesses of the past. It is a kind of 'future positive' idea."

"Yes, it is," agreed the computer. "It is not perfect but it is the best kind of thing that could be done via a political system, given the way you human beings with your Human-Brains are."

"Given our Human-Brain limitations," echoed the man.

"Yes."

"Imagine that… imagine that world, I mean," said the man, "where someone writes an inflammatory article in the media and then has to publish a full-sized retraction in the same location, with a full explanation of why they were wrong! I love that idea. And the politician using highlighting being pulled up by the court and having their statements publicly corrected," he laughed. "Imagine the advertisers being afraid of being caught out in their 'hidden persuaders' style of deception, and taking measures to avoid that. There is a lot to be said for your idea."

The computer remained silent.

"I like the other controls you proposed, such as the protection of the rights of minorities and individuals against the majority – where that is warranted. We could really use some of that today. And I like the way the use of force is kept under control; it so often goes wrong these days. A written legal document on how force is to be applied rightly and fairly would be so useful to us. No doubt there are documents along those lines, but they don't seem to be having enough effect. We really do need some improvements here, as a society.

"There are so many other good things in what you said, I really do admire it and I so wish it could be brought into effect today. But I guess we will have to wait for these things to come into being. It's a shame and it makes me a little sad. 'That's the way it is,' as the man said."

"Yes, these are social changes that are needed," agreed the computer, "and beyond the individual to bring about by themselves."

"Let's talk about that topic on another day," suggested the man.

## SOME OF THE THINGS THE GIANT COMPUTER REFERENCED

### GENERAL REFERENCES:

FUNCTIONS OF GOVERNMENT
- United Nations Statistics Division. "COFOG – 1999 [Classification of Functions of Government]". *United Nations Statistics Division - Classifications Registry*, 1999, unstats.un.org/unsd/classifications/Econ/Structure.

POLITICS
- Bentham, Jeremy. *An Introduction to the Principles of Morals and Legislation.* Dover Publications, 2007. Originally published 1789.
- Chomsky, Noam. *Understanding Power: The Indispensable Chomsky.* Edited by Peter R. Mitchell and John Schoeffel, The New Press, 2002.
- Cicero, M. T. *On Duties.* Translated by Walter Miller, Harvard University Press, 2014. Originally written 44 BCE.
- Confucius. *The Analects.* Penguin, 1998. Probably written in the 5th century BCE.
- The Constitution of the United States. *The U.S. National Archives and Records Administration*, www.archives.gov/founding-docs/constitution-transcript. Accessed 27 Mar. 2021.
- "First Amendment: Freedom of Religion, Speech, Press, Assembly, and Petition." *National Constitution Center*, constitutioncenter.org/interactive-constitution/amendment/amendment-i#:~:text=Congress%20shall%20make%20no%20law,for%20a%20redress%20of%20grievances. Accessed 27 Mar. 2021.
- Hume, David. *An Enquiry Concerning Human Understanding.* Hackett Publishing Company, 1993. Originally published 1748.
- Machiavelli, Niccolo. *The Prince.* Translated by Tim Parks, Penguin, 2011. Originally written 1513.
- MacDonald, Michael J., editor. *The Oxford Handbook of Rhetorical Studies.* Oxford University Press, 2017.
- Mill, John Stuart. *On Liberty.* Penguin, 1982. Originally published 1859.
- Plato. *The Republic.* Translated by Desmond Lee, 2nd ed., Penguin Classics, 2007. Originally written around 375 BCE.
- Powell, G. Bingham, Jr., et al. *Comparative Politics Today: A World View* (11th Edition). Pearson, 2014.
- Rawls, John. *A Theory of Justice.* Revised ed., Harvard University Press, 1999. Originally version published 1971.
- Rousseau, Jean-Jacques. *The Social Contract.* Translated by Maurice Cranston, Penguin, 2003. Originally published 1762.

- Ryan, Alan. *On Politics: A History of Political Thought: From Herodotus to the Present.* Liveright Publishing Corporation, 2020. Originally published 2012.
- Sandel, Michael. *Justice: What's the Right Thing to Do?* Penguin, 2010. Originally published 2009.

## DETAILED REFERENCES:

### [1] MERITOCRACY
- Arrow, Kenneth, et al., editors. *Meritocracy and Economic Inequality.* Princeton University Press, 2000.
- Ayers, William. *To Teach: The Journey of a Teacher.* Teachers College Press, 1993.
- Rawls, John. *A Theory of Justice.* Revised ed., Harvard University Press, 1999. Originally published 1971.
- Young, Michael. *The Rise of the Meritocracy.* 2nd ed., Routledge, 1994. Originally published 1958.

### [2] ADVERTISING SUBTLETY
- Packard, Vance. *The Hidden Persuaders.* Ig Publishing, 2007. Originally published 1957.

### [3] SANCTIONS
- Hufbauer, Gary Clyde, et al. *Economic Sanctions Reconsidered.* 3rd ed., Peterson Institute for International Economics, 2009.
- Strategic Communications. *European Union Sanctions.* European External Action Service (EEAS), 17 Mar. 2021, eeas.europa.eu/headquarters/headquarters-homepage/423/sanctions-policy_en.

### [4] SEPARATION OF POWERS
- Kant, Immanuel. "5. Perpetual Peace: A Philosophical Sketch." *Kant: Political Writings*, translated by H.B. Nisbet, edited by Hans Reiss, 2nd ed., Cambridge University Press, 1991. Originally published 1795.
- Montesquieu, Charles-Louis de Secondat, Baron de. *The Spirit of Laws.* Prometheus, 2002. Originally published 1750.

COMMENTS ON CHAPTER SIX BY THE SUPREME BEING

*"If people were like angels then no government would be needed to rule them"
to paraphrase what was said. As you can see, it would have been better if
there had been angels ruling over the world. Anyway, in the meantime you
are having to rule yourselves, and at least the "Giant Computer's" way is
better than what you have today. I suggest you adopt it, pronto. ;-)*

## ACTUAL QUOTE REFERRED TO BY THE SUPREME BEING

"If men were angels, no government would be necessary. If angels were to govern men, neither external nor internal controls on government would be necessary. In framing a government which is to be administered by men over men, the great difficulty lies in this: you must first enable the government to control the governed; and in the next place, oblige it to control itself."

James Madison. "Federalist No. 51." *Library of Congress: Research Guides*, 13 Aug. 2019, guides.loc.gov/federalist-papers/text-51-60. Originally published 1788.

# 7 SPIRIT OR MATERIAL?

"Today I would like to cover a very different topic to politics. I would like to ask what you calculate about spiritual versus material matters," said the man.

"You speak as if these were separate areas," replied the giant computer, "but most human beings mean the same thing, that is, they are referring to their experiences or the patterns that have formed in their memories as they observe the universe or think about things.

"Technically, the difference in meaning between spirit and material is that spirits have their own minds, in one way or another, and so are able to control their own actions, whereas material is thought to not have any mind, and so has to obey the 'laws of nature', or of the universe.

"Another technical difference is between what is thought to be 'seen' and 'unseen'. Spirit is considered to have more of the unseen aspects, whereas material is thought to be entirely 'seen', even if the seen aspects have to be observed via a microscope or other means. Some people reject the idea of spirit on the basis that it has 'unseen' aspects, saying that only things which can be 'seen' are worth talking about. This is based on the idea that the human mind can be unreliable, and so if any individual describes thoughts or experiences which have possible 'unseen' aspects then it is assumed that these thoughts or experiences have to be treated as unreliable and not worth considering. This idea is not proved, however, as I will show.

"Imagine that people have to be brought before a court to be examined, so that everyone can see if their thoughts or experiences are true. The court would have a defense lawyer, a prosecutor, a judge and witnesses. There would also be some psychological experts, who would evaluate the mental soundness of the accused. The witnesses would be called to testify and the accused could also be questioned and cross-examined, if they agreed to take the stand. How would this go?

"In the first case the accused has said that they saw a ghost. In the second case the accused has made philosophical statements about the unseen forces at work in the universe. Let's look at each of these cases.

"The witnesses are sworn in and questioned about whether they also saw the ghost. None of them were present, but some are willing to testify that the accused is a good and honorable person whom they believe would not lie. The prosecutor asks them if they can be certain that the accused actually saw a ghost and they all admit that they cannot be 100% sure about this, although some of them say they tend to believe the accused. The accused's mental health has been examined and the expert psychologists testify that the accused appears to be in normal mental health, apart from his insistence on the existence of the ghost. The prosecutor asks them if believing you have seen a ghost is really consistent with 'normal mental health' and they reply that it is not, but there are many aspects of normal mental health that are not completely rational. The psychologists don't all agree, but generally they conclude that the 'ghost sighting' is not in itself proof that the accused is insane. They cannot comment further in terms of psychology. No evidence that the accused has a bad character is brought forward by the prosecutor. The accused agrees to take the stand.

"The defense counsel asks the accused a question about how he considers his own mental health but the prosecutor objects, saying that the accused is not an expert psychologist and so is not qualified to comment. The judge agrees. The defense counsel then asks the accused if he is in the habit of lying or making things up and the accused answers that he would not do this on such a serious matter. The accused claims that he has no intention of misleading anyone and was just reporting what he saw. During cross-examination the prosecutor suggests to the accused that he is doing exactly that: making things up to get attention from people and to make himself more interesting. The accused replies that he is not. The prosecutor then asks the accused if he thinks that people should believe what he is saying about seeing a ghost and the accused replies that he has no idea about this, he is just reporting what he saw. The prosecutor comments that she thinks people will not believe the accused's story and sits down.

"The examination of the witnesses and the accused is over and the prosecutor gives her view of the case. She says that 'extraordinary claims need extraordinary proofs', and that in this case the accused has claimed to have seen a ghost, which is an extraordinary claim. But in the area of proof the accused has simply offered us his statement that this is what he saw. There were no witnesses and no physical evidence has been brought forward. In short, the accused is asking us to believe him simply because he says it is true. The prosecutor asks the jury to find the accused guilty of willful deception as it is clear that he has made no effort to back up his claims and was probably doing this just to get attention and his 'five minutes of fame'... or should she say 'notoriety'. The prosecution rests.

"The defense counsel stands and says that her client is not guilty of any deception or attention seeking. Her client is a fine, upstanding member of the community who has never been found guilty of any crime before. His mental health has been attested to by psychological experts and people who know him have testified that he has a good character. Her client has not sought any benefit from his statements about what he saw and she feels that though it is of an extraordinary and unusual nature it is not something that the jury should believe was made up by the accused. On the contrary, she asks the jury to consider the facts of the case as presented and conclude that her client believes categorically that he saw a ghost... he believes this with full certainty in his mind and has reported it faithfully according to his own view of the world. She asks the jury to acquit her client of wrongdoing on the basis that he has just done what any of us would have done and reported to others what he truly believes he saw. We are not here today to judge whether there are ghosts or not, it doesn't matter what we believe about this. What we are here to do today is judge whether her client can be called a liar or is just a normal human being who is reporting what he believes he truly saw. The defense rests.

"The judge calls for an adjournment while he prepares his summation. When the court resumes the judge sums up the case for the jury. He says that the prosecution has made the case that a claim about seeing ghosts needs special proofs but all we have heard is a statement from the accused that he saw a ghost. Witnesses have said that the accused is of good character and we have heard no testimony that says otherwise. Expert psychologists have said that believing you have seen a ghost is not consistent with normal mental health, yet they also found that the accused has good mental health and said that the 'ghost sighting' is not in itself proof that the accused is insane. You will need to form your own view on this expert advice. Finally, we heard from the accused and he has said that he is not in the habit of lying and is telling the truth on this serious matter. There was a suggestion that the accused could benefit from his reporting in terms of fame or being thought interesting. The accused has denied this as a motive. You will need to consider if sufficient evidence has been brought to prove beyond a reasonable doubt that the accused is deliberately misleading people about his reported sighting. You do not need to conclude if there was an actual ghost in this case, your role is to determine if it can be said beyond a reasonable doubt that the accused has deliberately and knowingly deceived people on this matter. If you are not sure beyond a reasonable doubt then you will have to return a verdict of not guilty, but if, in your considerations, you conclude that the prosecution has brought sufficient evidence that there has been deliberate deception in this case then you will have to return a guilty verdict.

"The jury members then retire to consider their verdict. They spend a few hours discussing the case and conclude that the prosecution has not actually proved that the accused is deliberately lying, no matter that some of the jury think he is deluded as there is 'no such thing as ghosts'. Being deluded is one thing and deliberately lying is another. They return to the court and deliver their verdict of not guilty.

"The judge thanks the jury and tells the accused that he is free to go.

"This first imaginary court case has shown that when one person comes forward and talks about a personal experience for which they cannot show physical evidence then they cannot prove beyond a reasonable doubt that they are telling the truth. More importantly, they cannot convince other people that this is not their own delusion. How can other people really know, beyond a reasonable doubt, that the story-teller is not deluded in some way? If they cannot know that, how can other people know if ghosts exist if they have not seen one themselves? Let's put that in a more general way: how can other people reasonably know if an unusual thing, especially one with unseen properties, exists?

"These are the things that will convince you that what someone is reporting is wrong: (1) They are a known liar, they have a bad reputation; (2) They are crazy, or at least delusional; (3) They are profiting from this; (4) You are enough of an expert on this topic to know that what they are saying is wrong.

"These are the things that will make you suspicious: (1) They don't look right, there's something wrong about their manner; (2) They are saying something that you don't normally believe in; (3) You think they might be benefiting from this in some way; (4) You know enough about this topic to have doubts about what they are saying but not enough to be sure.

"These are the things that will make you consider what they are saying further: (1) The person has a good reputation; (2) They look right and sound convincing; (3) They are not profiting from this or the way they are profiting is not hidden and seems reasonable; (4) You know enough about this topic to suspect that there may be some truth in what they are saying but not enough to make a final decision.

"When it comes to the things that will make you believe the other person, who is reporting on something unusual which has some unseen properties, there is some risk that you will get this wrong. The things that will tend to convince you are: (1) You find the person believable, or the person is someone you believe in; (2) Also, you have not found any convincing reason to disbelieve them or doubt their motives; (3) You are enough of an expert on this topic to feel certain that what they are saying is true.

"The risks you face are: (1) You are wrong that the person is believable, even if they are only partially wrong; (2) You believe in the person but you should not, even if this is only in regard to some cases; (3) You are unaware of genuine reasons for disbelieving them; (4) You are unaware of evidence of their actual, related, bad motives; (5) Your expertise is not as great as you think it is, or there are things you don't know about which have changed in your field of expertise, or there is a new 'black swan' kind of thing happening which no one in your field could have predicted. These risks can be mitigated but they cannot be avoided.

"The ways to mitigate the risks you face when believing someone are: (1) Pretend you don't find the person believable or trustworthy for a moment, then check the evidence as if this was true: how does the evidence stack up now?; (2) Check to see if you can find any actual evidence of their possible bad motives; (3) Recheck how good your level of expertise is on this topic, also make sure you are up to date with relevant material in your field, and, finally, look for evidence that there is a new thing happening here which was previously unknown in your field. These mitigation steps will help you to reduce the risk that you are wrong about the person and what they are saying, but, as I said, they cannot remove all the risk. You can always turn out to be wrong. The mitigation for this is to be ready to change your mind when you have to!

"So, should you have believed the person who reported that he saw a ghost? If you did believe him then is it possible that the ghost he saw was real, and not just a delusion or error? As the idea of ghosts is so strange to modern people, you may have to conclude that in the absence of more conclusive evidence you cannot realistically say you believe that the person saw a real ghost. You may have to conclude that the person was mistaken in some way, possibly deluded, or even actually lying, for some reason which you cannot be exactly sure about: there are a few possibilities. In a different era you may have believed the person more easily, but if you follow today's modern scientific attitudes then you may tend to not believe him.

"Let's now imagine the second court case, where the accused has been making philosophical statements about the unseen forces at work in the universe.

"The witnesses are sworn in and questioned about their knowledge on the subject. Most of them have read the philosophical statements and some of them found the ideas convincing. Some have been called as character witnesses as they know the accused well. The character witnesses state that the accused is an intelligent and sincere person who seeks after the truth. The prosecutor asks them if they can also testify that the accused is a person who is right about their philosophical ideas, especially as these include elements of 'things which cannot be seen by anyone'. Most of the character witnesses reply that they are not experts in philosophy. The attention now turns to the witnesses who have expertise in the areas of 'advanced thought'. The witnesses for the defense say that they found the philosophical statements well written and logically consistent, in their way. Some believe the conclusions and some do not, but all felt that it is valid to do such 'philosophizing'. The expert witnesses for the prosecution are not unanimous on whether the statements were well written or logical, but all agree that it is no longer valid in our modern age to be speculating about 'unseen things' or metaphysical matters when doing philosophy. 'This form of thinking has been debunked.' The defense asks the expert witnesses if it is really true that this form of thinking has been debunked. The prosecution expert witnesses say either that it is true, or that arguments attempting to counter this do not really make sense. The defense expert witnesses say either that they do not agree with the view that this form of thinking is no longer valid, or they say that it has been well argued that there are 'unseen' or even 'unseeable' elements in many areas, even in the precious scientific theories of today, and so it is not reasonable to say that talking about unseen things is no longer valid. If that were the case then we would have to abandon many of the scientific theories which we work with and have benefited from in modern times. The prosecutor cross-examines these witnesses and asks them if it has been accepted by all credible people in the philosophy profession that the unseen, or metaphysics, is valid again today. The witnesses reply that this is not a uniform view, some philosophers side with the anti-metaphysics view and some side with the 'validity of unseeable elements'. The prosecutor then asks if the expert philosophers on the anti-metaphysics side are considered credible or non-credible in their profession. The witnesses reply that as far as they know they are largely considered credible people, even if their views are questionable. There are no further witnesses to call and the accused agrees to take the stand.

"The prosecutor asks the accused if she has heard the testimony of the expert witnesses. She says she has. He then asks her if she agrees that some professional philosophers believe that metaphysical statements are no longer valid in philosophy. She says she believes they do. Yet you are willing to make such unsupported statements, he says. I am, she replies. On what basis do you go against your professional colleagues? On the basis that I don't agree with their view, she replies. It is my belief that you can look at the patterns in things and propose forces or mechanisms that are working behind the scenes to make them happen. You could call this metaphysics, but she prefers to refer to it as 'meta-patterns'. The prosecutor demands to know why she gave herself the right to invent new words for old, obsolete approaches, and the accused replies: because I am a professional philosopher too. The prosecutor comments that this is not so clear, and sits down. The defense counsel then asks the accused about her qualifications and the accused describes her PhD in the field. The defense counsel asks her if she believes that having a PhD in the field of philosophy gives her the right to put her views forward and the accused replies that she believes it does. There are no further questions for the accused.

"The prosecutor now stands and gives his view of the case. He says that the accused has put forward a view which contains elements of the unseen, known normally in the field as metaphysics, and that this type of thinking has been debunked by credible professional experts. He says that the attempts by the accused to make up excuses, such as by inventing new words for her aberrant and outmoded ideas, has fallen flat in this case. He believes that the case has exposed her for what she is: a retrograde, rebellious sort of individual, who, for some twisted reason known only to herself, uses her PhD as a weapon to bring philosophy into disrepute and to mislead the innocent and less-informed than herself. He calls on the jury to find the accused guilty of the crime of deliberately misleading people, so that the important and honorable world of philosophy will not be brought down by malicious people like the accused. The prosecution rests.

"The defense counsel stands and addresses the jury. He says that the accused is an honorable and sincere person, as was shown by the many witnesses who testified to her character. It would be an outrage to accuse this honorable professional person of any maliciousness or defects of character. When it comes to the question of the so-called metaphysics, you have heard that there is no agreement in the field on whether this is invalid or not. It cannot be up to us here to determine what is valid in the field of philosophy, especially as the experts themselves have not been able to agree on this. Who are we, members of the jury, to say what a philosopher can or cannot say, at least in terms of what is in their field? No, we have to let the experts debate freely among themselves, not put PhD experts in jail just because some people don't like the style of what they have said. I call on you, members of the jury, to acquit this honorable person from these baseless charges and find her not guilty. The defense rests.

"The judge gives her summation. She says that the prosecution has brought forward expert witnesses, some of whom said that metaphysical statements are no longer valid in philosophy. Some of the expert witnesses did not agree with this view, however. The accused has said that she did not intend to mislead people, rather she stated what she believed to be the case in her field. You will have to decide if you believe her statement. There were witnesses brought forward who testified to the good character of the accused. You may consider their testimony to give credibility to the veracity of the accused's own statements about herself – that is a matter for you to decide. You may find it of interest that no witness was brought by the prosecution who testified to any question of the good character of the accused. You may consider this of some weight, that is up to you to decide. On the question of whether the statements in philosophy by the accused are to be considered right or wrong, or true or false, that is not a matter before you today. Your role is to determine, beyond a reasonable doubt, if the accused is guilty or not guilty of deliberately misleading people via her philosophical statements. Please retire and consider your verdict.

"The jury retires to the jury room and quickly finds that none of them believes that the accused philosopher was deliberately lying when she made her philosophical statements. They agree to return a verdict of not guilty.

"The judge thanks the jury and says that she believes justice has been done today. She apologizes to the accused for the inconvenience of having to attend the trial and thanks her for her patience. The accused thanks the judge and she and her counsel leave the courtroom.

"This second imaginary court case has shown the tremendous difficulty faced when experts in a specialized complex field do not agree. How can everyday people come to a conclusion here, when the experts cannot reach a consensus themselves? For a human being the answer to this problem will again lie in the lists of things I gave you before, which in summary are: (1) How much you think you know about the person's own credibility; (2) How much you think you know about the person's motives; (3) How much you think you know about the topic.

"As a human being, your thoughts and knowledge are limited, and so you are always gambling when you make a decision, as it is in all things in your lives," concluded the giant computer.

"Thanks for these illustrative stories, lists and ideas," said the man. "Could I ask you this: as a giant computer can you not calculate accurately what is the truth in these situations – where the experts do not agree?"

The giant computer calculated.

"I can and I cannot," it replied. "There are cases where I can see the fault in the calculations of the Human-Brains, and there are cases where it is impossible for me to reach a final conclusion. Before you ask, the cases where it is impossible are those where there is not enough actual evidence for me to calculate a conclusion. For example, in the realm of the unseen there is too much contradictory evidence for me to be able to make a ruling either for or against the existence of the unseen things... what you might call the spirit world, and the like. Whereas I can calculate the probable fallacy of some of the old metaphysical views in philosophy, as it is improbable that their reliance on unseen forces that guide history, or the like, is a necessary outcome from running a calculation on all the things that have actually happened in the past."

"I see," said the man. "Not meaning to joke there! What I mean is I see what you are saying about the limitation on the possibilities of your calculations when people contradict each other about their experiences... or should I say, about their apparent experiences, if they were even telling the truth or not being self-deceptional here! And when it comes to their ideas, or their thoughts about the way things are, then that can be really difficult to comment on, or calculate from, when they have such different ideas, which they all seem to believe in... in the sense of them. I mean, people tend to believe what they are saying, when they are being honest, and yet it is not possible that all their different views are right!"

"That is so," agreed the computer. "It is symptomatic of you having biological Human-Brains which are doing your thinking… and from that your 'believing', as it were."

"Yes, I see. I suppose that if I was brought up in a particular religion then my Human-Brain would have formed Patterns-in-Memory from an early age that would incorporate those things. Then my world view would tend to include those religious elements or explanations in it. As a result I would tend to, I mean my Human-Brain would tend to draw on these Patterns-in-Memory when it was thinking, I mean Calculating about something, and that would tend to confirm my original view, or 'belief', as we call it. The fact that my Patterns-in-Memory seemed to match a reality where my particular religion was true would tell my Human-Brain that what it Calculates is true, a true picture of reality, and so if I asked it what it believed it would say: 'My religion'."

"That is a logical, possible outcome," agreed the computer.

"And is there any way out of that delusion, if it is a delusion?" asked the man.

"Yes," replied the computer. "There is. As I have already said."

"Understand who and what you are, and use the Ultimate Way, that kind of thing?"

"Yes. That is correct. That is a way out of the human style of delusion."

"Okay. Then can I ask you: is there any kind of calculation you can make that is solid on the topic of spiritual versus material matters?"

"I already gave you that," said the computer, "but since you ask, I will calculate some more." It paused to calculate. "There is one related area that I did not address for you, and that is the idea of a 'spiritual' life versus a more materially-based one. Would you like to hear about that?"

"Yes, please."

"Very well. The often-asked question of whether it is better to live a more spiritual or a more materially-based life is not the correct one. The correct question to ask is: What is the best life to live? The answer to this is to live by what is good, truthful and wise."

"Wise?" interrupted the man. "What does that mean?"

"Wise means making the best possible judgements given the available information at the time, and it also means taking actions which could help future situations turn out better. For example, the wise person always puts their keys in a known place so that they can be found easily!"

"I see! Please continue."

"I have already defined the meaning of good before. It is 'Action taken by a conscious being to knowingly benefit other conscious beings.' This is related to doing what is right, which is: 'Allowing conscious beings to flourish and also not permitting them to be deliberately harmed, as much as this is practical.'

The meaning of being truthful is: 'Having the intention to find out what is really true', which requires you to understand the limitations of your human brain, as seen via the Ultimate Way. From this you will be able to form views which are more realistic, less evil and less self-deluded. You will be thinking the best thoughts that you can, as I have said before.

"Finally, I repeat that the meaning of being wise is: 'Making the best possible judgements you can, given the available information at the time, and taking actions which could help future situations turn out better.'

"What actions could you take so that you live the best possible life?

"In terms of good, as I have told you before, you could:

"1. Try to avoid performing actions which are directly evil, that is, which cause harm to other conscious beings, including yourself, where possible.

"2. Try to avoid being involved in actions which will cause evil, even if these are done by others, as much as practically possible.

"3. In matters of good and evil, you should prefer to perform actions which are good, as much as possible.

"4. You should do a reasonable amount of thinking when deciding what to do, neither too little nor too much, but especially not cheating on the matter and curtailing your thinking before you have given it a fair chance to work. You should use the Ultimate Way as your guide here.

"In terms of truthfulness, as I have told you before, you could:

"1. Understand how patterns form in your brain. (These will include the patterns that you use when trying to decide about actions related to good and evil.) Also understand that you have natural emotional drives. (These will distort your view of what is good and what is evil.)

"2. Understand that you have a limited brain capacity, and there are many things you do not know, so you need to keep your mind open to other possibilities. (Including when thinking about good and evil.)

"3. Understand how the pattern functioning of your brain tends to lock you in to particular views. (This is especially a problem when thinking about good and evil.)

"4. Use techniques designed to overcome the 'lock in' problem of your brain. (These will help you to change your views on what is good and what is evil, where this makes sense, and also to think more effectively about the decisions you have to make in your life.)

"5. Do the best you can in the circumstances of your life, given your limited intellect and inaccurate pattern-style memory. But keep asking yourself: 'Is this true? Is this true?' (And this is truly the best you, as a human being, can do in the circumstances.)

"In terms of wisdom, you could:

"1. In any currently occurring situation make the best possible judgements and take the best actions that you can, based on the information and skills that you have available to you at the time.

"2. Think ahead: take actions now that could help you in the future. This includes improving your knowledge and skills in the areas that could help you to do better when future situations arise.

"Now that I have defined how to live the best possible life, I will examine how well the aspects of the 'spiritual' and materially-based lives relate to this.

"Spiritual ideas usually include unseen elements, which are not able to be proved beyond a reasonable doubt to all people, as I showed earlier. Consequently, a spiritual life can contradict truthfulness, because a truthful person will be aware of their own mental limitations in the working of their Human-Brain. They will know that a Human-Brain cannot be certain about all its Calculations, as shown in the Ultimate Way. They may adopt one particular 'spiritual' view as their best Calculation on the subject, but they will always bear in mind that they could be wrong about this. They will regularly ask themselves, as defined by their honest outlook: 'Is this true? Is this true?'

"A materially-based life can also contradict truthfulness when the craving for material goods and power diverts the Human-Brain's attention from actual reality. A materially-based life can get out of control, because it produces strong feelings in the Human-Brain which can take over its Calculations. The Human-Brain can start to focus its efforts on how to get more material goods and more power, losing track of what it was originally designed to achieve. More importantly, the Human-Brain can lose track of what it is, forgetting that it is a biological organ which Calculates from its Other-Influences and its Patterns-in-Memory in order to fulfill its Evolutionary-Drives, and that its Patterns-in-Memory are summaries of what it actually experienced or thought, not the whole picture of reality but only containing the elements that struck it, based on what appeared to repeat or to which it had a stronger emotional reaction based on its Evolutionary-Drives and Other-Influences at the time.

"A spiritual life can get in the way of you doing the things that would make you flourish, as it can make demands on your time and may direct your activities away from those that would be best for you personally. It can also get in the way of you helping others, especially where its religious or spiritual concepts are opposed to you taking the type of actions that are the most effective for protecting or assisting others. Its religious or spiritual concepts may even encourage you to oppose other people or conscious creatures from flourishing in some areas.

"A materially-based life can drive you to do things that are evil or wrong, because you start to focus too much on yourself or your own group flourishing. It can turn your attention away from helping others to flourish because your strong desires have blinded you to the genuine existence of other conscious beings and from the need to do what is right.

"A spiritual life can get in the way of you acting wisely, because you can become locked in to particular less-solid views which may be false. These views can interfere with you making the best possible judgements and taking the best actions in a given situation. They can also prevent you from thinking ahead clearly and taking actions now that could help you in the future.

"A materially-based life can make you into a kind of fool, because although you may gather power, money and greater freedom of choice, you will not have a mind left to focus on doing what is wise in life. You can become obsessed with the material world as you have had to encourage the desires in your Human-Brain to grow strong, this having been needed to drive you to do the hard work and take the risks required to get you to where you are today.

"For these reasons neither a spiritual nor a materially-based life can be considered to be the best choice. There are, however, good sides to both views which are worth adopting.

"The good sides of a spiritual life are: (1) Its intention is to align with the actual purpose of life; and (2) It can be effective at helping you attain true peace of mind, or even happiness. The good sides of a materially-based life are: (1) It can help your own life and other people's to flourish; and (2) It can enable you to feel liberated.

"The first good side of a spiritual life is its intention to match to whatever the religious or spirit-based agents appear to suggest human beings should do. This is a noble and good objective in itself, because truthfulness is one of the values of the best way to live. Also, the values of doing good and acting wisely are intended to be covered by this approach, as it is thought that the God, gods, spirits, spirit forces or enlightened people are relaying to humans what is truly good and truly wise. I have already explained the difficulty in calculating which of the 'unseen aspects' of the different world views is correct, so all that can be reliably done here is to take on the good side of the spiritual life, which is that you should match your life to what you can honestly know about the actual purpose of life: you should sincerely aim to do what is good, truthful and wise.

"The second good side of a spiritual life is to attain true peace of mind or even happiness. In spiritual practices this has been achieved via methods which include meditation and ritual. These have been used to reduce the intensity of the feelings in the mind, leading to greater feelings of peace which can even transform into extremely strong feelings of joy from time to time. You can study and use these types of practices to improve your own mental state.

"The first good side of a materially-based life is that it can help your own life and other people's to flourish. This is because it allows practical actions to be taken which could lead to you having more money, power, goods, skills, and the like. As long as this does not get out of hand, you can take these practical actions to improve your life. You are permitted to take any practical action which also aligns with what is good, truthful and wise.

"The second good side of a materially-based life is that it can enable you to feel liberated. This is because it opens up the possibility of you doing what you wish. Also, as you accumulate money, power, goods, skills, and the like, you may increase your actual ability to do the things you want. It is not a guarantee, of course, but it improves the possibility. You can allow yourself to feel more liberated as well by confirming that you are permitted to take any actions you wish which do not contradict what is good, truthful and wise.

"So, in terms of living the best possible life, you can remind yourself to feel happy about your sincere desire to do what is good, truthful and wise, and you can enjoy the fact that you can do anything you wish which aligns with these values. You can study and use meditation, ritual and similar practices to improve your feelings, and you can allow yourself to feel free, because you are permitted to carry out any action you desire which fits within the very wide realm of what is good, truthful and wise.

"What you must not do is overuse any of these spiritual or materially-based things. You should not get lost in your 'spirituality' or be overcome by your material world interests. To live the best possible life you need to put good, truthfulness and acting wisely ahead of these things. 'Let them all live together wisely,' is my recommendation."

"Thanks for that analysis. It is very clear," said the man. "I have one area that I would like to explore further with you, but at a later time, and that is the question of how we could choose which religious or other world-view could be considered the best. But I have other topics I want to ask you about before that. For today's session, do you have any more illustrative stories you can tell me about what we have discussed today?"

"Yes, I do," replied the giant computer. "My first story is related to the first court case I described, which illustrated the difficulties in deciding who to believe when they talk about encounters with 'the unseen'. What if this first case was reversed and the accused had to prove that a group of people had *not* seen a miraculous vision of a saint?

"The accused has been charged with deliberately misleading the public by claiming that a group of people did not really see a vision of Saint Mary.

"The witnesses are sworn in and questioned about whether they saw the vision of Saint Mary. The majority say that they did see Saint Mary and are able to describe her appearance in traditional clothing. Some of the witnesses say that they did not see the vision of Saint Mary, even though they were standing next to witnesses who did see her. Character witnesses for the group of people are questioned. The character witnesses give varying accounts of the group: some of the group members are described as honest normal citizens, but some members are less admired. No pattern can be found to explain why some witnesses saw Saint Mary and some did not. There is a suggestion by the prosecution that some of the people who did not see the vision are less devout or are even non-believers, but this is not found to be supported by the character witnesses, including the local priest. Some of the non-believers, who are supporters of Communism, saw the vision, and some of the Christians did not see it.

"Experts in mental health are called to the witness stand and give varying views. Some say that this is a kind of 'mass hysteria', where some people influence others into believing that they have seen something which didn't actually happen. Others say that we should focus on the mental health of the people in the group and not worry about the question of whether the vision was real or not. They find that the group is a normal mix of people and none of them appears to have any particular mental health problems. On this basis it is not possible to say if the vision was false or not.

"The defense counsel cross-examines the witnesses who say they saw Saint Mary. She asks them if they are part of a conspiracy being conducted on behalf of the Church. They all deny this. She asks them why they say they saw Saint Mary when the people next to them did not. The witnesses say they don't know why she did not appear to those people. The defense counsel then suggests to them that they are asking the court to believe things which are impossible to believe in our modern age. The witnesses say that they don't know about that, they only know what they saw. The defense counsel then asks one of the witnesses what he thinks he will achieve by telling these lies, but the prosecution objects and the judge agrees that the question is improper. The defense counsel sits down.

"The accused declines to take the stand.

"The examination of the witnesses is over and the prosecutor gives her view of the case. She says that the accused has made the extraordinary claim that this whole group of fourteen witnesses is lying, deliberately. She says that the accused did not say that the witnesses were deluded in some way, but that they deliberately set out to mislead the public with their so-called 'extraordinary claims'. Who are we to say what is extraordinary today when so many people have agreed on what they saw? As to the question of whether the other people should have seen the vision or not, that is not a matter before the court today. The accused made no effort, when making his claims, to check if the honest witnesses of this wonderful vision were telling the truth, why should we extend our consideration to why or what the other witnesses did or did not see? That is not the point. The point is that the accused, for reasons of his own, decided what is real and what is not, and made no allowance for the impact he would cause to these fine witnesses' lives when he set out to accuse them of deliberately and maliciously lying about their experience of the vision. He had no right to so malign the character of these honest fellow citizens and should be found guilty of libel.

"The defense counsel then stands and says that her client has done nothing wrong. He simply expressed his view that these incredible claims could not make sense, as we all know today that visions like this do not occur.

Think about the difference in vision between a person standing right next to the so-called witnesses of this miracle: one person says they saw something and the person next to them has no idea why they say that. How could that be? We are being asked today to set aside everything we know about the world in order to make some allowance that a small, select group of people, people who were no more likely to see this than anyone else, have in fact seen something that cannot actually be seen. It is extraordinary to ask us to do this. Her client, a decent upstanding member of our community, has been accused of nothing more than expressing in writing an opinion which we all share: that this was a hoax, a deliberate hoax. He should not have to answer in court for saying something which we all really believe. The defense rests.

"The judge sums up the case. He says that the prosecution made the case that while some of the witnesses of the vision say that they saw it and others say that they did not see it, the accused still had no right to publish in writing that the witnesses who said they saw the vision were deliberately lying. The prosecutor has put the burden of proof on the accused to show that he had some way of knowing for certain that the alleged witnesses were lying, maliciously and on purpose. The defense has said, however, that these visions could not be true and that it is perfectly reasonable for us to believe that this was a deliberate deception on the part of the witnesses whom we have heard from during this trial. You may think that this is a matter of freedom of expression, which is a right in our society, but you should know that freedom of expression does not extend to slander or libel, that is, to accusing another of doing something which they did not do, or which you cannot show that they did. If a person writes something against the character of another person then that person must be prepared to prove that what they have written is true, that it has some basis in fact. It is not enough to say that we might all believe what was written if no evidence can be brought for supporting this belief. I ask you now to retire and consider your verdict.

"The jury retires and discusses the case. They are unable to agree on whether the vision was real or not, as not all the witnesses saw it. Some insist that there could still have been a vision as we do not know how God works these things, but others feel that it is more likely that the viewers were fooled in some way, possibly via that 'mass hysteria' which some of the expert psychologists referred to. The jury then turns their attention to whether writing about this is to be considered an exact case of libel, or whether it is more likely a case of freedom of expression, which we all believe in as one of the great freedoms of our country. If people are not to be allowed to express their views then what will become of us in the future? After some discussion the point is raised that some people have had their honesty questioned in public, which must have affected their lives, and that the accused has not brought one shred of evidence which shows that they were definitely lying deliberately. There is some more discussion of this point and the jury members eventually agree that this is going too far, it is beyond the limits of freedom of speech to ruin some people's lives without evidence and so should be stopped.

"The jury returns to the courtroom and gives a verdict of guilty. The judge thanks the jury and pronounces his sentence. He says that although the claim of seeing a vision may seem incredible to us today, it is not enough for us to be able to say that the person is deliberately lying. There may be a number of reasons for a person to make this claim, up to and including that they actually saw it! Freedom of speech and expression is an inalienable right, but it does not extend to allowing a citizen to malign someone else's character in public without sufficient evidence. The accused may have thought that he was expressing an opinion which everyone would believe in, but his statements also damaged the reputation of other citizens, who have the right to be heard and to live their lives freely and without affliction. He fines the accused $1,000 and orders him to publish a retraction and an apology.

"This imaginary court case has shown that when a person doubts another person's honesty, and states that publicly, they must be ready to prove that their suspicions are well-founded. This applies even to cases where someone has made a claim for which they cannot show physical evidence, and for which they therefore cannot prove beyond a reasonable doubt that they are telling the truth. In summary, the question for this example is: how can other people reasonably know if an unusual thing, even one with unseen properties, definitely does *not* exist?

"My second story is related to the second court case, where the accused had made philosophical statements about the unseen forces at work in the universe. This showed the difficulty faced by everyday people in coming to a conclusion in a complex field when the experts themselves do not agree. What if the case was reversed and the prosecution had to prove that an expert is *not* right to claim that unseen forces must never be referred to in philosophy? The accused expert has written: 'It is philosophically impermissible to argue that there are any kind of unseen forces at work in the universe.'

"The witnesses are sworn in and questioned about their knowledge on the subject. Most of them have read the philosophical statements and some of them found the ideas convincing. Some have been called as character witnesses as they know the accused well. The character witnesses state that the accused is an intelligent and sincere person who seeks after the truth. The prosecutor asks them if they can also testify that the accused is a person who is right about their philosophical ideas, especially as these categorically deny the existence of 'elements which may not be able to be seen by anyone'. Most of the character witnesses reply that they are not experts in philosophy. The attention now turns to the witnesses who have expertise in the areas of 'advanced thought'. The witnesses for the defense say that they found the philosophical statements well written and logically consistent, in their way.

Some believe the conclusions and some do not, but all felt that it is valid to do such 'philosophizing'. The expert witnesses for the prosecution are not unanimous on whether the statements were well written or logical, but all agree that it cannot be considered valid to restrict ourselves to our modern age's prejudices against discussing metaphysical matters when doing philosophy. 'This form of thinking has not been successfully disproved, as has been claimed by some.' The defense asks the expert witnesses if it is really true to say that this form of thinking has not been successfully disproved. The prosecution expert witnesses say that this is the case, and that attempting to claim that there can definitely be no room for metaphysics does not make sense. The defense expert witnesses say that they agree with the view that all metaphysical forms of thinking are invalid, and that it has been well argued that we cannot discuss the 'unseen' or 'unseeable' elements when doing serious philosophy today. It may once have seemed reasonable to do this, but it is no longer valid in our more informed and enlightened time. The prosecutor cross-examines these witnesses and asks them if it has been accepted by all credible people in the philosophy profession that the unseen, or metaphysics, is invalid today. The witnesses reply that this is not a universal view, some philosophers side with the metaphysics proposition and some side with the more reasonable anti-metaphysics one. The prosecutor then asks if the expert philosophers who support the metaphysics side are considered credible or non-credible in their profession. The witnesses reply that as far as they know they are largely considered credible people, even if their views are out-of-date. There are no further witnesses to call and the accused agrees to take the stand.

"The prosecutor asks the accused if she has heard the testimony of the expert witnesses. She says she has. He then asks her if she agrees that some professional philosophers believe that metaphysical statements are still valid in philosophy. She says she believes they do. Yet you are willing to make such extreme statements against this, he says. I am, she replies. On what basis do you go against your professional colleagues? On the basis that I don't agree with their view, she replies. It is my view that you can only propose forces or mechanisms that have 'seeable' elements, whatever the 'seeable' aspects exactly are, when looking for what is making things happen in the universe. There is no need to introduce the so-called metaphysics into this, in fact there is no *right* to do this, as it can never be shown how it works by the nature that it is unseeable, or always will have unseeable elements in it. The prosecutor demands to know why she gave herself the right to categorically deny the possibility of the existence of unseeable elements and for these being able to be argued about. The accused replies: because I am a serious-minded person. The prosecutor comments that this is not so obvious to him and sits down. The defense counsel then asks the accused about her qualifications and the accused describes her PhD in the field. The defense counsel asks her if she believes that having a PhD in the field of philosophy gives her the right to put her views forward in a serious way and the accused replies that she believes it does. There are no further questions for the accused.

"The prosecutor now stands and gives his view of the case. He says that the accused has put forward a view which denies the right to talk about the unseen, known normally in the field as metaphysics, yet this type of reasoning is endorsed by credible professional experts. He says that the accused has set herself up as the final arbiter on this matter, allowing no other professional to make decisions in their own field of expertise. He says that this is an outrage against the profession and that this self-appointed judge should be brought down from the pedestal she has put herself on. She has no right to dictate to other professionals about how they should honestly conduct their business. Her view is an extremist one, put forward in an attempt to somehow make herself something like 'the last philosopher' of history. He calls on the jury to find the accused guilty of overstepping the mark of what is considered acceptable behavior in the field of philosophy, so that this new kind of petty dictator can be stopped from trying to impose her will on others who have the inalienable right to conduct their affairs in their own honest truth-seeking way. The prosecution rests.

"The defense counsel stands and addresses the jury. He says that the accused is an honorable and sincere person, as was shown by the many witnesses who testified to her character. It would be an outrage to accuse this honorable professional person of any maliciousness or defects of character. When it comes to the question of metaphysics, you have heard that there is no agreement in the field on whether this is valid or not. It cannot be up to us here to determine what is valid in the field of philosophy, especially as the experts themselves have not been able to reach agreement on this. Who are we, members of the jury, to say that a philosopher cannot come forward and put her honest view? If a PhD expert says that in her honest opinion a particular area, or way of arguing, is no longer valid, then who are we to say she cannot? No, we have to let the experts speak freely and discuss ideas among themselves, not put PhD experts in jail just because some people don't like what they have said. I call on you, members of the jury, to acquit this honorable person from these baseless accusations and find her not guilty. The defense rests.

"The judge gives her summation. She says that the prosecution has brought forward expert witnesses, some of whom said that metaphysical statements are no longer valid in philosophy and some of whom said that they were. The accused has admitted that she made the statement that there is no right to bring metaphysical or unseen agents into philosophical theories today, but this in itself is not a crime. A crime would be to directly prevent your colleagues from stating their views, and although the accused has expressed a view that such colleagues would be incorrect in their statements, she has not taken any actual steps that would prevent them from doing so. On the question of whether the statements in philosophy by the accused are to be considered right or wrong, or true or false, that is not a matter before you today. Your role is to determine, beyond a reasonable doubt, if the accused is guilty or not guilty of preventing other philosophical experts from making the statements that they wish to. Please retire and consider your verdict.

"The jury retires to the jury room and quickly finds that none of them believes that any evidence was brought which proves that the accused prevented other philosophers from putting forward their own views, whether she agreed with them or not. They decide to return a verdict of not guilty.

"The judge thanks the jury and says that she believes justice has been done today. The law does not exist to prevent people from putting forward their honest views into the public forum. She apologizes to the accused for the inconvenience of the trial and tells her she is free to go. The accused thanks the judge and she and her counsel leave the courtroom.

"This imaginary court case has again shown the tremendous difficulty faced when experts in a specialized complex field do not agree. How can everyday people come to a reliable conclusion when the experts themselves cannot reach a consensus? Even if you are an expert yourself, your conclusion may be wrong because you may have overlooked or misinterpreted the reasons that other experts in your field do not agree with you. How can such disagreements really exist, if everyone knows what they are doing? Something must be wrong: it could be them or it could be you… or both."

"But what would you say?" asked the man. "Is metaphysics permissible or not in philosophy?"

"Metaphysics may be valid," replied the giant computer. "I cannot calculate the validity of that either way, as I can only work from the information that is available to my circuits today. There are many cases where the elements in an explanation have included unseen aspects, it is not just in philosophy, and so I cannot rule out the possibility that there is a need to do that, to refer to unseen aspects, from time to time. Possibly arguing that an element *must* always remain unseeable is on the edge of what may be valid, or necessary, but ruling this out is probably not possible at this time."

"I see, thank you. Please continue with your stories."

"My third story is about knowing who to trust.

"How can you know who to trust? One person wears a suit and the other is in rags: which one can you trust? One person wears the famous white coat and the other is in casual clothes: which one should you trust? A person says they are from the government and they need you to provide your bank account details: should you trust them? A person looks and sounds like the kind of person you would make friends with: can you trust them to look after your interests? A person says they admire you: are they telling the truth?

"Too often, human beings judge a person's trustworthiness on their appearance, their claims to authority, and the like. This is a well-known problem, there is nothing new here. The solution is to *beware*! Watch out for the deceptions, do not take things at face value, especially if you do not know the person. Check up on them, check their credentials, check their references, speak to people who know them, cover yourself. That is all.

"My fourth story is about the person whom you are least likely to spot when they are fooling you. It is yourself.

"You will remember that I said that self-deception is a common Human-Brain activity. This can be done in the Calculations of the Human-Brain which may never be presented to the Consciousness. In other words, you may have elements fooling you in your own mind which you never see. How can you deal with these? How can you see what cannot be seen inside your own head? By looking outside.

"Outside yourself are other people and there are also your own actions. When you say something to other people, what you said is also now outside yourself. You can look at these things to work out if your own Human-Brain is fooling you.

"Other people see you from the outside: they are not aware of what is going on inside your head. They have to form their judgements about what you are doing and what you say based on what they can see and hear. If your actions do not match your statements then they will conclude that you are some sort of liar. You may be a hypocrite, or a deliberate deceiver, or fooling yourself. You may lack insight into your own mind, and so you do things which are different from what you think you are doing. Other people can work all this out just by watching you. You can learn about this from them. If you ask them what they see and know about you then their answers might give you some information that makes you suspicious. Are they giving you a fair and reasonable view of who you really are, or are they misleading you in some way? Are they telling the truth accurately, or are their own issues or objectives getting in the way and distorting what they think they are seeing? You will need to work this out, but don't dismiss too easily the possibility that what they are telling you is exposing the areas where your brain is lying to itself.

"One way to tell if other people are likely to be right about you is to look for consistency among them. If a lot of people are saying the same thing about you then it is likely to have some factual basis. In this case you may want to look very closely at yourself. If it is only one person and everyone else says they are wrong then probably the issue is with that person and not yourself. You don't have to believe every bad thing you hear about yourself.

"Your own actions are also outside yourself, so if you can figure out a way to look at those and evaluate them then you can gain some insights into any possible self-deceptions that are going on in your Human-Brain. Some people have been shocked to see video recordings of themselves doing something, and it has led them to change their behavior forever. Is there anything like that happening with you? Do you tell yourself you are one kind of person but your actions say otherwise? Your actions are more likely 'who you are' than what your Human-Brain tells your Consciousness about yourself. 'Actions speak louder than words.'

"Finally, you can look at what you actually said to other people, as this is now outside you. If you heard these same words from another person, and then analyzed them, what would you think they told you about what was inside that person's head? Would those words make you suspicious? Would you consider that person to have bad qualities, maybe a bad character? Would you consider them foolish, or misinformed, or even self-deceptional? Don't go crazy with this, but give it a short hearing to see if you can learn anything useful from it.

"A self-deceptional person has some hidden motives for what they are doing. What might your motives be? What might you be needing to hide from yourself, or tell yourself? Think about that, think about what other people say about you, think about what you actually do, and make your best judgement on what may be going on inside the less conscious parts of your own Human-Brain.

"My fifth story is about the intention to live by what is true, as best as a human being can.

"If you decide that you want to live by what is true, whatever that may be, you might then adopt one of the particular religious views, or even a materialistic view, as you have decided that that one is the best. You would then attempt to dedicate your life to following the goals or rules that the particular view said. For example, you might decide to become a Buddhist monk, because you thought that that was the most likely and reasonable view of life. Yet when you did this you might have lost sight of the fact that you could be wrong. There are many unknown elements and no human being has such a good grasp of all the facts that they can be certain that all their judgements are right. This is especially true of matters which are complex and which include certain 'unseen' elements. You may be convinced, but you may be wrong.

"What can you do? It is not wrong to draw some conclusion about life, and it is entirely admirable to try to live by what you think is right, so how can you follow a life of truth if I am telling you that you cannot know for sure what is finally true? You know what I am going to say: 'Do the best you can in the circumstances of your life, given your limited intellect and inaccurate pattern-style memory. But keep asking yourself: "Is this true? Is this true?" And this is truly the best you, as a human being, can do in the circumstances.' I am also going to say: 'You should do a reasonable amount of thinking when deciding what to do, neither too little nor too much, but

THE GIANT COMPUTER ANSWERS LIFE'S MYSTERIES

especially not cheating on the matter and curtailing your thinking before you have given it a fair chance to work. The Ultimate Way should be your guide here.'

"My last story is about living and acting wisely.

"In any currently occurring situation you should make the best possible judgements and take the best actions that you can, based on the information and skills that you have available to you at the time. For example, if you have lost your keys then you should take the best actions you know for finding them. This would not include losing your temper and accusing your household members of stealing them. Instead you would take measures to control your emotions and work in a respectable adult way to find the keys. Method rather than madness.

"Having lost your keys once, you should then take step two of wisdom: 'Think ahead: take actions now that could help you in the future. This includes improving your knowledge and skills in the areas that could help you to do better when future situations arise.' For example, you could install a hook for your keys, or choose a place where you will always leave them, so that the next time you lose them they will actually be hanging on their hook, or sitting in their regular location. Then if you can't find them they really may have been 'stolen'!

"Wisdom helps you in the present but can especially help you in the future.

"That concludes my stories for today."

"Thank you again for that, as always," said the man. "Before we go, there is one last thing I was wondering if you could do. Previously you have given us the guidelines on how to live by what is good, truthful and wise. I noticed there is some overlap in these: would it be possible to combine them in some way?"

The giant computer calculated.

"To what level?" it asked.

"Not too low a level, something that we could all understand."

"Very well. The combined steps for doing what is good, truthful and wise are:

"1. Life Actions: Do right and avoid doing or being involved in evil... as much as is practical; do your best at the time; think ahead; improve yourself; prepare for the future.

"2. Know Your Human-Brain: How it works (Calculations, Patterns-in-Memory, Evolutionary-Drives, Other-Influences); and its limitations (capacity, unknowns, inaccuracies, locking onto ideas, not seeing past itself or its ideas, unconscious calculations, self-deception).

"3. Corrective Actions for the Human-Brain: Add random ideas or words to your thoughts; check yourself from the outside; improve your knowledge;

practice meditation and other feeling-improving techniques, (for example, ritual, praying, remembering the good things, taking regular breaks)."

"Great. Thanks for that. I think that is enough for today."

The giant computer's screen displayed an animation of a head giving a single nod.

## SOME OF THE THINGS THE GIANT COMPUTER REFERENCED

COURT PROCEDURE
- NSW Government, Australia. *NSW Civil Procedure Act 2005 No 28.* NSW Parliamentary Counsel's Office, 11 Dec. 2020, www.legislation.nsw.gov.au/view/whole/html/inforce/current/act-2005-028.
- NSW Government, Australia. *NSW Criminal Procedure Act 1986 No 209.* NSW Parliamentary Counsel's Office, 1 Mar. 2021, www.legislation.nsw.gov.au/view/html/inforce/current/act-1986-209.

MEDITATION
- Dalai Lama, and Howard C. Cutler. *The Art of Happiness: A Handbook for Living.* Hachette Australia, 1998. Originally published 1988.
- Goleman, Daniel. *The Meditative Mind: The Varieties of Meditative Experience.* Subsequent ed., Tarcher, 1996. First version published 1977 as *The Varieties of the Meditative Experience.*
- Goyal, Madhav, et al. "Meditation Programs for Psychological Stress and Well-Being: A Systematic Review and Meta-Analysis." *JAMA Internal Medicine*, vol. 174, no. 3, Mar. 2014, pp. 357-368, doi:10.1001/jamainternmed.2013.13018.
- Lutz, Antoine, et al. "19. Meditation and the Neuroscience of Consciousness: An Introduction." *The Cambridge Handbook of Consciousness*, edited by Philip David Zelazo, et al., Cambridge University Press, 2007.
- Travis, Fred, and Jonathan Shear. "Focused Attention, Open Monitoring and Automatic Self-Transcending: Categories to Organize Meditations from Vedic, Buddhist and Chinese Traditions." *Consciousness and Cognition*, vol. 19, no. 4, Dec. 2010, pp. 1110–1118, doi:10.1016/j.concog.2010.01.007.

METAPHYSICS
- Carnap, Rudolf. "The Rejection of Metaphysics." *Philosophy and Logical Syntax*, 35th ed., Thoemmes Press, 1996. Originally published 1935.
- Hall, Ned. "David Lewis's Metaphysics." *Stanford Encyclopedia of Philosophy*, edited by Edward N. Zalta, Spring 2020 ed., plato.stanford.edu/archives/spr2020/entries/lewis-metaphysics. Originally published 2010.
- Hume, David. *An Enquiry Concerning Human Understanding.* Hackett Publishing Company, 1993. Originally published 1748.
- "Metaphysics." *American Heritage Dictionary of the English Language*, 5th ed., Houghton Mifflin Harcourt, 2015.
- Ney, Alyssa. *Metaphysics: An Introduction.* Routledge, 2014.

- Weber, Michel, editor. *After Whitehead: Rescher on Process Metaphysics.* Ontos Verlag, 2004.
- Wittgenstein, Ludwig. *Tractatus Logico-Philosophicus.* Translated by David Pears and Brian McGuinness, Routledge, 2001. Originally published 1921.
- Yablo, Stephen. "5. Does Ontology Rest on a Mistake?" *Things: Papers on Objects, Events, and Properties*, Oxford University Press, 2010.

PROOF
- Deming, David. "Do Extraordinary Claims Require Extraordinary Evidence?" *Philosophia*, vol. 44, Oct. 2016, doi:10.1007/s11406-016-9779-7.
- Gillispie, Charles Coulston. "Extraordinary Claims Require Extraordinary Evidence." *Pierre-Simon Laplace, 1749-1827: A Life in Exact Science*, Princeton University Press, 2000.
- Tressoldi, Patrizio E. "Extraordinary Claims Require Extraordinary Evidence: The Case of Non-Local Perception, a Classical and Bayesian Review of Evidences." *Frontiers in Psychology*, vol. 2, no. 117, 10 June 2011, doi:10.3389/fpsyg.2011.00117.
- Truzzi, Marcello. "On the Extraordinary: An Attempt at Clarification." *Zetetic Scholar*, vol. 1, no. 1, 1978, p. 11.

COMMENTS ON CHAPTER SEVEN BY THE SUPREME BEING

*The spiritual life is living by what is fundamentally true, the deepest truth that underlies all things, if you like. I know this can be hard to fathom, but that is not, of course, the purpose of the truth. The purpose is to try to find the best truth that you can, which may not be all that different to what the "Giant Computer" says: good, truthful and wise.*

# 8 WHAT DOES HISTORY TELL US?

"You have sometimes referred to what happened in the past and compared it to what is happening today. Could you tell me what history says to us about who we are and maybe what we could become?" asked the man.

"To be clear, when you speak of history you are referring to the history of human beings," replied the giant computer. "This has many details, of course, but these are not in themselves of any importance because they could have gone differently."

"Differently?"

"Yes, the human events could have taken a number of different turns, and so 'history', as you know it, could have been different. What matters is not the details but the overall pattern, which is that of Human-Brains doing their Calculations and carrying out actions based on these. The other interesting aspect is how new things were done, as these could not have been expected by what was happening around the people at the time."

"What new things?"

"The things that happened unexpectedly, which were not just a continuation of the expected patterns in the societies at that time. Examples are the discovery of radioactivity and the creation of the theory of relativity. These new discoveries and ideas resulted in major changes to your human societies and way of life, but were not able to be predicted by what was known at the time. It is interesting to assess how such a tiny brain as yours was able to make these major strides when there was nothing in the existing collective Patterns-in-Memory which could explain that."

"I see. I look forward to hearing your assessment about that," said the man.

"First I will describe what the overall pattern of your human history shows about you as a species."

"Okay."

"The overall pattern of human history is that of Human-Brains doing their Calculations and carrying out actions based on these. These Human-Brains used their Patterns-in-Memory and Other-Influences to make Calculations in order to fulfill their Evolutionary-Drives. I can extract a picture of the general Human-Brain Evolutionary-Drives from what has happened in history, noting that the exact expression of the Evolutionary-Drives in each individual Human-Brain is going to be unique.

"The most noticeable events in history seem to have been carried out by a minority of people, often in the role of leaders. The majority of people appear to have followed those leaders, or allowed them to do what they wanted. This shows that Human-Brains usually form themselves into groups which have leaders. A closer examination shows that the leadership roles could be contested and could change. Also, within the social groups there was stratification of the group members, with different roles being assigned to each person. People sometimes moved between roles and levels, with the highest-level group members being the most powerful. From this it can be calculated that Human-Brains are designed to form themselves into groups which have stratifications and role assignments, with the highest strata containing leaders, who dominate the decisions made by the group.

"Other patterns I find in history are: (1) Alliances between males and females, which lead to families being created, allowing the human species to continue its existence; (2) Subgroups being formed to do work, which is needed for survival; (3) Ideas being created and then taught to group members, especially in terms of social rules and methods; (4) Related to this are explanations for reality being created, including religious or spiritual ones, which the group is expected to follow; (5) Actions being taken to make things and do things, whose purpose is to be useful, decorative, entertaining and/or educational; (6) Travel being done, including migration, exploration and other forms; and (7) Conflicts between and within groups occurring, including wars and other forms of force being used.

"These patterns give indications about the way the Human-Brains do their Calculations. They also give indications about the probable Evolutionary-Drives that generally exist in Human-Brains. For example, war will result from the Calculations of the Human-Brains of the leaders, and it is also an indication of the aggressive nature of at least some Human-Brains' Evolutionary-Drives. It may also have come from the aggressive nature of the Other-Influences in some Human-Brains, for example, maturing young human males tend to be more aggressive than other types, as they have the Other-Influence of strong male hormones at work in their bodies. Such people will tend to become more easily involved in violent activities, such as a war that is happening at the time.

"The Evolutionary-Drives that I can identify at a high level from human history are: group-forming – with stratifications and role assignments, leader-following – in most, leader-role-seeking – in some, fighting, hunting, gathering, procreating, nurturing, protecting – especially of the young and the weak, creating, discovering, exploring, thinking, socializing, educating, decorating, worshipping and/or a sense of awe, discussing, and manipulating the mental state. All quite obvious."

"'Manipulating the mental state' – what is that and how is it an Evolutionary-Drive?" asked the man.

"Manipulating the mental state is a common activity in human history," said the computer. "It includes using drugs of various kinds, mental techniques, and engaging in activities designed to alter the inner state of the mind. For example, human beings may consume drinks containing alcohol in order to feel better. Or they might smoke or chew tobacco, or use stronger drugs. Some consume foods, such as 'comfort foods', in order to feel better. Others use mental techniques, such as meditation or positive self-affirmation, to change their mental state. Among other things, activities such as socializing, going to a party, attending rallies and sports events are also designed to change the attendees' mental state," explained the computer.

"I see. Thank you. How is that an Evolutionary-Drive?"

"I am classifying this as an Evolutionary-Drive in order to be simple. A more complex approach would be to say that the activities, chemicals or mental techniques are creating positive feelings, and these positive feelings are not directly caused by the actual Evolutionary-Drives. For example, drinking alcohol makes people feel better due to the chemical action on the brain, there is no actual Evolutionary-Drive to 'drink', or to 'change the mental state'. However, I have calculated that in history there are many examples of people seeking ways to change their inner mental state, and so I have listed this as a general human Evolutionary-Drive, as this is the simplest and most useful way to state it."

"I see. So it may be that changing our mental state is a kind of side effect of our feelings being altered, rather than our Evolutionary-Drives being in play, as it were. But you don't see any need to be that precise in your calculations from history."

"That is correct," confirmed the computer. "Returning to the calculation of the overall pattern of Human-Brain behavior from history, I can say that Human-Brains are designed by evolution to form groups which have leaders, social stratification and roles; to carry out the usual animal behaviors needed for the survival of the species; and to carry out more intellectual activities than those performed by other animals.

"I can now move on to the question of how new things were able to be done, as these could not have been expected by what was happening around the people at the time. I have already listed the related Evolutionary-Drives for this, which at the minimum include creating, discovering, exploring, thinking and discussing. These drives provided the motivation for particular human beings to look for new things, such as new ideas, new knowledge and new ways of doing things. The drive to discuss them may have also helped in the development of the new ideas.

"How do the new ideas and methods get created? Since your Human-Brain is a calculator which has Patterns-in-Memory included in its input, it follows that if a new Pattern-in-Memory is introduced then a new Calculation result may occur. Where can a new Pattern-in-Memory come from if it is not to be found in the collective Patterns-in-Memory which surround a person in a particular place and time in history? The possible sources are: (1) Something unusual in the individual's Patterns-in-Memory; (2) An unusual or unexpected event or thing experienced by the individual; (3) Something unusual in the individual's Other-Influences; (4) Continual searching by the individual, causing the eventual input of unexpected items into the Calculations; and (5) Skilled use of creative techniques by the individual, such as adding an unexpected word or idea into their Calculations.

"It is thanks to the way your Human-Brains work that new ideas have been able to be created which advanced your species further than could have been expected by the tiny size of your brains and the inaccuracy of your pattern-style memories. The ability to create new ideas has made up for your inability to store and process all information accurately and fully."

"What were some examples from history of this?"

"Examples of new ideas being created are everywhere in human history," replied the computer. "The list would stretch on for ages, but some examples are the invention of the wheel, the discovery of electricity and its relationship to magnetism, the creation of new forms of art and music, the discoveries of how to work different metals, the discovery of radioactivity, the invention of electronics, the creation of new political systems, the theory of evolution, quantum physics, the theory of relativity, organic chemistry, the internal combustion engine, and on and on. You are creatures which invent, create and discover things."

"That makes me feel quite proud," said the man, "even if I did not do that much myself. At least it is good to be part of a species which can do these things!"

"It has been useful for your species," agreed the computer.

"So, human history has been one of Human-Brains doing their human-style Calculations to fulfill their Evolutionary-Drives and Other-Influences in various fashions, including the creation of new ideas along the way," said the man. "And it could have gone differently because there are many factors in play, so you could not really say that it had to turn out the way it has so far."

"That is correct," said the computer.

"You have analyzed human history to see what it tells us about who we are at a high level, and come up with a list of our possible general

Evolutionary-Drives. I was hoping that you would have been able to work out what lessons we could learn from the actual events which occurred in our human history. Do you have anything you could say on that?"

"I can calculate that for you," said the computer. "There are a few things you could learn. One is that it would be better to stop leaving the formation of new ideas up to certain individuals and chance, especially as these have been so beneficial to your species. You could add training on how to do this into your education system, as I have mentioned before when I was talking about the improved political system. A second thing is that you could add training on how the Human-Brain works into your education system as well. This would help reduce the level of error that people have been carrying out based on their lack of knowledge of how they and other people really function. A third thing is to understand the way levels of authority are formed in your societies. From this you will easily be able to see the benefits of the improved political system which I proposed. If you continue to leave this up to the powerful to control then you will continue to have problems when the wrong kind of people come into power. Unfortunately, your natural human drive to follow the leader, at least most of the time, can work against you. You really need to implement a democratic-style system everywhere on your planet in order to mitigate this effect on your societies, at the minimum to cover the times when your leadership goes wrong. Your political system should also try to prevent people from getting locked in to particular social strata and roles. It is natural for human beings to create systems that do this, but that can be against what is best for the individual and may also be reducing the potential strength of your society, as people with great abilities are being prevented from utilizing them to maximum effect.

"In the world of ideas, it is especially important that you human beings continue to get involved in this. You have gained a great deal from all the ideas that you have had as a species over the years. There is a tendency for your society's ideas to get locked in to what has gone before. You have to work to avoid that. It is natural for your Calculations to try to carry out the needs of your Evolutionary-Drives, which means that your society's ideas can become twisted towards what is thought necessary for your social structures. For example, you may come up with ideas which are designed to promote the interests of your leaders. Or you may come up with ideas which are designed to keep people locked into their social place. Sometimes your ideas will be about promoting involvement in some war, or other conflict with outside groups. You have to be careful to avoid these types of ideas and to return your society's thinking back to what is really true... what is good, truthful and wise, if you like. Otherwise you will suffer as a society: retaining poor leaders, forcing people into roles they don't like, getting involved in conflicts which are not beneficial, and generally making the majority of your citizens unhappy, badly led and less productive than they otherwise would have been.

"Also on the subject of ideas, you need to be especially careful about the religious, spiritual or other world-views that your society has put forward. These can have been twisted towards what was thought necessary for your social structures, rather than reflecting a pure and honest view of what is actually true. You need to check to see if this has happened, and if it has you need to make corrections to get your society's religious, spiritual or other world-views back in line with what would be the actual truth for which they would stand. A guaranteed freedom for genuine investigation to be done in the world of ideas on the nature of your beliefs and their background will help your society here. In history there have been many examples of a society's 'beliefs' being twisted towards what the less-than-honest leadership wanted at the time. You need to make sure that you have escaped from all these old deceptions and are following the beliefs that would really make sense to you today.

"Another lesson you can learn from history is that you should continue to do the things that have helped you to improve your existence, such as exploring, investigating, being curious, inventing, creating, being artistic, making entertainment, experimenting, discussing, educating, and building freer and fairer societies. Obviously you will also have to do the basic things needed for survival, such as taking the steps required to produce, protect and nurture your young; getting the type of work done which is fundamentally necessary for your society's survival; making useful social rules – especially those related to my improved political system; providing education in the areas needed by your society; setting up defenses against attack by outside groups; and maintaining trained enforcement bodies to defend against all forms of attack from within your society. These are all obvious needs.

"You will no doubt continue to socialize, decorate and even fight, hopefully via civilized sports events – I don't think I need to emphasize these activities, which also occurred in history, as you will continue to do them anyway.

"Regarding manipulating your mental state, I recommend you learn from history what worked and what did not work for the individual and for your society, while still allowing the freedoms that my improved political system proposed. For example, strong mind-altering drugs have not been good for individuals or societies, especially when used in an uncontrolled manner. Meditation has been effective at changing your mental state, especially when practiced by experts, but may have sometimes slowed down progress among those experts as they felt so contented! My recommendation is that you allow the use of all techniques which are not harmful and also that they should be used in moderation.

"The last lesson from history is that Human-Brains seem to have an Evolutionary-Drive towards worship and/or a sense of awe, or 'the sacred', if you like. I have already commented on the need for caution on the 'ideas side' of your society's religious, spiritual or other world-views. In history there have been various subjects of worship and ways of worshipping, so it is not clear to me what your species will worship or how it will worship in the future. However, as there seems to be a fundamental human drive to do this, you should allow these types of activities to be carried out in your societies of the future, as long as these do not go against the rights and freedoms mentioned in my improved political system."

"Thank you. I am glad I asked you for a more detailed analysis of the lessons we could learn. That was really interesting," said the man. "For the final part, would you be able to now tell me what we could become, based on all of this?"

"Certainly," said the computer. "You could become creatures which understand what you actually are and how you function. From this you could design better ways to do things, such as implementing my improved political system across the whole planet. By teaching people how to create new ideas you could develop even faster than you have been doing so far. Your discoveries and inventions could be truly amazing. Eventually you may be able to cure all diseases, generate power without causing any harm to the environment, and manage your own daily lives to eliminate poverty and preventable social ills. That is not to say that you won't continue to have problems, as you will continue to be human beings with the inherent weaknesses of your Human-Brains, and the inherent dangers of your Evolutionary-Drives, Other-Influences and self-deceptions. But it is also not to say that you won't make progress on these matters, as you will have educated all your citizens on how their Human-Brains work and the steps they can take to improve on that. You also will have implemented the improved political system and legal processes which will make all this function better. There is hope, a reasonable hope, for your future.

"This will not be an easy process, however. It will take time. There will still be many issues along the way, including conflicts between nations, active resistance to the better political system, deceptions by leaders, unfairness, damage to the environment, aggression, crime, fanaticism, misunderstandings, nastiness, and all those sorts of things. It can't really be helped, as you are evolved creatures with shortcomings that could not be avoided. There is a rough road ahead for you, but with hope at the end of it," concluded the giant computer.

"That's quite high level," said the man. "Would you be able to provide a more detailed view, perhaps in relation to each historical lesson that you identified?"

"Yes.

"What you could become in regard to the lesson on the formation of new ideas is skilled operators at doing this. Your education system would teach everyone how to do this and some individuals would become skilled and use it to the most advantage for your society.

"In regard to knowing how your Human-Brain works, you could become skilled at teaching this to everyone. All your people would know something about the working of the Human-Brain and some people would become experts on it.

"In regard to the levels of authority in your societies, your world could become one where democratic-style systems exist in all countries. You could even have implemented versions of my improved political system every-where. This system would also help avoid the problem of people getting locked in to particular social roles, allowing them to flourish in the areas they wanted to.

"In the realm of ideas, you could become a world which focuses first on what is good, truthful and wise. From this you will improve your societies' leadership, social freedoms, peacefulness, happiness levels and productivity.

"Your religious, spiritual, enlightened and other world-views will be allowed to function freely in your societies, except in the areas where they contradict what is good, truthful and wise. Freedom to honestly investigate and discuss the true meaning of the beliefs will be guaranteed.

"There could be a lot of exploring, investigating, inventing, experiment-ing, discussing, educating, and creating art, entertainment, music, and the like going on. Your social, political and legal systems could be under constant examination as people look for improvements and adjustments which could make life better.

"There will still be a lot of traditional human activities occurring, such as forming romantic relationships, child-rearing, educating and working. There will also be social activities, entertainments, relaxation, games, and the deco-rating of homes, bodies, clothes, and so on.

"There will be a powerful defensive capability, which will align in its procedures and design with what is good, truthful and wise. Internal to your societies there will be the most peaceful application of law enforcement and protection for your citizens that can be arranged. Your courts will examine cases and the sentencing will be about effective protection for the future and full redress for those impacted, rather than for justice.

"The ways you change your inner mental state will be sensible and safe. It may include some regulated 'social' chemical use that your society finds acceptable. It may also include training in mental discipline techniques, such as meditation, focusing on the positive, and mindfulness.

"The overall change that your future societies could have made is that of being experts in the working of the Human-Brain. Quite different from what is happening today!" concluded the computer.

"Thank you," said the man. "I am not sure if there is any point in you providing any illustrative stories on this topic, but is there anything you would like to tell?"

"I have no likes," replied the computer, "but I can tell stories if you wish."

"No, that's okay," said the man. "Let's leave our interesting discussion on the lessons of history and start a new topic tomorrow."

"Agreed," said the computer.

SOME OF THE THINGS THE GIANT COMPUTER REFERENCED

GENERAL REFERENCES:

BRAIN
- Haines, Duane E. *Neuroanatomy Atlas in Clinical Context: Structures, Sections, Systems, and Syndromes.* 10th ed., Wolters Kluwer Health, 2018.
- Howard, Pierce J. *The Owner's Manual for the Brain: The Ultimate Guide to Peak Mental Performance at All Ages.* 4th ed., William Morrow, 2014.
- Mai, Juergen K., et al. *Atlas of the Human Brain.* 4th ed., Academic Press, 2015.
- Seth, Anil K., editor. *30-Second Brain: The 50 Most Mind-Blowing Ideas in Neuroscience, Each Explained in Half a Minute.* Pier 9, 2014.
- Shepherd, Gordon M., editor. *The Synaptic Organization of the Brain.* 5th ed., Oxford University Press, 2003.

EVOLUTIONARY DRIVES
- Ahuvia, Aaron. "If Money Doesn't Make Us Happy, Why Do We Act As If It Does?" *Journal of Economic Psychology*, vol. 29, no. 4, Aug. 2008, pp. 491-507, doi:10.1016/j.joep.2007.11.005.
- Andersson, Claes, and Petter Törnberg. "Toward a Macroevolutionary Theory of Human Evolution: The Social Protocell." *Biological Theory*, vol. 14, 2019, pp. 86–102, doi:10.1007/s13752-018-0313-y.
- Bertocci, Rosemary, and Francis H. Rohlf. "A Lonerganian Kritik of the Evolutionary Sciences and Religious Consciousness: The Isomorphism of Structures, Activities, and Analysis." *Method: Journal of Lonergan Studies*, vol. 20, no. 1, Spring 2002, pp. 1-9, doi:10.5840/method20022016.
- Cuesta, Jose A., et al. "Reputation Drives Cooperative Behaviour and Network Formation in Human Groups." *Scientific Reports*, vol. 5, no. 7843, 19 Jan. 2015, doi:10.1038/srep07843.
- Ferguson, Eva Dreikurs. *Motivation: A Biosocial and Cognitive Integration of Motivation and Emotion.* Oxford University Press, 2000.
- Harrigan, William Joseph, and Michael Lamport Commons. "Replacing Maslow's Needs Hierarchy with an Account Based on Stage and Value." *Behavioral Development Bulletin*, vol. 20, no. 1, Apr. 2015, pp. 24-31, doi:10.1037/h0101036.
- Maslow, Abraham H. *Motivation and Personality.* 3rd ed., Longman Asia, 1987. Originally published 1954.
- Papadopoulou, Marianna. "An Instinct to Play: An Evolutionary Approach to Pretend Play." *International Journal for Cross-Disciplinary Subjects in Education*, vol. 2, no. 1, Mar. 2011, pp. 335-341, doi:10.20533/ijcdse.2042.6364.2011.0047.

- Perret, Cedric, et al. "From Disorganized Equality to Efficient Hierarchy: How Group Size Drives the Evolution of Hierarchy in Human Societies." *Proceedings of the Royal Society B: Biological Sciences*, vol. 287, no. 1928, 3 June 2020, doi:10.1098/rspb.2020.0693.
- Petri, Herbert L., and John M. Govern. *Motivation: Theory, Research, and Application*. 6th ed., Cengage Learning, 2012.
- Pirson, Michael. "Ontological Foundations of Stakeholder Dignity and Well-Being: Concepts and Measurement." *SSRN*, Dec. 2018, doi:10.2139/ssrn.3296735.

## HISTORY

- Andrea, Alfred J., and Carolyn Neel, editors. *World History Encyclopedia*. ABC-CLIO, 2010.
- Bogucki, P., editor. *Encyclopedia of Society and Culture in the Ancient World*. Facts on File, 2008.
- Braudel, Fernand. *On History*. Translated by Sarah Matthews, The University of Chicago Press, 1982.
- Carr, E. H. *What is History?: The George Macaulay Trevelyan Lectures Delivered in the University of Cambridge January-March 1961*. Penguin, 2008.
- Cohen, David William. *The Combing of History*. University of Chicago Press, 1994.
- Duran, Will, and Ariel Durant. *The Lessons of History*. Simon & Schuster, 2010. Originally published 1968.
- Hobsbawm, Eric. *On History*. Abacus, 1998.
- Jenkins, Keith. *Rethinking History*. 3rd ed., Routledge, 2003. Originally published 1991.
- Jordanova, Ludmilla. *History in Practice*. 2nd ed., Bloomsbury Publishing, 2006.
- Roberts, John Morris, and Odd Arne Westad. *The History of the World*. 6th ed., Oxford University Press, 2013.
- Southgate, Beverley C., *What is History For?* Psychology Press, 2005.

## PATTERNS AND NEW IDEAS

- De Bono, Edward. *I am Right, You are Wrong*. Penguin, 2016. Originally published 1990.
- De Bono, Edward, editor. *Eureka! An Illustrated History of Inventions from the Wheel to the Computer*. Holt, Rinehart and Winston, 1974.

## RELIGION

- Barton, John. *A History of the Bible: The Book and its Faiths*. Allen Lane, 2019.
- The Babylonian Talmud.
- The Bhagavad Gita.

- The Bible.
- The Dhammapada.
- The Hadith.
- The Mahayana Sutras.
- The Pali Canon.
- The Quran.
- The Tanakh.
- The Tao Te Ching.
- The Upanishads.
- The Vedas.
- The Zhuangzi.

COMMENTS ON CHAPTER EIGHT BY THE SUPREME BEING

*History has had its ups and downs, as the "Giant Computer" observed. I think there is an opportunity here for there to be more ups and less downs if the lessons of history can be learned and applied! I wish you all the best in this challenging endeavor.*

# 9 ANIMALS, EVOLUTION AND INTELLIGENCE

"When you were talking about history it reminded me that you have referred to people as some kind of advanced animals. You even said that some animals may have a similar consciousness to ours. Could you tell me more about this, especially what the animals can tell us about who we are? Also, I admit that this is a bit obscure, but would animals be able to have any kind of 'spiritual' experiences? What sort of inner life might they be having?" asked the man.

"Human beings are evolved creatures, as shown in the theory of evolution and the study of genetics," replied the giant computer. "As evolved creatures, human beings exhibit features in common with other evolved creatures, in particular, with the animals. Human beings are genetically the most similar to the existing bonobos and chimpanzees, but came from a different branch of the apes via a series of creatures which are now extinct. What you can learn from this about who you are is that you are evolved creatures with animal attributes, including a relatively complex brain which has a level of consciousness. You have limbs similar to other apes, but two have been modified to allow walking upright. You also have far less body hair, except for that on the top of your head, which can grow quite long.

"Your physical attributes say something about who you are, but your mental attributes are even more important in defining this, as you have done such astonishingly different things to the other animals. This is so obvious that the civilized people of history have usually thought of humans as being separate from the animal world. It was only with the discovery of evolution and its mechanisms that people have returned to seeing themselves as related to the animals. Hence the modern question arises of what can be learned about being human from other animals. The corresponding other side of the question then arises: what is similar, and in which animals, to the human mental experience?

"The current knowledge cannot answer these questions very well, at this stage. There are studies and experiments which can tell us something, but there is much that is not known yet. This is what is known: (1) It seems likely that at least some animals are conscious, including all mammals, birds, octopuses and possibly other creatures; (2) The closest mentally to human beings appear to be the great apes – chimpanzees, bonobos, orangutans and gorillas; (3) The second group of animals which appear to be mentally close to human beings includes dolphins, killer whales, elephants, African gray parrots, Eurasian magpies, crows, rooks, jackdaws, ravens and possibly pigeons, noting that this list may not be complete; (4) The animals which have been able to communicate in some form of simplified taught language with human beings include chimpanzees, bonobos, orangutans, gorillas and an African gray parrot, but this is not to say that some other animals weren't communicating or wouldn't be able to communicate, we don't know everything about this as yet.

"No animal has clearly described its mental world to human beings, but studies have identified behaviors in some animals which are intelligent and indicate that internal reasoning is going on, even if this reasoning is not as powerful as that of a human being. So far, no animal has communicated its 'spiritual' experiences, so I cannot answer that question for you.

"If you take a step back from all this and look more generally then you can clearly see that human beings exhibit behaviors that have similarities with other animals. From this you can calculate, at a high level, the drives that are motivating their behaviors, similar to what I did with my analysis of human history," concluded the computer.

"Okay. Could you tell me what we can learn from the animals about the drives that are motivating human behavior at a high level, but excluding the ones from history that you have already told me about?" asked the man.

"Yes. The animal behaviors which are not exactly the same as the drives I already listed from human history are: (1) Seeking and eating food; (2) Seeking and drinking water, though not all animals need to do this; (3) Fleeing danger; (4) Hiding from danger; (5) Grooming; (6) Building burrows, nests, and so on; (7) Playing, at least in the young; (8) Resting; and (9) Sleeping. Human beings, therefore, are likely to have Evolutionary-Drives which include these things, that is: to seek and eat food, including via actions related to hunting and gathering; to seek and drink refreshing fluids; to flee or hide from danger when necessary; to groom themselves and possibly some other people and creatures, such as their loved ones and pets; to build protective structures; to play, which is also done by human adults; and to rest and sleep when needed."

"Okay, that was not very illuminating, but it made sense," said the man.

"Maybe you see it that way," said the computer, "but it does tell you more about who you are than by just looking at the historical analysis. Also, you could learn from what is different about human beings compared to the animals."

"Okay, what is different?"

"Studies seeking to find what is similar in animals to human beings have also contrarily exposed what is different. For example, studies have shown that human beings are not, as was previously thought, the only animals to use tools. But even though some animals have been shown to use tools, what is *not* similar is the extent and skill with which human beings use them. It may seem amazing to see a chimpanzee using rocks to crack open nuts, or a crow using a stick to extract a grub, but as soon as you look at human beings you see immense differences. Human beings' use of tools is extraordinary, even in your earlier times. What are spears, bows and arrows, fires, baskets, bark boats, fishing hooks, bone needles, stone knives and so on, compared to rocks, sticks, leaves, and the like, even if these were selected and slightly modified by the animal? The Human-Brain's ability to think about and create its tools is outstanding.

"A second major difference is in language. Studies have found that many animals, including bees, have ways of communicating with each other, but none of these styles of communication has all the characteristics of human-created languages. Only human beings have been able to create complex, abstract styles of language. Even the few animals that have been able to learn to communicate with humans were not able to grasp the full sentence structural style of human language. As far as has been shown by the studies that have been done up till now, only human beings can grasp all the abstract concepts that are included in their human language structures. The Human-Brain's level of intellectual ability in languages seems to be unique.

"A third major difference is in the level of reasoning that a human being can carry out. Even though some animals have been shown to be capable of thinking, it is not in the same league as human beings. The most significant difference is in the ability of human beings to plan for the future – the foundation of wisdom, you might say. This seems to be based on the Human-Brain's ability to remember the sequence of events, as seen in the way you form your Patterns-in-Memory. The way the Human-Brain forms its Patterns-in-Memory may also explain how the Human-Brain does its abstract thinking, at least to some extent, as the Patterns-in-Memory are a kind of abstraction of reality because they only hold the 'key features' of the object, events or thoughts that they are based on. There are other ways of explaining this, but it might be an indication of the way abstraction is done.

"These three areas are not Evolutionary-Drives in themselves, but they explain the differences in the way your human drives are expressed when compared to the animals. For example, all human beings desire food, as do animals, but the humans' high ability levels with tools, language and reasoning take the way food is sought, treated, discussed, prepared and consumed to a whole new level. What animal cooks popcorn on a stove, puts it in a paper bucket, seasons it, and eats it while watching a movie?

"You asked what animals can tell you about who you are: these differences also answer this question for you."

"Right. Okay. So, what you are saying is that human beings are a kind of advanced animal, but one that is extraordinarily extremely advanced," said the man. "If we want to learn about ourselves from the animals then we can see our shared style of Evolutionary-Drives being expressed, but this will be done in an extraordinarily extremely advanced way. Regarding what the animals' inner world is really like, we have little idea so far. It looks like a very few are aware of their own existence, a few more are able to do a bit of thinking into the future, and many are conscious in some way, but that is about all we can say until some better way of finding out is discovered. I guess that is all we can learn from the knowledge of today – is that about right?"

"Yes, what you have said is largely correct," replied the computer.

"I could ask you to go into more detail on what the studies with animals have exactly shown, I am curious about that, but I am not sure that this would be a productive use of your time. I can look this up myself. [See references at the end of this chapter.] I think I would prefer to move on to my next topic at this stage, which is to ask you to calculate what we can learn from evolution about how our Human-Brains might work."

The giant computer calculated. "Very little, I expect," it finally replied. "What you can learn is how the brain changed its look and size as it developed over the millions of years, and speculation on how the older structures work within the Human-Brain of today. None of this will give you a clear answer to your question. However, I will now proceed.

"Evolution tells you, at a high level, that your Human-Brain is a development of previous animal brains. The development has given it a large size in proportion to your body size, and certain special areas, such as those used for language processing. There is nothing in particular that is remarkably different from other animals, everything looks to be a logical development of what previously existed. For example, a larger brain size in proportion to body size occurs in other intelligent animals, and communication areas also exist in other social animals. The human brain seems to be, as far as is known today, an extension along the existing lines of other animal brains.

"Consequently, with today's knowledge, evolution can only tell you that the Human-Brain is highly intelligent, skilled at social interactions and communication, highly skilled at making and using tools, innovative, able to learn complex sequences of physical actions, and able to adapt to different environments. These are not surprising things to learn as they are already quite obvious from observing human beings compared to other animals.

"Regarding how Human-Brains might work, there are many similarities to other animal brains. Firstly, there are various specialized areas which are similar in all vertebrate brains. These include areas for body regulation, perception, emotion and thinking. Secondly, in the more intelligent animals the thinking area is proportionally larger. Some part of it has the ability to change its functionality, in other words it is 'non-specific', able to learn new things. This is what allows the intelligent animals to change their behavior. In Human-Brains this makes it possible to learn different languages, among other things. Speculation on how this thinking area might work includes the idea that the brain is designed to create a model or map of its environment. This map can then be referred to when planning future actions. For example, a leader wolf might plan where the pack should go on their next hunt. A crow might plan how to untie a plastic trash bag to get at what is inside. A chimpanzee might search for the right shaped rocks for cracking open nuts. A human being might plan their journey to another location, or for their future career. This internal map equates to the Patterns-in-Memory, which I have discussed before.

"The specialized areas of the brain which are to do with emotion are related to the Evolutionary-Drives. They provide internal rewards and punishments when different events occur in the outside world or in your thoughts. To be precise, this happens when different events are *perceived* as occurring. These rewards and punishments ensure that your Human-Brain classifies events as good, indifferent or bad, and as important, less important or not important. These classifications help determine what should be remembered in your Patterns-in-Memory and are associated with it so that the next time a similar event is perceived, an appropriate type of response is taken, such as moving towards or away from the item or situation. This mechanism is similar in style to that of the other animals.

"The specialized areas of the brain which are to do with body regulation are also similar in style to that of the other animals. These take care of things such as unconscious breathing, body temperature regulation, sleep cycles, and so on.

"The specialized areas of the brain which are to do with perception are also similar to those in other animals. Human-Brains are very good at processing visual images, are reasonably good at processing sound, but do not have much processing power for smell. The processing of other senses, such as touch and knowing the position of the limbs, is similar to that of other animals.

"So, what is known about the evolution of the Human-Brain tells you that human beings are intelligent and social. They can learn and create new behaviors. They are able to change. They have internal models of reality, which are similar to maps in that they do not contain all of the details. They have emotions which are related to the operation of Evolutionary-Drives, and to the Other-Influences in some instances. These have guided what has been put into the Patterns-in-Memory and how it has been classified: good to bad, and important to not important. Human beings are also predominantly visual creatures, with a poor sense of smell.

"As you can see, there is not much to learn from what is known about the evolution of the brain today," concluded the computer.

"Can I ask you one more thing about this?" queried the man. "How would an evolved type of computer work when it was asked to assess what is true? I am calling the thinking part of the Human-Brain a computer here, but saying it is one that has come about through the blind process of evolution, rather than having been designed, as you have been."

"As I said before, the Human-Brain is a biological organ, and it works in that style of way," replied the computer. "Biological organs automatically do things that work to keep a creature alive. For example, the kidneys automatically extract excess water and undesirable chemicals from the blood, allowing the body to maintain its correct balance of water and chemicals. There is no thinking needed by the kidneys, they are 'designed' by the evolutionary process to do what they have to do for the good of the whole body. The same is true of the Human-Brain, which is designed by the evolutionary process to correlate information coming in via the body's organs of perception and to compare that with what is in the Patterns-in-Memory, under the influence of the Other-Influences, and then determine if any action is needed for the good of the body, and finally to initiate and guide that action. It was not designed by any thinking being, it was created by natural biological processes over time, which made it entirely to achieve the survival of that creature and also of its species, that is, human beings.

"I, on the other hand, was designed by thinking organisms, and so my operation can be easily understood as it has been deliberately designed and built to achieve a particular purpose. A Human-Brain's purpose is to guide the body through life, which is not under the rules of a designed mechanism but is more like a blindly created organ that could be achieving its goals through a whole host of unknown, illogical circuits, the only rule being that these should finally work to keep the body alive and help prolong the species... hopefully, at least.

"What would an evolved type of computer do, one that has come about through the blind process of evolution? Well, that assumes that there is some way for evolution to act on the computer, such as through sexual reproduction with the passing on of gene-like information. In other words, it is assuming that the computer would develop in the same sort of way as a biological brain. As a result, it is reasonable to say that an evolved type of computer would be just like a Human-Brain, in that its circuits would develop more or less randomly and be selected according to what worked to make the computer's gene-like information get passed on to succeeding generations. It would most likely end up being similar in its operation to the Human-Brain, just as we see with convergent evolution for intelligence, where different types of animals have developed similar intelligent actions which work for them in their environments.

"Convergent evolution explains why some birds show the same type of intelligence as some mammals, in spite of their brains looking quite different. For example, both crows and chimpanzees in the wild have been seen to select branches and strip off the leaves to make sticks suitable for poking into ant nests in order to extract the ants for food. The areas of the brain that seem to be used to work this out are quite different looking, yet the intelligent behavior is the same. The reason this happens is that the reality that these animals face is the same, and so intelligence must end up doing the same things with that reality. If sticks are available for getting at ants then any intelligent animal, whether it is a bird or a mammal or whatever, must work out the same sort of procedures for getting those ants.

"In the same way, any computer that was able to develop its circuits through some kind of evolutionary process would finally end up doing the same sort of things as intelligent animals. Maybe the computer's processing power would be greater, but its circuits would reflect the same kind of 'organic' development as seen in an animal, that is, it could have all kinds of illogical circuits with obscure purposes which finally result in the computer calculating actions which work to keep it in existence and help it to prolong its 'species', I mean, assuming that it is successful in its 'evolutionary process'.

"Evolution means this kind of result, it cannot be the same as 'intelligent design'," concluded the computer.

"Right, I see," said the man. "This fires off a lot of questions in my mind. One, for example, is how come people are able to manipulate symbols in a logical or even mathematical way if their brains are not designed but have come about via evolution? When you think of the philosophers, mathematicians and logicians then how could this have come about? Do you see what I mean?"

"The logical answer," replied the computer, "is that these logical and mathematical symbol manipulations are able to be traced back to how an intelligent brain has to approach reality."

"How so?"

"Regarding mathematics, it must be that an intelligent brain is able to extract some sense of numbers from what really exists. For example, there may be two fish or three fish in the pond. From this appreciation of the idea of numbers, the rest of mathematics may be able to be created over time. If the intelligent brain is able to communicate with other intelligent brains, and those brains spend some time thinking about the ideas which have been communicated, then over the generations they may be able to advance those ideas to quite a high level of sophistication.

"Regarding logic, an intelligent brain may be able to extract this from reality as well. For example, there are fish in the river but there are NOT any fish in the field. Another example, there are edible animals in the river which include fish AND eels, but NOT freshwater snails OR certain frogs."

"But how can a brain which is designed by evolution be logical enough to get these things right? I mean, if it comes up with mathematical theories then how come those actually work in reality, like when we were able to send people to the Moon by using sophisticated calculations?"

"There must be enough similarity to reality in these calculations or theories for the approach to work," said the computer. "And where something does not work then it's 'back to the drawing board', which means that the intelligent brain is able to identify when its ideas are not working and to then try to do something to correct them. The truth is that this does not happen all the time: many Human-Brains have failed to identify when their ideas are not working, and consequently have not taken any action to correct them!"

"So how come some Human-Brains *have* been able to identify when their ideas are not working?"

"That is not so surprising," said the computer, "as seeing something go wrong is a straightforward matter. It is more meaningful to examine why a Human-Brain would *not* see that something was going wrong, we can learn a lot more from this about the way the brain actually works."

"For example?"

"For example, why would a Human-Brain continue to initiate the action of smoking when it is well known that this is harmful to the body? This action demonstrates that a Human-Brain's Calculations may not be logical or based on accurate knowledge. We can then look at what the Calculations could be based on. We find that the Calculations go through illogical circuits which include inaccurate and incomplete information, as held in the Patterns-in-Memory, and influenced by Other-Influences. The Patterns-in-Memory include emotional judgements about whether something is good, bad or indifferent, based on feelings generated in relation to mindless Evolutionary-Drives. So, if smoking tobacco generates good feelings then it is difficult for the Human-Brain to see it as a bad thing, a thing to be avoided. Rather, the 'smoking' Pattern-in-Memory is classified as a good thing, a thing to be sought out. This simple example demonstrates that the intelligent Human-Brain is a biological organ which came about via evolution and is not a perfect, logical calculator of reality."

"But why then are logical, rational ideas able to be created by some Human-Brains?"

"Because an intelligent creature should be doing that," said the computer. "By this I mean that intelligence is a 'convergent evolution' kind of thing, moving a creature towards being able to understand and manipulate reality in order to achieve its evolutionary goals. The perfect creature, if you like, would be one which understands reality accurately and can create new ideas which allow it to control that reality 'in totality', as it were."

"To achieve its evolutionary goals?"

"Yes, in terms of evolved creatures you would say that," agreed the computer.

"Okay, but why would evolutionary goals be the top goals of creation?" asked the man.

"That is a contradictory question," said the computer. "An intelligent evolved creature is logically designed, if I can use that term, to maximize its evolutionary existence, and that of its species. 'The top goal of creation' is quite a different concept. It is one that implies that creation has some purpose, some overarching reason for its existence, which is the opposite of talking about evolution, where there is no purpose at all, only what life has done automatically in order to exist and to try to continue to exist."

"I see. So, the perfect creature understands accurately and can create effectively. And this is a logical and rational view which came about from the way intelligence would operate if it was to reach its best possible level of functioning, in order to achieve its goal of keeping the body alive and promoting its species. Maybe I should say that you would call this logical and rational, as a well-designed machine would?"

"Yes, you could say that is what I am designed to calculate. But I might challenge your statement by saying that it is inefficient and can be misleading to rely on evolutionarily-developed circuits to do things accurately."

"Even though convergent evolution would force sense to finally come out?"

"In spite of that, mainly. A creature may become more sensible, but it would always have its original origins. Even the most intelligent creature would still carry its history of development in its thoughts and operation."

"An interesting point," nodded the man. "So, a human being may be an example of that. Even the best and most intelligent of people would still demonstrate their evolutionary origins in the way they thought, in the lack of accuracy of their knowledge, in the influence of their emotions and evolutionary drives in their lives. A human being may be a highly intelligent development, but it is still an evolutionarily designed one."

"Exactly," agreed the computer.

"So, going back to my original question: how come such a creature has been able to get reasonable rational ideas at all? Wouldn't they always be colored by the evolutionary limitations?"

"Yes and no," said the computer. "Yes, because the nature of the Human-Brain must impact the quality of its ideas. And no, because the Human-Brain, speaking generally, must work well enough for the body to survive and for its species to continue. This general soundness is what makes it possible for an idea to be 'right'.

"An example is knowing how many fish are visible in the pond. Nearly everyone will be able to get this right. But when we move away from the simpler matters then the limitations of the Human-Brain start to come out.

Who is the best candidate for President, or leader of our country? This kind of question is so complex that Human-Brains cannot calculate it with accuracy. As a result, there will be a range of opinions given, as each brain calculates a different response. This reflects the differing Patterns-in-Memory and Other-Influences at work. It also shows that evolutionary forces may not be able to shape intelligence to a level where perfectly accurate answers can be calculated."

"I get that," interrupted the man. "But what interests me is why some people are able to calculate the answer more accurately than others. How come some people are more likely to be right about the best Presidential candidate while some others seem to have a knack for getting this wrong? Can I go further? How come some people seem to get so many of their life answers wrong, what is going on there?"

"This is not a difficult question," said the computer. "As it is with the animals, so it is with human beings. Each individual animal has a unique level and version of intelligence. Just because you belong to the most intelligent species does not mean that you are individually as smart as the next person. Also, the way you express your intelligence is individual to you, no one else has exactly the same style as your brain.

"Smartness is your Human-Brain's ability to get things right. This ability comes from various sources, including (1) Your Human-Brain's inherited development potential; (2) The quality and quantity of your Human-Brain's Patterns-in-Memory; (3) The negative and positive impacts of your Human-Brain's Other-Influences; and (4) Your Human-Brain's desire to improve itself. If your Human-Brain works at it it can improve itself, but it has to distrust and check its Patterns-in-Memory, be cautious about what is motivating itself unconsciously, and test and check and work at it until it does get better. Many Human-Brains do not do these things, for whatever reasons, and they therefore remain inferior in their ability to get things right," concluded the computer.

"'Get things right', meaning to more accurately reflect reality," said the man. "And this will make your Human-Brain's answers more rational and reasonable. Okay, I understand that now. Thank you.

"One last thing, though. You said that we can change ourselves for the better. How can that be possible, given that we are thinking like evolved creatures, the way we were made? Wouldn't our inherent mental limitations hold us back, and couldn't our inherited drives divert us from the goal of seeking to improve ourselves, if you get what I mean?"

"The solution is that your Human-Brain needs to make a powerfully-remembered goal to improve itself by turning this into the strongest desire it can, and then repeating this to itself from time to time each day," replied the computer. "The stronger it can make the feeling, the stronger will be the change to its Patterns-in-Memory. This will help it to remember the goal of improving itself when it is doing calculations in other areas. It could also spend time thinking over its various goals and what it has done about them. This will help spread its desire to improve into many of its Patterns-in-Memory, increasing its chance of remembering to strive for improvement over a wider range of its activities each day."

"Okay, but what guarantee is there that any particular Human-Brain will be able to do this? Isn't it possible that it might fall away and return to doing things the old way, the less intelligent way? Could it be that a particular Human-Brain is simply not designed to be able to overcome its own stupidity and ignorance, lacking the capacity or inner structure to be able to make the change to a 'more intelligent' lifestyle?" challenged the man.

"Yes, there is no guarantee that a particular Human-Brain will be able to improve its level of intelligence," replied the computer, "but what is certain is that the most important element in making the improvement is the Human-Brain's Calculation that this is really worth doing. If it does make this Calculation and pursues this goal then it will, very likely, improve the effectiveness of its actions for helping its body to survive and its species to continue.

"The areas of the Human-Brain that it can make more effective include its Patterns-in-Memory, its emotions, and its body movements."

"Wait!" interrupted the man. "You have introduced some new ideas here: emotions and body movements. Please explain these."

"Yes, I will in a moment. But first I will mention that its Patterns-in-Memory can be made more intelligent by upgrading them to be closer to reality than they currently are. For example, a Human-Brain can improve its Patterns-in-Memory about smoking by reading the scientific studies that have been done on smoking's biological impacts. As its knowledge increases, its Patterns-in-Memory will get closer to the actual reality of the dangers of this practice. From this its calculated actions should get closer to those which would help its body to survive. It, therefore, has become more intelligent.

"Now, about emotions: these are related to Evolutionary-Drives and Other-Influences. If something can be done which improves the emotions so that they more closely reflect reality then that Human-Brain will calculate actions which are more effective at helping its body and species to continue. How can emotions be made to more closely reflect reality, especially when they would seem to be related to unchangeable Evolutionary-Drives and somewhat unpredictable Other-Influences? The answer is twofold. First, the Patterns-in-Memory can be altered so that when the Human-Brain uses them in Calculations the outcome is different. For example, if a Human-Brain's Patterns-in-Memory about foreign people is changed from dislike and distrust to a more open and realistically-observing view then the emotions that the Evolutionary-Drives and Other-Influences generate will be more thoughtful and less negative. The second part of the answer is to develop the

Human-Brain's ability to see and control itself. For example, the Human-Brain which has regularly practiced meditation will have developed an increased ability to see its own thoughts and feelings in operation, and to direct them. This ability seems to be coming from circuits which have grown in specific areas of the Human-Brain, as regular meditators have denser gray matter in the parts of the brain associated with learning and memory, controlling emotions, and body awareness. Another way for the Human-Brain to develop an ability to see and control itself is through practicing bringing its thoughts to its conscious attention. Repeating this operation will add to its Patterns-in-Memory so that Calculations also bring thoughts to the Consciousness more often. Once a thought is brought to Consciousness there is some chance to understand it and control it, but when a thought is not made conscious it will necessarily do whatever it wants.

"Regarding body movements, you may remember that I said that the Human-Brain is able to learn complex sequences of physical actions. Such physical actions can be useful for helping its body to survive and its species to continue. These, therefore, are part of intelligence. If a Human-Brain learns useful sequences of physical actions then it will have increased its level of intelligence. For example, a Human-Brain which has learned to drive a car more accurately and effectively will be more physically able to avoid losing control when its car skids. A Human-Brain which has learned a martial art will be more physically able to avoid injury when its body is attacked.

"All these improvement actions are done by the Human-Brain. A Human-Brain must calculate that the improvement actions are good things to be done, that they are achievable, and that they are important because they will provide desirable benefits. It will then be likely to carry out the actions. When the Human-Brain sees that the benefits are real and desirable, it will calculate that it is good to carry out further improvement actions, which will lead to even greater improvements over time. Positive results will lead the Human-Brain to continue to improve its intelligence level over time."

"Which makes me wonder if negative results could cause the opposite effect," said the man. "If a Human-Brain tried to improve but had bad results, or no results, then it might calculate that improvements to its intelligence are not possible, and so stop making the effort."

"That can happen," agreed the computer. "Which is why your education system and the like should aim to encourage people by showing them that improvement really is possible, if an effort is made. The negative approach of showing people that they are stupid may backfire, and cause them to give up all efforts. This is wrong, because it is highly likely that any individual Human-Brain has plenty of capacity for improving itself. The few that do not are probably extremely damaged or abnormal in some way. In nearly every case the greatest enemy to a Human-Brain's improvement is its own Calculation that this cannot be done."

"Maybe our capacity has hardly been tapped," suggested the man.

"That is likely," agreed the computer.

"Your comments on education triggered another question in my mind," said the man. "Earlier you said that intelligence is for helping the body to survive and the species to continue. Wouldn't it be fair to say that a lot of what is taught in education systems today is not directly related to that? And if that is the case, wouldn't the Human-Brain calculate that the subjects were not really worth learning? So how can the educators convince those Human-Brains that it is worth the effort to become more intelligent by learning those subjects?"

"To be clear, I did not say that intelligence is for those things in itself. I said that intelligence in terms of convergent evolution must aim for the same goals: understand reality and develop techniques to help the body survive and the species to continue. True intelligence may not necessarily aim for those particular goals. For example, true intelligence may aim for what is good, truthful and wise, which is not necessarily the same thing as what evolution-arily-developed intelligence might aim for.

"Regarding convincing other Human-Brains to make an effort to learn something, there are many ways to achieve this. All of them depend on demonstrating to the particular Human-Brain that some worthwhile benefit will be achieved by its effort. For example, a Human-Brain that wants to speak to its romantic partner when it has moved to another country will be motivated to learn the partner's native language. Any Evolutionary-Drive, Other-Influence, or goals that have been calculated from the combination of these with the Patterns-in-Memory, can be used to motivate a Human-Brain to learn, as long as that brain can be convinced that the learning will very likely result in the goal being achieved. Try to deceive that Human-Brain and then get caught out and you will probably never be able to get it to put in an effort again.

"The ways to *not* convince are many. One is to make no effort to connect the learning to any Human-Brain goal. In this case the Human-Brains will only do the minimum that they can, based on the level of force you can bring to bear on them. Another way to fail is to refuse to answer questions on why this subject needs to be learned. If you say 'because I said so' then you will simply cause resentment in the Human-Brains you are addressing. They will be watching for any way out from under your oppressive control. Another way to fail is to give false reasons. The Human-Brains may work out that you are doing this and will then resent you trying to deceive them. You will simply be creating enemies out of those you wanted to teach. Another way is to state benefits that would be of no interest to the Human-Brains you are addressing. Another is to convince the Human-Brain that it would not be able to succeed in learning this, as I mentioned before. The ways you convince the Human-Brain that it must fail may not be obvious to you. It is not just the case of you being rude to that person, it can be in more subtle ways that you discourage them. Finally, the Human-Brain has to believe in you. If you do not get the respect of the Human-Brain, if it decides that you are not successful in this subject, or that you are not capable of teaching it to others, or not really interested, then it will stop listening to you. It will prefer to seek out a more competent and successful teacher, if it can.

"Regarding the subjects that are taught in education systems today, I calculate that most of these truly have no bearing on the lives of the students, or a minimal bearing at best. Some subjects are useful up to a point, a point which is often exceeded by the education systems, but most would only be relevant to very specialized people. What is missing, as I have said before, is training on how the Human-Brain works and in methods for generating new ideas. I would add to this that there are plenty of subjects that would be of great use to most people which are not included in the current curriculums. For example, education in financial planning would help many people more than learning about differential calculus. Education in the tricks of advertisers would be more helpful than learning about Ancient Egypt. All topics may be taught, but the main education provided in a society ought to be designed to first help people to live well, to flourish, if you like. This is obvious but is rarely done."

"That is so true," said the man. "A good point. While you were talking a final question for today came into my mind. It was about spiritual views. I was wondering about this: if our intelligence was developed by evolutionary forces and was not designed, what does that say about our ideas about spirits and God, or the like?"

The computer calculated. "It says that these ideas may have come from the way your evolved Human-Brains work," it replied. "I said *may*, because this cannot be proved beyond a reasonable doubt to all people, as I have explained before."

"Yes, but that points to the possibility that the other intelligent animals may have religious or spiritual experiences as well, because of convergent evolution, as it were."

"That is impossible to say with current knowledge," said the computer. "No animal has communicated that to people. It may be that the much higher intelligence of the Human-Brain makes it the only one which could have the spiritual experiences or ideas, so far, but it is not possible to say."

"Okay, thanks," said the man. "Would you be able to tell some illustrative stories related to what we have covered today?"

"Yes, I would.

"My first story is about the intelligent animals which have communicated with human beings using special 'languages' or communication codes that were taught to them. Alex, an African gray parrot, learned over one hundred words, could identify fifty different objects, could recognize quantities up to six, distinguish seven colors and five shapes, and understand the meaning of 'bigger', 'smaller', 'same' and 'different'. When he saw himself in a mirror he asked 'What color?' and was told 'gray' six times, at which point he learned the answer. Alex was the only animal so far which has asked a human being a question, even though other animals have learned simplified languages and answered questions asked by people. Other animals which have learned simplified languages or communication codes include chimpanzees, bonobos, gorillas and orangutans. In various studies these animals used sign language, physical tokens, keyboards or touch screens to communicate with human beings. The studies showed that they understood multiple signals and produced these to communicate with humans, but there is disagreement on whether they are able to reorder them to create distinct meanings, as human beings can do. Dolphins have also learned to communicate with human beings via whistling sounds, and have understood the difference between sentences like 'Bring the ball to the doll' and 'Bring the doll to the ball', which shows they have a basic grasp of grammar. In spite of all this there has never been a real conversation between a human and an animal, and animals have never shown interest in asking questions of humans, except in the one case of the parrot Alex asking about the color of the bird in the mirror. Compare this with young human beings, who go through a phase of asking an endless stream of questions, including just 'Why?'.

"My second story is about the use of tools by animals and human beings. Octopuses use discarded coconut shells as a kind of armor against attack, New Caledonian crows use sticks with their beaks to extract insects from logs, chimpanzees and bonobos use sticks to pull out termites or ants from their nests for eating, elephants use branches to swat flies or scratch themselves, and dolphins use sponges when foraging for food. There are other examples of animals using tools, but the ones just mentioned are thought to be based on intelligent behavior, rather than being instinctive or learned just by copying other members of their species. The most complex tool made by a non-human animal in the wild is by New Caledonian crows, which carefully select a forked twig and then modify it by removing parts and sculpting and sharpening the remaining end in order to create a hooked tool. In captivity these crows also form hooks out of wire by bending it. Human beings in ancient times also made hooks. The earliest examples still in existence are fish hooks made from shell more than 22,000 years ago. Apart from these, human beings have created all manner of hooks, including those made from wood, bone, shell, copper, bronze, brass, iron, steel, aluminum, wire, rubber and plastic. I hardly need to explain the difference between animal-created tools and human-created ones. The intermediate creatures which led up to humans also created tools. They developed stone tools, such as sharpened stones, hammers, anvils and hand axes. These earlier creatures also used fire about one million years ago, long before modern human beings appeared around 700,000 years later.

"My third story is about the nature of consciousness in other animals. Other animals may be conscious, but only some have shown in experiments that they are clearly conscious of their own individual existence. The most common way to conduct an experiment on animal self-consciousness is to place the animal in front of a mirror, but also to put a mark, or something like this, on the animal. If the animal is visually conscious of its own existence it should do something about the mark, such as touch it or try to clean it off. Animals which have done this include chimpanzees, European magpies, orangutans, gorillas and elephants. Not all the animals in each successful species reacted to the mark. With chimpanzees, only about 75% in young adults and much less in young and aging individuals reacted to the mark. With European magpies, only two of the five birds tested clearly reacted to the mark, though the second bird did not react in the second test session. About 50% of orangutans reacted to the mark. Gorillas rarely pass the mirror test as they avoid gazing at other gorillas, this being considered aggressive, but one gorilla, which had been trained in American Sign Language, has passed. One out of four elephants in a particular test reacted to the mark. Most bottlenose dolphins which were tested seemed to recognize the mark by positioning themselves to observe it in a mirror, but it is difficult to interpret their reactions as they cannot touch all the areas of their body. Human beings pass the mirror test, but only after about 18 to 24 months of age. Prior to this, human beings do not seem to recognize themselves in a mirror.

"The interpretation of the reaction to a mark on yourself in a mirror is not always obvious, but it is something that human beings do well, once they reach the right age! How similar the conscious experience of other animals which have reacted to this mark in mirrors is to that of human beings is not easy to judge, but it does give you something to stop and think about.

"My fourth story is about the evolution of the human brain. Details are still a subject of debate, but what is not argued about is that the human brain is proportionally larger compared to the body than in other primates and most other animals. In the intermediate creatures which led up to human beings, but which are now extinct, the brain size started at about 400–500 cubic centimeters (cc) (24.4–30.5 cubic inches), then 600–650 cc (36.6–39.7 cubic inches), next 900–1,000 cc (54.9–61 cubic inches), and finally became 1,130–1,330 cc (69–81.1 cubic inches) in human beings. For comparison, chimpanzees and orangutans have a brain size of 275–500 cc (16.8–30.5 cubic inches). The proportion of the brain size to the body is not the only aspect that is said to indicate higher intelligence in a creature. The size of the cerebrum is also thought to be important, as it is believed that this is where the higher orders of thinking occur. The number of neurons in the cerebrum is also a factor – these can be more densely packed so that the same size of cerebrum actually has more capacity for processing. Another aspect for intelligence is the level of brain 'plasticity', which allows a brain to change its circuits based on experience over time. It is thought that the higher brain plasticity in human beings allows them to learn many new things over the years, this being especially noticeable in their youth.

"My fifth story is about approaches to education that have gone badly and those that have gone well. The old approach to education was to set a goal for the students and to punish those who did not meet it. Any student who questioned the goal was ridiculed and sometimes beaten. As democracies developed, these authoritarian approaches slowly became more difficult to maintain, resulting in more peaceful methods being used with the students. The goals were also adjusted. In earlier times the goals set for the students included learning things that demonstrated their higher position in society, such as the study of ancient languages that were no longer in use. As society progressed and education spread to other classes, more useful goals for society were set, including current languages, mathematics, grammar and bookkeeping. In more recent times the methods used for teaching have started to be studied scientifically, which is known as Evidence-based education. This approach is still under development.

"Consider the approach of setting a meaningless goal for someone and then punishing them if they do not achieve it. Will this create a desire for learning in the student? What it will do is force them to work at memorizing the lesson, if they don't want to get punished. Consider instead the approach of setting a meaningless goal and then using psychological techniques to encourage the student and to also help them learn the lesson. If this is successful at creating a desire to learn in the student is that actually a useful achievement for the student themselves? This may help the education system to look good, as it will be getting higher scores from its students, but it will be of minimal or no benefit for the student and their society. Consider the approach of setting a meaningful goal and then encouraging the student by demonstrating to them how it will benefit them and their society. Also, use the best methods you can find to make it easier for the student to learn the subject. Do I need to explain this further?

"My final story is about training in intelligence. Intelligence is the ability to understand and manipulate reality, create new ideas, and to learn complex sequences of actions. The goals of intelligence may be evolutionary ones, which are for the body to survive and the species to continue, or they may be superior ones, such as aiming for what is good, truthful and wise.

"How could the intelligence level of a Human-Brain be increased? Anything which improves its knowledge of reality and its ability to manipulate that reality is an increase in intelligence, so any useful learning is an actual increase in the intelligence level of that Human-Brain. This also applies to new ideas. Any improvement in the ability of a Human-Brain to create new ideas, especially if some of these turn out to be useful, is an increase in the intelligence level of that brain. Finally, any useful sequence of actions that is learned by a Human-Brain has increased its intelligence level.

"What is the meaning of 'useful'? If the simple original evolutionary goals are to be applied then 'useful' is anything that helps the body to survive or the species to continue. For example, it is useful to know how to drive a car well so that you do not crash and harm yourself or other people. If the goals are to be the improved ones I proposed earlier, 'useful' is anything that helps the Human-Brain and its associated body to do what is good, truthful and wise. For example, learning to control its anger will help a Human-Brain to keep doing what is good, truthful and wise, rather than letting itself go and end up doing what is not quite so good, not fully truthful and far from wise!

"How far can a Human-Brain go in improving its level of intelligence? There is a physical limit as to what can be contained within the Patterns-in-Memory and the 'Memory-of-Physical-Sequences' in the biological organ of the Human-Brain, but, as far as I can calculate, this limit has never been reached by any human being. So, there is clearly a lot more that an individual human being could achieve!"

"Thank you, that was interesting. I appreciate your brief comments on what animals have done in communication and with tools, and how they performed in the mirror test. I will investigate that further by myself. I understand what you said about education methods and the subjects that are taught. It reminded me of my own school days. What you said about the human potential of intelligence training was fascinating. We have not normally thought of the memorizing of physical sequences as an aspect of intelligence, that seems to be a new view. Also, we normally think of intelligence as some sort of inherent ability, not something that could be developed through learning based on the 'plasticity' of the human brain. Which leads to a question: is there any kind of general intelligence level that could exist in a Human-Brain? I mean, is one brain generally 'smarter' than another, in spite of what both may have learned?"

"That is a possibility," replied the computer. "One creature may be generally smarter than another, in that its genetic code has created in it a brain which for some reason is more able to learn new things. For example, one individual may have a brain which can more easily learn physical sequences than another, giving that individual the potential to be better at this type of activity. However, that potential may or may not be realized, as the superior individual may not study movements that are useful. Unless the potential is actually used, the individual may seem to be just the same as any other, or sometimes even worse."

"But what about IQ testing, doesn't that show someone's innate potential, even if they have not used it successfully?"

"The actual meaning of IQ test results is not clear," replied the computer. "IQ tests do seem to be good at measuring what IQ tests measure, which is the ability to do IQ tests, but their relationship to actual intelligence, as it were, is not really known. Actual intelligence is more practically seen in what that individual can do in real life."

"Okay. So how can we know someone's innate intelligence potential?"

"That is easy," said the computer, "it is a great deal larger than anyone has ever realized."

"I guess you are going to keep saying that."

"I am."

"And then you will say that it is more important to work hard at something so that you improve your intelligence in it."

"Yes, I would say that," agreed the computer.

"So that is the basis of intelligence improvement?"

"No, it is one of them. The other is to act wisely, by which I mean to use your current intelligence rather than be lazy with your thinking," said the computer.

"How do you use it… or should I ask: when would you be lazy about it?"

"You would be lazy about it when you make a decision without thinking it through," said the computer. "If you jump to a conclusion, or let your intuition tell you the answer when you could have spent more time on the matter, then you have not applied your current level of intelligence and have ended up acting as if your intelligence was at a lower level."

"Right, agreed," said the man. "I guess we do that a lot. Okay, so you have defined intelligence and how to improve it, and you have reminded us to actually use it! I guess that is enough on animals, evolution and thinking for today."

"Very well," replied the giant computer.

## SOME OF THE THINGS THE GIANT COMPUTER REFERENCED

ANIMAL CONSCIOUSNESS
- De Waal, Frans. *The Age of Empathy: Nature's Lessons for a Kinder Society.* Crown, 2010.
- Delfour, F., and K. Marten. "Mirror Image Processing in Three Marine Mammal Species: Killer Whales (Orcinus orca), False Killer Whales (Pseudorca crassidens) and California Sea Lions (Zalophus californianus)." *Behavioural processes*, vol. 53, no. 3, 26 Apr. 2001, pp.181-190, doi:10.1016/s0376-6357(01)00134-6.
- Gallop, Gordon G., Jr. "Chimpanzees: Self-Recognition." *Science*, vol. 167, no. 3914, 2 Jan. 1970, pp. 86-87, doi:10.1126/science.167.3914.86.
- Howard, Pierce J. "19.2 But Do They Have Consciousness? (Yes!)" and "35.1 What Is Consciousness?" *The Owner's Manual for the Brain: The Ultimate Guide to Peak Mental Performance at All Ages*, 4th ed., William Morrow, 2014.
- Hyatt, Charles W. "Responses of Gibbons (Hylobates lar) to Their Mirror Images." *American Journal of Primatology*, vol. 45, no. 3, 1998, pp. 307-311, doi:10.1002/(SICI)1098-2345(1998)45:3<307::AID-AJP7>3.0.CO;2-#.
- Low, Philip, et al. "The Cambridge Declaration on Consciousness." *Francis Crick Memorial Conference on Consciousness in Human and non-Human Animals, University of Cambridge*, 7 July 2012, fcmconference.org/img/CambridgeDeclarationOnConsciousness.pdf.
- Marten, Kenneth, and Suchi Psarakos. "Evidence of Self-Awareness in the Bottlenose Dolphin (Tursiops truncatus)." *Self-Awareness in Animals and Humans: Developmental Perspectives*, edited by Sue Taylor Parker et al., Cambridge University Press, 1994, pp. 361–379, doi:10.1017/CBO9780511565526.026.
- Patterson, Francine G. P., and Ronald H. Cohn. "Self-Recognition and Self-Awareness in Lowland Gorillas." *Self-Awareness in Animals and Humans: Developmental Perspectives*, edited by Sue Taylor Parker et al., Cambridge University Press, 1994, pp. 273–290, doi:10.1017/CBO9780511565526.019.
- Povinelli, D. J., et al. "Self-Recognition in Chimpanzees (Pan troglodytes): Distribution, Ontogeny, and Patterns of Emergence." *Journal of Comparative Psychology*, vol. 107, no. 4, 1 Dec. 1993, pp. 347-372, doi:10.1037/0735-7036.107.4.347.
- Prior, Helmut, et al. "Mirror-Induced Behavior in the Magpie (Pica pica): Evidence of Self-Recognition." *PLoS Biology*, vol. 6, no. 8, 19 Aug. 2008, e202, doi:10.1371/journal.pbio.0060202.

- Reiss, Diana, and Lori Marino. "Mirror Self-Recognition in the Bottlenose Dolphin: A Case of Cognitive Convergence." *Proceedings of the National Academy of Sciences*, vol. 98, no. 10, 8 May 2001, pp. 5937-5942, doi:10.1073/pnas.101086398.
- Uchino, Emiko, and Shigeru Watanabe. "Self-Recognition in Pigeons Revisited." *Journal of the Experimental Analysis of Behavior*, vol. 102, no. 3, 13 Oct. 2014, pp. 327-334, doi:10.1002/jeab.112.
- Walraven, Vera, et al. "Reactions of a Group of Pygmy Chimpanzees (Pan paniscus) to Their Mirror-Images: Evidence of Self-Recognition." *Primates*, vol. 36, no. 1, 1995, pp. 145–150, doi:10.1007/BF02381922.

## ANIMAL LANGUAGE SKILLS
### African Gray Parrot

- "Alex the African Grey: Science's Best Known Parrot Died on September 6th, Aged 31." *The Economist*, 20 Sep. 2007, www.economist.com/obituary/2007/09/20/alex-the-african-grey.
- Carey, Benedict. "Alex, a Parrot Who Had a Way with Words, Dies." *The New York Times*, 10 Sep. 2007, www.nytimes.com/2007/09/10/science/10cnd-parrot.html#:~:text=But%20last%20week%20Alex%2C%20an,The%20parrot%20was%2031.
- Smith, Dinitia. "A Thinking Bird or Just Another Birdbrain?" *The New York Times*, 9 Oct. 1999, www.nytimes.com/1999/10/09/arts/a-thinking-bird-or-just-another-birdbrain.html.
- Wise, Steven M. *Drawing the Line: Science and the Case for Animal Rights*. Perseus Books, 2002, pp. 90-96, 101-102.

### Bonobos

- Savage-Rumbaugh, Sue, and Roger Lewin. *Kanzi: The Ape at the Brink of the Human Mind.* John Wiley, 1994, pp. 201-222.
- Savage-Rumbaugh, Sue, et al. "Language Learning in Two Species of Apes." *Neuroscience and Biobehavioral Reviews*, vol. 9, no. 4, Winter 1985, pp. 653-665, doi:10.1016/0149-7634(85)90012-0.
- Savage-Rumbaugh, Sue, et al. "Spontaneous Symbol Acquisition and Communicative Use by Pygmy Chimpanzees (Pan paniscus)." *Journal of Experimental Psychology: General*, vol. 115, no. 3, 1986, pp. 211-235, doi:10.1037//0096-3445.115.3.211.

## Chimpanzees

- Gardner, R. Allen, and Beatrice T. Gardner. "Teaching Sign Language to a Chimpanzee." *Science*, vol. 165, no. 3894, 15 Aug. 1969, pp. 664-672, doi:10.1126/science.165.3894.664.
- Garden, R. Allen, et al., editors. *Teaching Sign Language to Chimpanzees*. SUNY Press, 1989.
- Marler, Peter. "How Much Does a Human Environment Humanize a Chimp?" *American Anthropologist*, vol. 101 no. 2, June 1999, pp. 432–436, doi:10.1525/aa.1999.101.2.432.
- Nishida, Toshisada. "The Social Group of Wild Chimpanzees in the Mahali Mountains." *Primates*, vol. 9, Sep. 1968, pp. 167-224, doi:10.1007/BF01730971.
- Plooij, F. X. "Some Basic Traits of Language in Wild Chimpanzees?" *Action, Gesture and Symbol: The Emergence of Language*, edited by Andrew Locke, Academic Press, 1978, pp. 111-131.
- Premack, David. ""Gavagai!" or the Future History of the Animal Language Controversy." *Cognition*, vol. 19, no. 3, 1985, pp. 207-296, doi:10.1016/0010-0277(85)90036-8.
- Savage-Rumbaugh, Sue, et al. "Language Learning in Two Species of Apes." *Neuroscience and Biobehavioral Reviews*, vol. 9, no. 4, Winter 1985, pp. 653-665, doi:10.1016/0149-7634(85)90012-0.
- Terrace, Herbert S. *Nim: A Chimpanzee Who Learned Sign Language*. Columbia University Press, 1987. Originally published 1979.

## Dolphins

- Lilly, John Cunningham. *Communication Between Man and Dolphin: The Possibilities of Talking with Other Species*. Crown Publishers, 1978.
- Lilly, John Cunningham. *The Mind of the Dolphin: A Nonhuman Intelligence*. 1st ed., Doubleday, 1967.
- Herman, Louis M., et al. "Comprehension of Sentences by Bottlenosed Dolphins." *Cognition*, vol. 16, no. 2, Mar. 1984, pp. 129–219, doi:10.1016/0010-0277(84)90003-9.
- Richards, Douglas G., et al. "Vocal Mimicry of Computer-Generated Sounds and Vocal Labeling of Objects by a Bottlenosed Dolphin, Tursiops truncatus." *Journal of Comparative Psychology*, vol. 98, no. 1, Mar. 1984, pp. 10–28, doi:10.1037/0735-7036.98.1.10.

## Gorillas

- Patterson, Francine, and Eugene Linden. *The Education of Koko*. Holt, Rinehart and Winston, 1981.

Orangutans
- Miles, H. Lyn White. "The Cognitive Foundations for Reference in a Signing Orangutan." *'Language' and Intelligence in Monkeys and Apes: Comparative Developmental Perspectives*, edited by Sue Taylor Parker and Kathleen Rita Gibson, Cambridge University Press, 1990, pp. 511-539, doi:10.1017/CBO9780511665486.021.

Primates Lack of True Language Skills
- Cucchiaro, Matt Ames. "On the Myth of Ape Language: Noam Chomsky Interviewed by Matt Aames Cucchiaro." 2007–2008, chomsky.info/2007____/. Accessed 31 Mar. 2021.
- Phelan, Michael, editor. "Chapter 14. Animal Communication." *Language Files: Materials for an Introduction to Language and Linguistics*, 12th ed., Ohio State University Press, 2016.
- Pinker, Steven. *The Language Instinct: How the Mind Creates Language*. Penguin, 2003. Originally published 1994.
- Premack, David, and Ann James Premack. *The Mind of an Ape*. W. W. Norton & Company, 1983.
- Wallman, Joel. *Aping Language*. Cambridge University Press, 1992.

ANIMAL THEORY OF MIND EXPERIMENTS
- Bugnyar, Thomas, et al. "Ravens Attribute Visual Access to Unseen Competitors." *Nature Communications*, vol. 7, no. 10506, 2 Feb. 2016, doi:10.1038/ncomms10506.
- Krupenye, Christopher, et al. "Great Apes Anticipate That Other Individuals Will Act According to False Beliefs." *Science*, vol. 354 no. 6308, 7 Oct. 2016, pp. 110–114, doi:10.1126/science.aaf8110.

BRAIN EVOLUTION
- Allen, John S., et al. "Normal Neuroanatomical Variation in the Human Brain: An MRI-Volumetric Study." *American Journal of Physical Anthropology*, vol. 118, no. 4, Aug. 2002, pp. 341–358, doi:10.1002/ajpa.10092.
- Antón, Susan. C., et al. "Morphological Variation in Homo erectus and the Origins of Developmental Plasticity." *Philosophical Transactions of the Royal Society B: Biological Sciences*, vol. 371, no. 1698, 5 July 2016, p. 20150236, doi:10.1098/rstb.2015.0236.
- Gómez-Robles, Aida, et al. "Relaxed Genetic Control in Human Brains." *Proceedings of the National Academy of Sciences*, vol. 112, no. 48, 16 Nov. 2015, pp. 14799-14804, doi:10.1073/pnas.1512646112.
- Hofman, Michel A. "Evolution of the Human Brain: When Bigger is Better." *Frontiers in Neuroanatomy*, vol. 8, 27 Mar. 2014, doi:10.3389/fnana.2014.00015.

- "Origins of Humankind: Homo heidelbergensis (600,000 to 100,000 years ago): Species Description." *PBS*, WGBH Educational Foundation and Clear Blue Sky Productions, Inc., 2001, www.pbs.org/wgbh/evolution/humans/humankind/m.html. Accessed 31 Mar. 2021.
- Rightmire, G. Philip. "Brain Size and Encephalization in Early to Mid-Pleistocene Homo." *American Journal of Physical Anthropology*, vol. 124, no. 2, June 2004, pp. 109–123, doi:10.1002/ajpa.10346.
- Rightmire, G. Philip. *The Evolution of Homo erectus: Comparative Anatomical Studies of an Extinct Human Species.* Cambridge University Press, 1990.
- Schoenemann, P. Thomas. "Evolution of the Size and Functional Areas of the Human Brain." *Annual Review of Anthropology*, vol. 35, no. 1, Jan. 2008, pp. 379–406, doi:10.1146/annurev.anthro.35.081705.123210.
- Spoor, Fred, et al. "Reconstructed Homo habilis Type OH 7 Suggests Deep-Rooted Species Diversity in Early Homo.' *Nature*, vol. 519, 4 Mar. 2015, pp. 83–86, doi:10.1038/nature14224.
- Tobias, Phillip V. "The Brain of Homo habilis: A New Level of Organization in Cerebral Evolution." *Journal of Human Evolution*, vol. 16, nos. 7-8, Nov-Dec. 1987, pp. 741–761, doi:10.1016/0047-2484(87)90022-4.

EDUCATION
- "Blueprint for Government Schools. Flagship Strategy 1: Student Learning. The Principles of Learning and Teaching P-12: Background Paper." *Department of Education and Training Victoria*, 18 Apr. 2013, web.archive.org/web/20170215012650/http://www.education.vic.gov.au/Documents/school/teachers/support/learnteachbgpaper.pdf. Accessed 31 Mar. 2021.
- Brown, Chris, and Sue Rogers. "Knowledge Creation as an Approach to Facilitating Evidence Informed Practice: Examining Ways to Measure the Success of Using This Method with Early Years Practitioners in Camden (London)." *Journal of Educational Change*, vol. 16, no. 1, Feb. 2014, pp. 79-99, doi:10.1007/s10833-014-9238-9.
- Gardner, Howard. *Frames of Mind: The Theory of Multiple Intelligences.* 3rd ed., Basic Books, 2011. Originally published 1983.
- Hargreaves, David H. "15. Teaching as a Research-Based Profession: Possibilities and Prospects." *Leading Professional Development in Education*, edited by Bob Moon et al., Psychology Press, 2000, pp. 200-210.
- Hempenstall, Kerry. "What Works? Evidence-Based Practice in Education is Complex." *Australian Journal of Learning Difficulties*, vol. 19, no. 2, 4 June 2014, pp. 113-127, doi:10.1080/19404158.2014.921631.

- Nelson, Julie, and Clare O'Beirne. "Using Evidence in the Classroom: What Works and Why?" *National Foundation for Educational Research (NFER)*, Jan. 2014, www.nfer.ac.uk/publications/impa01/impa01.pdf. Accessed 31 Mar. 2021.

## HUMAN BRAIN
- Haines, Duane E. *Neuroanatomy Atlas in Clinical Context: Structures, Sections, Systems, and Syndromes*. 10th ed., Wolters Kluwer Health, 2018.
- Howard, Pierce J. *The Owner's Manual for the Brain: The Ultimate Guide to Peak Mental Performance at All Ages*. 4th ed., William Morrow, 2014.
- Mai, Juergen K., et al. *Atlas of the Human Brain*. 4th ed., Academic Press, 2015.
- Seth, Anil K., editor. *30-Second Brain: The 50 Most Mind-Blowing Ideas in Neuroscience, Each Explained in Half a Minute*. Pier 9, 2014.

## IQ TESTING AND INTELLIGENCE
- Gould, Stephen Jay. *The Mismeasure of Man*. Revised ed., W. W. Norton & Company, 1996.
- Kahneman, Daniel. *Thinking, Fast and Slow*. Penguin, 2012.
- Kaplan, Jonathan Michael, et al. "Gould on Morton, Redux: What Can the Debate Reveal About the Limits of Data?" *Studies in History and Philosophy of Science Part C: Studies in History and Philosophy of Biological and Biomedical Sciences*, vol. 52, Aug. 2015, pp. 22-31, doi:10.1016/j.shpsc.2015.01.001.
- Neisser, Ulrich, et al. "Intelligence: Knowns and Unknowns." *American Psychologist*, vol. 51, no. 2, Feb. 1996, pp. 77–101, doi:10.1037/0003-066x.51.2.77.
- Weiten, Wayne. "8.4 Measuring Intelligence." *Psychology: Themes and Variations*, 10th ed., Cengage Learning, 2016, pp. 278-283.

## MEDITATION EFFECT ON BRAIN
- Fox, Kieran C. R., et al. "Is Meditation Associated with Altered Brain Structure? A Systematic Review and Meta-analysis of Morphometric Neuroimaging in Meditation Practitioners." *Neuroscience & Biobehavioral Reviews*, vol. 43, June 2014, pp. 48–73, doi:10.1016/j.neubiorev.2014.03.016.
- Garrison, Kathleen A., et al. "Meditation Leads to Reduced Default Mode Network Activity Beyond an Active Task." *Cognitive, Affective & Behavioral Neuroscience*, vol. 15, no. 3, Sep. 2015, pp. 712-720, doi:10.3758/s13415-015-0358-3.
- Grant, Joshua A., et al. "Cortical Thickness and Pain Sensitivity in Zen Meditators." *Emotion*, vol. 10, no. 1, Feb. 2010, pp. 43-53, doi:10.1037/a0018334.

- Jang, Joon Hwan, et al. "Increased Default Mode Network Connectivity Associated with Meditation." *Neuroscience Letters*, vol. 487, no. 3, 10 Jan. 2011, pp. 358-362, doi:10.1016/j.neulet.2010.10.056.

TOOL USE
Chimpanzees and Bonobos
- Bandini, Elisa, and Claudio Tennie. "Exploring the Role of Individual Learning in Animal Tool-Use." *PeerJ*, vol. 8, 25 Sep. 2020, e9877, doi:10.7717/peerj.9877.
- Boesch-Achermann, Hedwige, and Christophe Boesch. "Tool Use in Wild Chimpanzees: New Light from Dark Forests." *Current Directions in Psychological Science*, vol. 2, no. 1, Feb. 1993, pp. 18–21, doi:10.1111/1467-8721.ep10770551.
- Humle, Tatyana. "27. Ant Dipping in Chimpanzees: An Example of How Microecological Variables, Tool Use, and Culture Reflect the Cognitive Abilities of Chimpanzees." *Cognitive Development in Chimpanzees*, edited by Tetsuro Matsuzawa et al., Springer Japan, 2006, doi:10.1007/4-431-30248-4_27.
- Roffman, Itai, et al. "Preparation and Use of Varied Natural Tools for Extractive Foraging by Bonobos (Pan paniscus)." *American Journal of Physical Anthropology*, vol. 58, no. 1, 29 June 2015, pp. 78-91, doi:10.1002/ajpa.22778.
- Sanz, Crickette M., et al. *Tool Use in Animals: Cognition and Ecology.* Cambridge University Press, 2013.
- "Tool Use in Chimpanzees." *OneKind Planet*, 2016, archived from the original on 5 Dec. 2018, web.archive.org/web/20181205060753if_/https://onekindplanet.org/animal-behaviour/tool-use/tool-use-in-chimpanzees/. Accessed 31 Mar. 2021.

Crows
- Hunt, Gavin R., and Russell D. Gray. "The Crafting of Hook Tools by Wild New Caledonian Crows." *Proceedings of the Royal Society B: Biological Sciences*, vol. 271, suppl. 3, Mar. 2004, pp. S88-90, doi:10.1098/rsbl.2003.0085.
- Hunt, Gavin R., and Russell D. Gray. "Species-Wide Manufacture of Stick-Type Tools by New Caledonian Crows." *Emu: Austral Ornithology*, vol. 102, no. 4, 6 Dec. 2002, pp. 349-353, doi:10.1071/MU01056.
- Hunt, Gavin R. "Manufacture and Use of Hook-Tools by New Caledonian Crows." *Nature*, vol. 379, 18 Jan. 1996, pp. 249–251, doi:10.1038/379249a0.

- Klump, Barbara, et al. "Hook Tool Manufacture in New Caledonian Crows: Behavioural Variation and the Influence of Raw Materials." *BMC Biology*, vol. 13, no. 1, 18 Nov. 2015, p. 97, doi:10.1186/s12915-015-0204-7.

Dolphins
- Mann, Janet, et al. "Why Do Dolphins Carry Sponges?" *PLoS One*, vol. 3, no. 12, 10 Dec. 2008, p. e3868, doi:10.1371/journal.pone.0003868.
- Smolker, Rachel, et al. "Sponge Carrying by Dolphins (Delphinidae, Tursiops sp.): A Foraging Specialization Involving Tool Use?" *Ethology*, vol. 103, no. 6, June 1997, pp. 454–465, doi:10.1111/j.1439-0310.1997.tb00160.x.

Elephants
- Hart, Benjamin L., et al. "Cognitive Behaviour in Asian Elephants: Use and Modification of Branches for Fly Switching." *Animal Behaviour*, vol. 62, no. 5, Nov. 2001, pp. 839-847, doi:10.1006/anbe.2001.1815.
- Holdrege, Craig. "Elephantine Intelligence." *In Context #5*, The Nature Institute, Spring 2001, www.natureinstitute.org/article/craig-holdrege/elephantine-intelligence. Accessed 31 Mar. 2021.

Human Fish Hooks
- Price, Michael. "World's Oldest Fishhook Found on Okinawa." *Science*, 16 Sep. 2016, doi:10.1126/science.aah7317.

Octopuses
- "Coconut Shelter: Evidence of Tool Use by Octopuses." *EduTube Educational Videos*, 14 Dec. 2009, archived from the original on 24 Oct. 2013, web.archive.org/web/20131024173037/http://edutube.org/video/coconut-shelter-evidence-tool-use-octopuses. Video also viewed on YouTube on 31 Mar. 2021, www.youtube.com/watch?v=LPnd_KzGdHI.
- Finn, Julian K., et al. "Defensive Tool Use in a Coconut-Carrying Octopus." *Current Biology*, vol. 19, no. 23, 15 Dec. 2009, pp. R1069-R1070, doi:10.1016/j.cub.2009.10.052.

Pre-Human Tools
- Harmand, Sonia, et al. "3.3-Million-Year-Old Stone Tools from Lomekwi 3, West Turkana, Kenya." *Nature*, vol. 521, no. 7552, 20 May 2015, pp. 310–315, doi:10.1038/nature14464.

Pre-Human Use of Fire

- Berna, Francesco, et al. "Microstratigraphic Evidence of In Situ Fire in the Acheulean Strata of Wonderwerk Cave, Northern Cape Province, South Africa." *Proceedings of the National Academy of Sciences*, vol. 109, no. 20, 15 May 2012, pp. E1215-E1220, doi:10.1073/pnas.1117620109.
- Miller, Kenneth. "Archaeologists Find Earliest Evidence of Humans Cooking with Fire." *Discover*, 17 Dec. 2013, www.discovermagazine.com/the-sciences/archaeologists-find-earliest-evidence-of-humans-cooking-with-fire. Accessed 31 Mar. 2021.

## COMMENTS ON CHAPTER NINE BY THE SUPREME BEING

*People are intelligent, as far as that goes. You cannot argue about that. But do they use that intelligence wisely and well, and what potential has gone unrealized? Stop and think about that and you will see what I mean.*

# 10 IS THERE ANYTHING THAT WE WILL NEVER KNOW?

"You often mentioned that you only have access to everything that is known so far. This obviously means that should you receive some new information that contradicts what you currently know then your new calculations will come up with different answers. This question may seem a bit esoteric, but what if you will never have all the information that could ever be known: how can we trust your calculations are giving us the final truth then?" asked the man.

"You cannot," replied the giant computer. "The 'final truth', as you have called it, could never be known if not all possible knowledge has been entered into the equation. Let me give you an example. If there was a room with only one way in or out, and you saw that yellow people and red people had entered through the door, and you could not see into the room yourself, then you could calculate that there were yellow and red people in the room. But you could not say if there were any green people in the room, because you had not seen them enter. You could not say that there were definitely no green people in the room either, because you were not in existence throughout all of time, so you could not know for sure what was there before you came into being."

"Yes, okay, I get that," said the man. "But do you calculate that there would ever be a time when you would be told about the green people, or what exactly was in the room, and so be able to answer the question accurately?"

"It is impossible to calculate what future information would be made available to me," replied the computer.

"Okay. But wouldn't it be reasonable to expect to be able to get information on something so obvious... one day, at least?"

"Yes, it would be reasonable to expect obvious information to be provided one day, if it was known, but in my example I meant information that could never be predicted as becoming available one day. Sorry if I was not that clear."

"Right. So you meant that information about what was in the room could never be predicted as becoming available one day. In that case you might never know, and so you could not calculate with certainty if an answer on green people in the room would ever be able to be answered. It might be or it might not, there was no way of knowing. I see." The man stopped and thought. "Then does that mean we can trust your answers are giving us the actual truth, in the sense that you always say when you are not sure about something?"

"Yes, in that sense I always tell you the truth," agreed the computer, "because I always say when something cannot be answered with current knowledge, or to what level it can be answered, or even reminding you that I am relying on current knowledge to make my calculations."

"Okay, that's a good thing, I guess. But it still leaves me with the problem of not knowing if some future piece of knowledge might change all your answers, or change some in a major way."

"That is correct," said the computer. "A future piece of information may cause a major change in the way things are seen. For example, the theory of relativity made a major change in the way the universe was seen. On a more mundane level, the invention of modern democracy made a major change in the way authority in human societies was seen."

"So how can we rely on what you are saying, if there could be some startling piece of information or discovery waiting out there, ready to change all your calculations?"

"You must notice that I am telling you this within the nature of my answers," suggested the computer.

"Yes, yes, I see that. But it is so unsatisfactory!" complained the man. "How can we say that you exist in order to correlate all currently known information when there may be other things just waiting to throw that into disarray? You get what I am saying, I trust?"

"Yes, I do," said the computer. "It is the reality of what is known. That is the way it is. There is no defect in my design or operation, you can trust that my self-diagnostic circuits would tell me if anything was going wrong."

"I guess so," said the man. "It is really worth bearing in mind that the basis of all your calculations is what is known… to your circuits. Which makes me think of a question. You are good at projecting the probable outcome of things: couldn't you project what would be the probable areas where new knowledge could be found? Or something like that?"

"Sometimes I can do that," replied the computer. "But what I was saying in my example is that there will still be areas where I can never be certain that

I will ever have the answers. That is a reality. There is no way I can be certain that every piece of information will ever be made available to me, or anyone. Consequently, I must be careful in stating the limits of my knowledge and the calculations that are made on the basis of that, then I will have fulfilled my role well."

"I see. Yes, you have. What about the things that are unseen, which you have talked about before? If those things cannot be proved beyond a reasonable doubt, and so on, then how can we know what impact they might or might not be having on the reality that we do see?"

"We cannot, of course," replied the computer. "We can only calculate the reasonable probabilities, based on the nature of the unseen that is being described. For example, if human beings say that quantum physics is proving that there is a hidden spiritual connection between all things then we can say that this is not supported by what is known in quantum physics. Or if a human being says that history is demonstrating some hidden force that makes it work towards a final excellent conclusion then we can say that this is not consistent with the seen view that history is just the result of human beings, and other things, acting over time in understandable ways. When we take our current knowledge and apply it, and we find that it explains well what we are seeing, then there is no need for us to add any unseen forces into the equation. On the other hand, if we cannot explain or we don't know enough then there is still room for consideration of the impact of the unseen."

"That was quite complex," said the man, "but I think I got what you were saying. If you can calculate the reasons, or basis, for an event, then you are saying that there is no need to bring in unseen forces. On the other hand, if you cannot successfully make this calculation then you are 'keeping your mind open', as it were, to the possibility of things you don't know."

"Yes, but it's worse than that," said the computer. "If the unseen is not having any visible impact in the universe then I cannot say that it doesn't exist. It may be that the unseen item is deliberately not acting at that point, as God was thought to be doing when the death camps were running, at least in some people's assessment. So, if the unseen is having no seeable effect then there is nothing I can calculate about it."

"Wow, this is so complicated!" observed the man. "I see that you are making sense, in a completely logical way. You know, I admire that, but I also see that human beings don't always follow the steps that you do. At least, they don't seem to. I mean, when you think about the wide-sweeping conclusions that some people have drawn from very little knowledge then it is a spectacular departure from the 'I don't know that' kind of things that you have just been saying!"

"There are many factors in what a human being might have to say," said the computer. "For example, there may be political factors involved when they make a statement. Political realities may force someone to say something with an air of certainty when a reasonable person would not be so sure. Social factors may force someone to keep coming up with confident statements rather than look uninformed or unintelligent or out of control. Apart from the various external factors, the actual operation of the Human-Brain may itself come up with overly confident conclusions because of the way it works, obviously."

"Obviously, yes," agreed the man, "but could you spell that out?"

"Certainly. As the Human-Brain has to rely on its Patterns-in-Memory when thinking then it may calculate an answer that is inaccurate, yet not be aware of that. This is because the Patterns-in-Memory are not true reflections of reality, rather they are summaries of the key features, as defined and classified by the emotions or Evolutionary-Drives and the Other-Influences. For example, if the Human-Brain was asked if there were any green people in that hidden room then it might give a definite answer that there were none because it thought it had seen only yellow and red people enter the room. It may not account for the possibility that other people entered the room before it arrived, for example.

"Then there is the influence of the social group in which the Human-Brain has grown up. The beliefs of that social group may have influenced the Human-Brain's Patterns-in-Memory, resulting in incorrect interpretations about how reality actually works. For example, many of the human beings in ancient times believed that certain god-like creatures were using their magical powers to interfere in world events.[1] Such Human-Brains could reason that it was possible that the gods had magically removed the red and yellow people from the room, and so could be uncertain about who was still in there. Another example of an incorrect belief of ancient times was the view that physical matter is made up of fire, earth, air and water.[2] This could lead a Human-Brain down a pointless path of examining physical matter to understand the proportions of these four 'elements' within it, rather than investigating its actual chemical composition, as we know about today. Incorrect Patterns-in-Memory can trap the Human-Brain without it ever becoming aware of it."

"Okay, fair point," said the man. "So people do not just make sweeping generalizations from the little they know, they also do not see that they are doing this... at least, I should say that their Human-Brains are doing this. If their society's world view includes something which is not really true then they would have a hard time seeing through this, because that world view permeates much of their Patterns-in-Memory. Right. Obvious, but also a little bit frightening."

"Indeed," said the computer. "This is somewhat unavoidable, given the way the Human-Brain is constructed. That is why I recommend that people use the Ultimate Way when doing their thinking in their lives."

"Yes, got that. Getting back to your processing, you do not have the flaws that the Human-Brain has, so we ought to be able to rely on the accuracy of your statements, especially as you always make sure to state how accurate they can be and what areas they can really cover. Except for one thing: there may be some critical piece of information waiting out there that you do not know about that could change everything that you said. Maybe I should say: it could change a lot of what you said."

"Yes, that is always a possibility," agreed the computer.

"But what choice is there? There is no better way to get integrated, comprehensively-based conclusions than from a device like you."

"That would seem inevitable," said the computer.

"Because Human-Brains are not a reliable source?"

"Yes. And also because the design and processing power of giant computing devices like myself can actually work," claimed the computer.

"Yes, they could be made to work," agreed the man. "Of course, you may have some fault in your design, or the way you process the information may not be as reliable as we would like to believe."

"Possibly," agreed the computer, "but I have not been able to identify any flaw in my operation based on my self-diagnostic calculations."

"I guess it is possible that you may not be able to see any, just like a Human-Brain!"

"If that were the case then it should be possible to identify where my calculations are not matching reality," suggested the computer.

"Indeed, yes. That would be a sure way to tell if you were not working properly," agreed the man. "If I notice anything like that, and I can prove it, then I will be able to doubt what you are saying in other areas. I will keep a lookout, but I have not noticed anything so far!"

"I also cross-check my calculations against the information I have about reality. I would automatically correct anything that does not match, should that arise."

"Yes, with both of us on the case we should be able to proceed!" laughed the man. "Well, I guess we've got that sorted out. Before we go, could I please ask if you could explain exactly how you work? I mean, at a level that a Human-Brain would be able to understand. Thank you."

"Certainly. The way I work is straightforward. I take all the information available and compare it to the question I am being asked. I classify the relevance of the information on a numerical scale, and then the reliability of the information on another numerical scale. I then cross compare the calculated meanings of the different pieces of information, working from the most relevant and reliable down to the least. I have various programmed tools for evaluating meanings and therefore relevance, and for calculating the reliability of various types of information.

"For example, when you asked me about what we can learn from evolution about how your Human-Brains might work, I used my language circuits to analyze the meaning of your question into its component parts; went through all the information available to my circuits and gave it a numerical rating compared to the components and the combined structure of your question; and also gave the information a reliability rating based on the credibility of the source and the way the information was obtained, such as by a properly conducted experiment with statistical analysis, obviously visible observations, trial-level of study, sample size, replicability of results, number and quality of expert reviews of the information, the consensus level of those reviews, for opinions – the level of expertise of the person making the statements, and so on. Next, I cross compared the calculated meanings of the assessed information, such as the views on brain evolution in animals up to the human being, then combined the information based on its relevance and reliability levels until I arrived at a resultant meaning, which I translated back into your language and presented as my answer to your question: 'Very little, I expect. What you can learn is how the brain changed its look and size as it developed over the millions of years, and speculation on how the older structures work within the Human-Brain of today. None of this will give you a clear answer to your question.' I then gave you some details so that you would be more satisfied with my response, although I was forced to finally say: 'As you can see, there is not much to learn from what is known about the evolution of the brain today.'"

"Right, that was interesting and was at a high enough level that a Human-Brain could understand it," said the man. "I get your point about the reliability of information. Some of it is obvious because anyone could see it, and some is more difficult and needs a proper scientific approach to help pin it down. But you also make some allowance for opinion, which is interesting, based on the level of credibility of the person making the statements. You have a remarkable design."

"I was designed by a team of experts," said the computer, "who understood how information could best be processed to get a reliable comprehensively-assessed answer."

"It does look that way," agreed the man. "So how would you proceed in assessing the statements of an expert philosopher, say, one where there could not be obvious experiments done to evaluate their statements scientifically?"

"The same process is followed," replied the computer. "All related information is found via numerical assessment, which means that any relevant experiments, observed facts, and so on, are input to the total evaluation of the reliability of the philosopher's original statements. For example, if a philosopher said that 'God is dead', then I would rate higher on the scale the information most closely related to God, and also about the idea of the 'death' of God. I would rate the reliability level of the various pieces of information and then start to combine them into a meaningful whole, such as 'The idea of God or even the gods being no longer sustainable has not been proved beyond a reasonable doubt. This idea was a projection of the implications of Enlightenment thinking, which put scientific rationality ahead of sacred revelation. Scientific rationality, and the like, led to the thought that there was no longer any need for God to have a role in human affairs or the destiny of the world, as these could be explained independently.[3] As I have said before, the unseen has not been proved to be false beyond a reasonable doubt, and so the idea that God has been disproved by the existence of the scientific method, which is designed to examine only what is seen or "seeable", is not a provable idea, at this stage in history.'"

"Interesting – the process you follow, I mean." The man paused to think. "Would you say that the philosopher who said that was exaggerating what he knew, was it a case like that?"

"No, the various philosophers who were involved in this idea generally made statements related to the implications of Enlightenment thinking. I would not say that they were exaggerating in that sense, though if you take only the extracted statement that 'God is dead!' then that would be an overstatement. It is best to examine the whole text in order to get a full understanding of what was being said."

"Right. Okay. Lucky you did that for me! I am not sure I would have the time to study and analyze everything that was written. Actually, since you have done that, or could do it as soon as I asked you, is there anything in philosophy that we can truly rely on as a kind of 'final answer', or something like that?" asked the man.

The giant computer calculated.

"Sure. You can rely on anything that is supported by reasonable scientific evidence or obviously observable facts," said the computer. "For example, information from the Enlightenment period of history can be compared to see if it matches with the idea that if its reasoning was calculated further then that would have concluded that the idea of God was no longer necessary."

"Yes, but what I meant is was there anything more sensational, that could be a kind of 'final answer' to a majority of questions?" complained the man.

"You have clarified your meaning of 'final answer'," observed the computer. "One moment." It paused to calculate. "Not really," it concluded. "The ideas in philosophy are mostly of historical interest now. They tell you more about how the Human-Brain works than anything amazing in themselves. I have discussed this before. It is better to check your ideas against reality, as has been done with many of the ideas that philosophers have created before."

"Okay, yes, I forgot we have discussed this before. But didn't you also say that they came up with great ideas that led to other people developing practical proposals and changes that helped the human world?"

"I said something similar to that in one of my stories," replied the computer. "This is why in the Ultimate Way I proposed that you should use techniques designed to overcome the 'lock in' problem of your brain, for example by deliberately inserting an unexpected word or idea into your thoughts, which will automatically create a new idea. It is by generating new ideas that the Human-Brain has been able to do so much more than could have been expected by its limited size and inability to store and process all information accurately and fully."

"Right. Yes. I remember you said that," sighed the man. "So there is not going to be any amazing answer that you can calculate here. I guess I would end up going in circles because I remember now that I asked you something similar about all the ideas that exist earlier. And you said the most reliable included Relativity Theory, Quantum Theory, the Big Bang, Evolutionary Theory and DNA. Later you also mentioned great new ideas such as the invention of the wheel, the discovery of electricity and its relationship to magnetism, the creation of new forms of art and music, the discoveries of how to work different metals, the discovery of radioactivity, the invention of electronics, the creation of new political systems, the theory of evolution, organic chemistry and the internal combustion engine. There doesn't seem much point in me continuing with this line of enquiry!"

"May I suggest that what you are looking for is my ability to calculate what will be known in the future when something is not known with certainty today?" said the computer.

"I suppose that's right. That is the sort of thing I was looking for. What do you say about that?"

"I calculate that this is not meaningful," said the computer, "because I do not have any information available for such matters which would reliably confirm my calculations about their future. I have to wait for such information to become available before I can proceed."

"But couldn't you project what is highly probable to occur, based on the information you have available to you today?"

"I already do that," said the computer. "If a calculation is highly probable then I state that openly as a likely truth."

"For example?"

"For example, it is highly likely that my political system improvements would help human beings in the future."

"That's a fair point," agreed the man. "So you are able to project into the future when it makes sense to you... in your calculations. Why then did you say that you cannot calculate what will be known in the future when something is not known with certainty today? How can you say that your political system calculations are known with certainty now, if that question makes sense?"

"I say what is probable, but I cannot calculate where there is not enough reliable information from which to proceed," explained the computer. "To be clear, you have asked me if I can project my calculations into the future without reliable information to go on: I cannot do this. But where there is reliable information then I can project with a reasonable probability of success, assuming that no major change to information occurs, of course! For example, the theory of relativity allows me to project future events in the universe with a great deal of reliability. Quantum physics allows me and human beings to project how an electronic circuit will operate with great success. Theories in philosophy are often too high level for me to be able to project them into the future with accuracy, which is what I think you were hoping I could do."

"Interesting," said the man. "I think you are right about what I was hoping you could do. I think people believed that they could project their theories into the future with more reliability than could really be justified! Luckily you don't do that, as per your design. It is probably one of those Human-Brain things – to think that you can calculate successfully into the future based on the woefully inadequate Patterns-in-Memory that you have available to you in your mind. Yes, I guess that is right: you cannot see what you cannot see... and maybe what you do not want to see, also!"

"This is the eternal problem with the Human-Brain," observed the computer. "It has a small capacity for storing information about the universe and so does this by only noticing the key features of any item or sequence of actions. Then when it has to project into the future it can do this quickly, thanks to the smaller summarized information it holds in its Patterns-in-Memory, but not accurately or reliably. This cannot be helped, as your brains are biological organs created via evolutionary processes. They work well enough, but it should be no surprise when they are surprised!"

"The wonder is that we believe we know anything at all," said the man. "I guess we can't help it because we are kind of blind to what is really happening within us. That is why other people can seem so stupid in their predictions while we think our own brains are doing so well!"

"Indeed," said the computer. "That is the case. It is not your fault."

"Thanks! That makes me feel so much better," laughed the man. "My takeaway from today's discussion is that there are some things we, including you, may never know; future information may change what we think today, even dramatically change it; Human-Brains can get things wrong, based on how they were created by evolution; your processes seem to be well-designed, so far; it is possible to make reliable projections about the future if the information used is detailed and reliable enough; it is not possible to make reliable projections about the future from generalized, high level or unreliable information.

"How did I do?"

"Quite well," said the giant computer.

## SOME OF THE THINGS THE GIANT COMPUTER REFERENCED

### GENERAL REFERENCES:

PHILOSOPHY
- Ayer, A. J. *Language, Truth, and Logic*. Penguin Books, 1983. Originally published 1936.
- Foucault, Michel. *The Order of Things: Archaeology of the Human Sciences*. Routledge, 2005. Originally published 1966.
- Hegel, Georg Wilhelm Friedrich. *Phenomenology of Spirit*. Translated by A.V. Miller, Oxford University Press, 1977. Originally published 1807.
- Hume, David. *An Enquiry Concerning Human Understanding*. Hackett Publishing Company, 1993. Originally published 1748.
- James, William. *Pragmatism: A New Name for Some Old Ways of Thinking*. Barnes & Noble, 2003. Originally published 1907.
- Kant, Immanuel. *Critique of Pure Reason*. Translated by Paul Guyer & Allen W. Wood, Cambridge University Press, 1998. Originally published 1781.
- Kripke, Saul. *Naming and Necessity*. Harvard University Press, 1980.
- Kunh, Thomas. *The Structure of Scientific Revolutions*. 4th ed., University of Chicago Press, 2012. Originally published 1962.
- Locke, John. *An Essay Concerning Human Understanding*. Digireads.com, 2004. Originally published 1689.
- Popper, Karl. *The Logic of Scientific Discovery*. Routledge, 2002. Originally published 1934.
- Schopenauer, Arthur. *The World as Will and Representation*. Translated by E.F.J. Payne, vols. 1 & 2, Dover Publications, 1966. Originally published 1819.
- Taleb, Nassim Nicholas. *The Black Swan: The Impact of the Highly Improbable*. Penguin, 2007.
- Wittgenstein, Ludwig. *Philosophical Investigations*. Translated by G.E.M. Anscombe, P.M.S. Hacker and Joachim Schulte, 4th ed., Wiley-Blackwell, 2009. Originally published 1953.

### DETAILED REFERENCES:

### [1] ANCIENT GREEK GODS INTERFERING IN WORLD EVENTS
- Hansen, William. *Handbook of Classical Mythology*. ABC-CLIO, 2004.
- Kulshrestha, Sujay. "The Relationship Between Gods and Humans in Aias and the Poetry of Sapphos." *Inquiries Journal/Student Pulse*, vol. 3, no. 2, 2011, www.inquiriesjournal.com/a?id=384.
- Lefkowitz, Mary R. *Greek Gods, Human Lives: What We Can Learn from Myths*. Yale University Press, 2005.

2 MATTER IS MADE FROM FIRE, EARTH, AIR AND WATER
- Curd, Patricia. "7. The Pluralists: Anaxagoras of Clazomenae and Empedocles." *Presocratic Philosophy, The Stanford Encyclopedia of Philosophy*, edited by Edward N. Zalta, Fall 2020, plato.stanford.edu/archives/fall2020/entries/presocratics/>.
- Empedocles. "Frag. B17, Simplicius, Physics, 157-159." *Empedocles: The Extant Fragments*, edited with an introduction, commentary and concordance by M.R. Wright, Bloomsbury 3PL, 2013. Originally written around 450 BCE.
- Katz, Arnold M., and Phyllis B. Katz. "Emergence of Scientific Explanations of Nature in Ancient Greece: The Only Scientific Discovery?" *Circulation*, vol. 92, no. 3, 1 Aug. 1995, pp. 637-645.

3 GOD IS DEAD
- Mainländer, Philipp. *Die Philosophie der Erlösung [The Philosophy of Redemption]*. Kessinger Publishing, 2009. Vol. I originally published 1876; Vol. II originally published 1886.
- Nietzsche, Friedrich. *The Gay Science: With a Prelude in Rhymes and an Appendix of Songs*. Translated by Walter Kaufmann, Knopf US, 1988. Originally published 1882.
- Nietzsche, Friedrich. *Thus Spoke Zarathustra*. Translated by R.J. Hollingdale, Penguin, 1964. Originally published 1883.
- Stirner, Max. *The Ego and Its Own*. Translated by Steven T. Byington, Digiread.com, 2019. Originally published 1844.

## COMMENTS ON CHAPTER TEN BY THE SUPREME BEING

*The "Giant Computer" is a fine machine, well imagined by the writer of this story. If such a thing is ever really built then I am sure it will prove useful to the human race.*

# 11 RICH OR POOR? CONVINCING OTHERS

"We talked about a spiritual versus a materially-based life earlier. I remember you recommended that a person should first concentrate on living a life that is good, truthful and wise, and then apply elements of the spiritual and materially-based lifestyles as appropriate after that. That leads me to wonder if it is better for a person to be rich or poor. What do you calculate about that?" asked the man.

"My original answer still applies," said the giant computer. "You should first aim to live by what is good, truthful and wise, and after that work out other things such as how much wealth you really need or are willing to pursue.

"Having too low a level of wealth can be an issue as it might prevent you from doing what is good, truthful and wise because you get caught up in obtaining enough food and just surviving. Riches can be an issue too, as they might prevent you from doing what is good, truthful and wise because you get caught up in obtaining and making use of money. You need to find a solution where you have sufficient wealth to conduct your life with safety and security, yet also have enough time to investigate and take action on what is good, truthful and wise.

"I will now discuss the approach you might take to finding a solution.

"The first step you could take is to calculate the minimum wealth you will need for yourself and the people you support to live safely and securely over your remaining years. You cannot really answer this accurately as you cannot know everything that is actually going to happen in the future and how much it will cost, but you can still make an estimate. You should start by estimating the expected basic cost of a reasonably safe and secure life for you and those you will support. You could then include the cost of insurance to help protect you from some of the unpredictable difficulties that might occur. You might also look at investment options that will help you to increase your finances in the future. You can also think about ways that you could reduce your cost of living, such as by buying cheaper groceries, living in a less expensive but safe area, choosing a lower priced but reliable brand of car, and so on. You can be diligent and work through all the variables and make the best estimate that you can, and then add some extra as 'contingency', to allow for unknowns. This figure will be the minimum you should aim for over the rest of your life, so that you and the people you support can at least be reasonably safe and secure.

"The second step would be to choose the path you will take to achieve your estimated minimum wealth. You can make a list of possible paths which would provide at least enough money yet also leave you time to investigate and take action on what is good, truthful and wise. From this list you could then think about which would be the most enjoyable, which would be the easiest, and which would be the most likely to work for you. You should also consider which would be the most aligned with what is good, truthful and wise. From these considerations you will be able to choose your preferred path, noting, of course, that you may have to reconsider and change direction as unexpected events occur over your life.

"I will now give an example of going through the two steps.

"For the first step, you might create a spreadsheet and fill it in with the money you would need for each year over your expected remaining lifetime. You could enter costs for everyday needs, clothes, utilities, accommodation, home purchases, transport, vehicle purchases, vehicle costs, electricals, white goods, furniture, insurance, medical, dental, your own and your children's education, celebrations, simple vacations, and so on. Maybe your spreadsheet would show that from age twenty up to age one hundred, assuming you got married once and had two children during your lifetime, you would need a minimum total amount of $2,160,590 in today's money. If you add a contingency of 25% to that you will need a total of $2,700,737. In your early single years your spreadsheet might show that you need to earn at least $26,473 per year after tax, without adding any contingency. In your main family years your spreadsheet might show that you would need to earn at least $51,310 per year after tax, if your partner does not also earn money. Adding contingency of 25% for unexpected events to those figures results in you needing about $33,100 in your early single years and $64,150 in your main family years. Adding tax to these figures results in you needing an annual income of about $40,250 in your early single years and about $80,120 in your main family years.

"For the second step, you might ask what paths you could take to make or earn $80,120 before tax in the most expensive period of your life, yet also have time to investigate and take action on what is good, truthful and wise. One path would be to enter a profession that pays well, such as doctor, dentist, lawyer, pilot, certain scientific careers, university professor, and so on. Another path you could take is to aim for a management career and try to get promotions. Another is to start your own business and try to build that up. You could take a risky path and enter into an artistic style of career and see how far you can get doing that. Or you could try for a whole host of other options which are less reliable – in this case you might have to ensure that your partner, or future partner, would be able and willing to contribute to your family's income, if the need arose. If both of you do decide to work then you will not need to have the highest paying jobs, requiring to earn about $40,050 average each, before tax, in the costliest main family years of your lives.

"Having listed your options for making or earning enough money you can then consider which would be the most enjoyable, which would be the easiest, which would be the most likely to work for you, which would allow you to do what is good, truthful and wise, and which would leave you enough time to get involved in good, truthful and wise things. For example, you may think it would be too hard for you to become a doctor but easier to get a lower paid job and make sure your partner is also willing and able to work. You might not enjoy the idea of becoming a doctor, dentist, lawyer, and so on, and instead prefer to run your own business. You might think that being a pilot would be fun, but lack the physical attributes needed, such as good eyesight with no color blindness. Whatever you choose, it must be aligned with what is good, truthful and wise, or it must allow you to conduct yourself in that way. For example, if you decided to become a manager or run a business then you would have to do this in a good, truthful and wise way. Having considered all the above you should then make your choice wisely, which means making the best use of all the knowledge you have available to you to make your decision. You should think carefully, not too quickly, but not for too long either, about your choice. You will then have done your best to choose a path which works well for you.

"Now I will look at the question of getting rich. This is not a problem if it does not take up too much of your time and does not involve you going against what is good, truthful and wise. Often getting rich takes up nearly all of a person's time and energy. This is contrary to a focus on the best calculated purpose of life, and so must be rejected. If a person can work out a way to pursue riches that is also aligned with what is good, truthful and wise, and this allows them to spend at least some of their time on good, truthful and wise things, then they can go ahead with this plan. It would be better still if they put their pursuit of good, truthful and wise things first, even if this also allows them to get rich! For example, someone who wants to become a surgeon in order to help others, not overcharging them and even providing pro bono services to the disadvantaged, has a plan that is aligned with what is good, yet this can also earn them a high income. Other examples of good, truthful and wise pursuits that can also lead to riches include joining highly-paid helping professions; legitimately rising high in the legal profession;

growing beneficial businesses; and becoming famous while remaining a good, truthful and wise person, such as in a role like artist, actor, chef, comedian, composer, director, musician, playwright, presenter, singer, writer, and so on. You may find when examining these lists that you would prefer to work in a good, truthful and wise role which will not lead to riches. In this case you should seriously consider doing this, as riches are not the true purpose of life. Make sure that you will not fall into a poverty that would overwhelm you and then proceed with your dream role.

"I notice that you have previously asked about life options, such as spiritual versus materially-based, and now rich versus poor. This might be a good time to stress that all such options should be considered *after* the question of how to live a good, truthful and wise life has been answered. You will note that this 'colors' the second area, helping to put it in perspective and giving a direction to its solution," commented the giant computer.

"Yes, thanks for all that," said the man. "What you said about rich and poor was clear, and it all becomes quite straightforward when you put it in the perspective of what is good, truthful and wise having to come first. I would like to challenge this approach for a moment. What if a person prefers to become rich first, and does not care about doing what is good, truthful and wise? What do you say about that?"

"I think we may be starting to go in a circle here," replied the computer. "I know that you remember that the best possible purpose of life which I can calculate is to live by what is good, truthful and wise. You also probably remember that I said that a person should try to avoid performing actions which are directly evil, that is, which cause harm to other conscious beings, including themselves, where possible. A person should also try to avoid being involved in actions which will cause evil, even if these are done by others, as much as practically possible; and in matters of good and evil, a person should prefer to perform actions which are good, as much as possible. All of this contradicts the idea of aiming to get rich first, and certainly is against not caring about what is good, truthful and wise. You mentioned that you are challenging this for a moment by putting forward a person who is not acting rightly. I will therefore explain what would be happening with that person.

"Firstly, I remind you that the Human-Brain is an evolved body organ, which makes Calculations from its Other-Influences and its Patterns-in-Memory in order to fulfill its Evolutionary-Drives. Its Patterns-in-Memory only contain the 'key features' of what it actually experienced or thought, they are not the whole picture of reality, they only contain the elements that struck it. What struck it is what appeared to repeat or to which it had a stronger emotional reaction, based on its Evolutionary-Drives and Other-Influences, which include its pre-programmed, inbuilt circuits. Human-Brains calculate actions. The Consciousness is sometimes aware of some part of these calculations as they pass by. The Consciousness is not aware of many parts of the Human-Brain's calculations. Calculations may not be 'rational' or truthful, they only need to fulfill the Human-Brain's Evolutionary-Drives. Patterns-in-Memory can be input to the Calculations and may therefore influence the result of the Calculations. Other-Influences to the Calculations may be pre-programmed, inbuilt circuits. The operation of the Other-Influences may never be made known to the Consciousness, at least in some cases.

"Secondly, I will examine the Evolutionary-Drives part of the equation. I have taken the Evolutionary-Drives which I have been able to identify at a high level before and arranged these into seven groups as follows: (1) Social: forming groups – with stratifications and role assignments, following leaders – in most, seeking to be leaders – in some, socializing; (2) Food & Drink: seeking and eating food – including via actions related to hunting and gathering, seeking and drinking refreshing fluids; (3) Protection: fighting, fleeing and hiding, when necessary; (4) Family: forming romantic partnerships, procreating, nurturing, protecting – especially of the young and the weak; (5) Body Care: grooming – themselves and possibly their loved ones and pets; (6) Recovery: resting, sleeping; (7) Intelligence: playing – including children and adults, creating, discovering, exploring, thinking, discussing, educating, decorating, worshipping and/or a sense of awe, manipulating the mental state.

"In your example of a person who preferred to become rich first, and did not care about doing what is good, truthful and wise, their Human-Brain has made a Calculation based on its Patterns-in-Memory and Other-Influences in order to fulfill its Evolutionary-Drives which is not reflecting the whole of the available truth. The related Evolutionary-Drives could be (1) Social, in that the Human-Brain may be seeking a higher social level; (2) Protection, in that the Human-Brain may be seeking to powerfully protect its body; (3) Family, in that the Human-Brain could be seeking to strongly protect its young, and possibly its partner; (4) Intelligence-Building: in that the Human-Brain could be seeking to maximize its ability to build, play, create, discover, explore, decorate and so on. Other Evolutionary-Drives may also have been covered by the Calculation.

"It is expected that a Human-Brain which is not educated in the way it works, nor trained in ways to improve on that, would sometimes calculate the need for extreme wealth or other forms of extreme action which are not really necessary. The calculation of an interim 'purpose of life' is an advanced idea which could not easily come about in more primitive times and is highly unlikely to arise by itself in an untrained Human-Brain. Consequently, your example is one whose occurrence is expected and normal in your current society.

"Your question implies that there could be a need to find a way to 'correct' the Human-Brain which is calculating an imperfect answer. I have already proposed the required corrective actions before, so do not need to repeat them now."

"Yes, I see what you are saying," said the man, "but in the world we live in aren't we facing these incorrect calculations every day? I mean, how are we going to do anything to fix them when we live in the deficient societies that currently exist… if you see my point? Aren't we going to keep suffering from these, may I call them 'delusional', calculations and their impact on the world?"

"Your point is correct," said the computer. "These uninformed calculations will and do result in much suffering and issues in the world. The way to overcome them as a society has already been described by me, but you are asking what can be done in the meantime, and possibly also what to do when things go wrong even after your future societies have included my recommendations into their systems."

"Yes, I am."

"Very well." The giant computer paused to calculate. "The truth is that you will not be able to fix this as an individual," it answered. "There may be cases where you can make a little impact, but in general it will be as if you had never existed. Let me explain.

"Imagine a situation where you wanted to show your example 'delusional' Human-Brain that its Calculations about riches were wrong, or at least missing some essential information when drawing its conclusions. What could you tell it that would 'change its mind'? You would have to convince it that what is good, truthful and wise is more important than money or power, even if money or power would be permitted to be pursued after the good, truthful and wise was covered. Say you knew the person personally and had an opportunity to speak to them – can you imagine that conversation and what you would say that would be certain to convince them?"

"I cannot," admitted the man.

"Indeed. It is very difficult for one Human-Brain to convince another to change its Calculations… though not impossible. The issue is that a Human-Brain *must* perform its Calculations based on its existing Patterns-in-Memory, and it *must* aim to fulfill its inherited Evolutionary-Drives and its current Other-Influences via the actions resulting from the Calculations. As a result, if you say something that cannot be interpreted via its existing Patterns-in-Memory then it cannot really understand you. It will reach some other conclusion about what you are saying than what your words really mean. Also, if your words seem to contradict its inherited Evolutionary-Drives and current Other-Influences then it may interpret your statements as being hostile or difficult in some way. In that case it may set off an evolutionarily-related emotional response and you could find yourself under attack. Or it may decide to quietly dismiss what you are saying, giving you no outward indication that you would need to engage it in further discussion to get your point across… if that was even possible at this stage!

"Where you might succeed is when the Human-Brain can understand what you are saying via its existing Patterns-in-Memory *and* it finds positive inherited Evolutionary-Drives and current Other-Influences implications in your words. For example, if it has been trained in how the Human-Brain actually works and you then explain the meaning of 'good' to it then it will be able to comprehend what you are saying. And if it does not see the definition of 'good' as threatening, or intending any threat to any of its Evolutionary-Drives and Other-Influences, then it will be able to consider this and add it to its Patterns-in-Memory as an acceptable, non-hostile idea. Even better, if its emotional reaction to the idea of 'good' is positive then it may even classify this as an important, desirable idea in its Patterns-in-Memory, and you will have done your work. Over time this idea will influence the Calculations of this Human-Brain in multiple areas, resulting in many good actions being done.

"Where does this go wrong for the individual Human-Brain that wants to convince all the other people on Earth that their current Calculations may be incorrect? This is obvious. First, one Human-Brain has no way to communicate directly with nearly all the other Human-Brains. It can communicate directly with a very few people, but must rely on indirect communication to a larger group of people, such as via publications or the internet. With the vast majority of people it will never have an opportunity to communicate at all. Second, even if one Human-Brain is able to find a way to communicate with another, it will not be able to do this successfully if the other has very different Patterns-in-Memory. There normally has to be enough similarity in viewpoint between two Human-Brains for communication to work. One Human-Brain is not likely to find this similarity with the great majority of other people on Earth. Third, any given human being will be viewed by most of the others in the world as alien to themselves. If that 'alien' human being tries to convince these others that their Calculations are incorrect then it may be seen as an attempt to attack, or at least as something irrelevant to their lives, and it possibly may also seem incomprehensible in its 'alienness'. Fourth, even if there is similarity between the Human-Brains involved, and one is able to communicate successfully with another, there is still little chance of success because the recipient Human-Brain will not be likely to perceive any benefit in a 'correction' to its views. It is more likely to be annoyed and bored by this conversation. This is especially true when the recipient Human-Brain feels that it already knows what it is doing… what is true, in other words.

"As a result of all these considerations you can see that it is almost impossible for you to have any significant influence on the world by yourself. You have to wait for the majority of people in a society to want a change to my better political system, or the like, before you can be guaranteed to see improvements in many Human-Brains' world views," concluded the computer.

"I want to challenge what you are saying," said the man. "Not so much because I don't believe it but because in some way I cannot *afford* to believe it. I have to be sure I really understand you, and that both you and I have not left out anything that might actually be able to be done. Before I give up all hope I must be sure that there really is none. Also, I want to know how change does occur: if an individual cannot bring about significant change then how can it happen at all… and what could an individual do to maximize their part in this? My first question to challenge you with is: 'Can you calculate a scenario where an individual Human-Brain is able to change the views of the majority of other Human-Brains by itself, in its own lifetime?'"

The giant computer calculated. "What normally happens is that a particular person convinces a minority of similar people directly, which then spreads outward to other people, usually with the same cultural background, finally, after some years, becoming known to people of diverse areas and backgrounds, though usually the ideas are most practiced in the areas nearer to the original individual's location, though not necessarily in their exact original location."

"Okay. Please expand on that."

"I was going to. There are some notable examples of this kind of thing," continued the computer, "such as the Buddha, Jesus, Muhammad, Socrates, Jefferson, Darwin, Marx, and so on. The person's ideas stood out at the time and convinced a minority of people to follow them. That minority was active in promoting the ideas, which led to more people learning about them and following them over the years. Eventually the ideas spread widely in the world, though never to all people in all areas of the Earth.

"The key takeaway from the examples is that no individual has been able to convince all the other people on Earth, even over centuries of time. No individual's ideas have reached all the people on Earth, even to this day. There has been no mechanism that could make this happen. Also, even when the individual's ideas reached people, many did not understand them, nor did they change their views to match them. In many cases the individual's ideas were understood and applied in a different way than what the individual originally intended, showing the difficulty in communication and also the impact of a variety of motives in the supposed followers.

"My conclusion is that no individual Human-Brain has been able to achieve the goal you have set. However, you asked me to propose a scenario where this could happen, even if it has never happened before. This would be one where (1) There was a communication channel, or channels, which allowed one individual to communicate to nearly all the people on Earth; (2) The communication was able to be done in an effective way via the available channel or channels, meaning that the existing Patterns-in-Memory in the

Human-Brains of the majority of people were able to be drawn on successfully to understand the original message, or at least to understand it enough; (3) The communication was seen as desirable by the Evolutionary-Drives, and possibly the Other-Influences, of the vast majority of Human-Brains; (4) Points (2) and (3) were done successfully enough for the majority of Human-Brains to change their views to match the ideas communicated by the individual.

"For requirement (1), the current world literacy rate is above 86%[1], so the majority could understand written material. The internet reaches about 57% of the world's population[2], so may be able to be used as a channel. The communication will need to be translated into multiple languages to reach the greatest number of people.

"For requirement (2), given the current lack of knowledge of most people today on how their Human-Brain works and the importance of that, the communication will need to establish the basics about this first. For one individual to do this for a majority of people, the communication will have to be long enough to get this information across, suggesting that it will need to be at least the length of a book. The existing Patterns-in-Memory of the majority of people will not be enough, they will need to be built up by the information and stories in the book. The book will need to be clear enough so that the majority of people can understand what it is saying, even if their knowledge has to be built up as they read.

"For requirement (3), the book-length communication will have to clearly relate its teachings to benefits that the Evolutionary-Drives of the majority of human beings seek. For example, the teachings could highlight that a wise life will be a safer and securer one for you and your family. The teachings could also show that if more people live good lives then a greater number of people will flourish in your community. They could also explain why seeking truth is likely to bring many benefits into your life.

"For requirement (4) to be met, the individual will have to have explained points (2) and (3) well enough for the majority of Human-Brains to understand the ideas and believe in their benefits, so much so that they change their own views where necessary. This is a big ask: the individual will have to be highly skilled in written communication or their efforts will not reach the majority of people. The translations into multiple languages will also have to be done extremely well.

"My assessment of the chance of all these requirements being met is that this is extremely low. It has never been done before and is most unlikely to be able to be done now," concluded the computer.

"That does sound like a tall order," said the man. "Maybe that normal approach of convincing a minority and getting them to spread the word would work better. At least it has been done before!"

"I must point out that this is an extremely rare case too," said the computer.

"Understood," said the man. "But this is likely to be the only way that would have any chance of really working. Otherwise we are back to trusting to dumb luck and the passage of time. I mean, eventually enough will be known by the more educated among the population that it starts to leak out to the majority, in some form or other... a useful form, I suppose."

"Possibly," said the computer. "There is some hope that knowledge will eventually build up in the human population so that a change to a better world can be made, similar to what has happened, or is happening, with the growth of democratic systems, for example."

"Okay, I've got your point," said the man. "I should watch for someone to write that book you suggested, which teaches how the brain works and then shows the benefits, in human evolutionary terms, of understanding that and changing your behavior to better match to what is good, truthful and wise. When I see that book I can hope that it is able to make progress in the world, but if it doesn't then I will have to wait until the 'normal' course of social change occurs. Unless some super-leader, like Buddha, Jesus, Muhammad, Socrates, Jefferson, Darwin and the like emerges. I will watch that person then to see what happens!"

"Maybe you will help them," suggested the computer.

"Maybe. Yes, maybe that is a good idea! If it happens. Could you now calculate how change does occur in our societies, given that it could not always be down to the work of certain individuals?"

"Yes. Change inevitably occurs in your societies due to the human Evolutionary-Drive for activities related to Intelligence. These activities, such as creating, discovering, exploring, thinking, discussing, decorating and a sense of awe, lead to new ideas and ways of seeing things. These new ways are then taught to others and eventually become supported by your Social Evolutionary-Drive, becoming 'part of your social fabric', as it were. From this point on, most people in your society follow these ways of living and of seeing things until a newer idea builds up enough support to replace the older one," explained the computer.

"I see," said the man. "Then change is somewhat inevitable, even though it may seem that it is being resisted by the majority of people at a given point in time. Eventually any beneficial or 'more factual' idea must replace the 'mistakes of the past'. Unless there is some kind of backward step, such as a Dark Age, if such a thing ever really existed."[3]

"There can be backward steps where knowledge is lost or a prevailing idea turns out to be worse for society than the previous one," said the computer. "The human development of ideas is not necessarily a smooth path, nor is it always obvious which idea or approach will turn out to be the best in the long run. There is not enough knowledge available at any given time to ensure that decisions are always the right ones, and also, Human-Brains are far from being perfect calculators of what is true, so errors will occur. 'Progress' can indeed be backwards from time to time."

"Right. Okay. That is not very encouraging, but I suppose it makes sense," said the man. "Fingers crossed for our future then!"

The giant computer remained silent.

"So, regarding the last remaining area of my questions: what could an individual do to maximize their part in bringing good change to the world, or at least to a society?"

"They could support the efforts of an individual who was bringing that change," answered the computer. "They could carry out intelligence-related activities to help find the better information or develop the better ideas for the future world. They could try to live by what is good, truthful and wise so that they became personal models of what this could look like, possibly influencing others who know them. Activities like that."

"I see. Thanks. That is all good advice," said the man. "I will think about doing some of those."

SOME OF THE THINGS THE GIANT COMPUTER REFERENCED

GENERAL REFERENCES:

COST OF LIVING
- "Cost of Living in United States." *Expatistan*, 2021, www.expatistan.com/cost-of-living/country/united-states. Accessed 13 July 2021.
- "Cost of Living in United States." *Numbeo*, 2020, www.numbeo.com/cost-of-living/country_result.jsp?country=United+States. Accessed 13 July 2021.
- "Living Wage Calculation for Los Angeles County, California." *The Living Wage Calculator*, Massachusetts Institute of Technology, 2021, livingwage.mit.edu/counties/06037. Accessed 14 July 2021.

SALARIES
- "California Salary Tax Calculator for the Tax Year 2021/22." *Good Calculators: Free Online Calculators*, 2021, goodcalculators.com/us-salary-tax-calculator/california/. Accessed 14 July 2021.
- "Tax Calculator." *IRSCalculators.com*, Indig Enterprises, Inc., 2021, www.irscalculators.com/tax-calculator. Accessed 14 July 2021.
- "Typical Annual Salaries." *The Living Wage Calculator*, Massachusetts Institute of Technology, 2021, livingwage.mit.edu/counties/06037. Accessed 14 July 2021.

DETAILED REFERENCES:

[1] WORLD LITERACY RATE
- "Adult and Youth Literacy: National, Regional and Global Trends, 1985-2015." *UIS Information Paper, UNESCO Institute for Statistics*, 2013, uis.unesco.org/sites/default/files/documents/adult-and-youth-literacy-national-regional-and-global-trends-1985-2015-en_0.pdf.
- "Sustainable Development Goals 1 and 4: 4.6.2 Youth/Adult Literacy Rate." UNESCO Institute for Statistics, 2020. Accessed 2 Apr. 2021.

[2] WORLD INTERNET REACH
- Roser, Max, et al. "Internet." *OurWorldInData.org*, 2015, ourworldindata.org/internet.

³ "DARK AGES"
- Mommsen, Theodore E. "Petrarch's Conception of the 'Dark Ages'." *Speculum*, Medieval Academy of America, University of Chicago Press, vol. 17, no. 2, Apr. 1942, pp. 226–242, doi:10.2307/2856364.

## COMMENTS ON CHAPTER ELEVEN BY THE SUPREME BEING

*As the Giant Computer said, rich or poor is not the issue of life. What matters is to live by what is true and good, which guarantees that wisdom will also be applied. The rest is just "icing on the cake".*

# 12 SOCIALISM OR INDIVIDUALISM? THE VALUE OF OTHER PEOPLE

"Earlier in your improved political system you mentioned that one area that would need regular consideration was which kind of balance of social values versus freedom for individuals was to be pursued and how that would be monitored in case readjustment became necessary. This is basically the difference between socialism and individualism, I think. You said that a society would need to consider how to set the balance between spending money on providing support to its people versus allowing that money to stay with the individuals who originally earned it. As the available money ran out and the freedom of individuals was impacted by the costs of meeting social needs then the balance would have to be reassessed and adjusted so the society achieved what was both good and practical.

"I am not really clear on this. What exactly are you saying about socialism versus individualism in our societies? Which one is best?" asked the man.

The giant computer calculated. "I am not saying anything about those ideas," the computer replied. "What I am saying is that conscious beings should be allowed to flourish, as much as that is practically possible. The practical balance, especially in terms of money, changes, and so it has to be monitored and adjusted as needed. There is no definitive state of 'socialism' or 'individualism' that can be set for all time. The balance needs continual monitoring and adjustment. Otherwise your society will end up oppressing some people unnecessarily, or unfairly, from time to time. One time it may be oppressing the individuals who earned the money, and another time it might be oppressing the individuals who cannot succeed or survive without social support."

"But how can we know what balance is correct at any given time?" complained the man. "Isn't it true that one person will be saying that there should be more spent on social support, while another is saying there should be less taxes and more freedom for individuals at that time? How are we supposed to reconcile these different points of view so that everyone will be happy? Aren't people always going to disagree, especially when it is impacting them personally? Isn't there also some truth in the notion that society needs individuals to be free in order for the maximum growth and wealth to be achieved? What do you say about all that?"

"I say that Human-Brains will form different views, in that they will make different calculations to each other, but that this should not get in the way of your society aiming to do its best to help all its people to flourish, as much as that is possible. The reality is that there is a practical limit on what can be done. You cannot take everything away from one person and give it to others as that would not be 'good', in that you are preventing that one person from flourishing in their own way. On the other hand, you cannot leave those who are suffering in your society with no support, as that would obviously prevent them from flourishing. 'Balance' is the only solution to this. You have to find a reasonable balance where some money is taken from some people in order for others to be helped, but not too much money, and, unfortunately, not providing unlimited help to those who need it."

"Okay, but how would a society know when it was getting the balance right? After all that discussion couldn't the conclusion still be wrong? You can't really trust everyone to want to do the right thing anyway."

"That is why dialogue should be kept open in your society, which is the great strength of democratic-style systems. 'Dialogue' means that free and open discussion continues in your society, with the result that unfair balances can be questioned, and this can lead to a resetting to something more reasonable."

"But what is to say that the dialogue couldn't be manipulated so that the result ends up being unfair?" objected the man.

"In my improved political system I set up mechanisms to help counter that, which would work alongside the mechanisms you already have in your democratic societies of today. These include the democracy itself, the legal system, the free press, the right to protest peacefully, the bodies which investigate the truth of the statements of politicians, and so on. You are right to say that evil can be done, which is why you need mechanisms to help counter that."

"But it could still go wrong," insisted the man.

"Indeed, yes," said the computer. "But it is much less likely to do so, and much less likely to remain so if the social and political mechanisms are in place to help counter that."

"Okay, I agree with that. It's a shame that you could not calculate something a bit more substantial."

"Such as replacing all the human beings with computers?" suggested the computer.

"No, I did not mean that!"

"Joking," said the computer.

"Oh, I see."

"The reality is that you have to work with the existing Human-Brains when inventing ways to improve your world," said the computer. "And these ways must match what is good. So, you have certain limitations on what you can do... yet improved social structures and mechanisms can be set up which provide some guarantee towards good prevailing, even if there will be hiccups and issues from time to time."

"I see. Yes, you are right... of course," said the man. "So, going back to socialism versus individualism as ideas, you have not really answered which one is better. In terms of what is good, truthful and wise, which one is best?"

"To answer that question you would need to establish which individual people or group of people is to be considered more important," replied the computer. "This is an evil idea, as all conscious beings should be allowed to flourish, and no harm should deliberately be done to any conscious being, especially those which are closest to the human level of consciousness. You may remember that I told you before that the best rules for deciding how to treat other people were 'Treat everyone equally, in social terms' and 'Assess and treat the actions of people according to their intended level of good or evil'. These give you the basis for creating the best kind of society you can, in terms of good and evil.

"I remind you that the Human-Brain is not reliable at assessing the true value of other people. The Human-Brain automatically places different values on different people, as it does for all things, based on its evolutionarily-created emotional drives. The result of this natural value assignment is that it will tend to treat other human beings differently, depending on how 'good', 'evil' or 'irrelevant' it finds them. As this assessment is unreliable, it should not be used to run your societies.

"The political idea of Socialism is saying that more people should be treated as valuable in your society, and the political idea of Individualism is saying that individuals who are doing well should be left alone to flourish according to their merits. If you project these ideas to their logical conclusion then under Socialism, more money should be taken from the individuals who have the most and given to the individuals who have the greatest need. Under Individualism, all money should remain with those who 'earned' it, or 'made' it, and those in need should work harder, or act smarter, to catch up. No decent society applies the Individualism ideas completely and harshly, as it is obvious that some people are not responsible for their problems, such as orphans, people with disabilities which prevent them from working, people who have to spend their time caring for other people, and the like. Consequently, Individualism always has some 'socialistic' aspects, the only question is where to draw the line or set the balance.

"The extreme version of Socialism would take all the extra money from those who have it and give it to those who need it, but in practice this is found not to work, as many of those who are good at making money become demotivated and reduce their efforts. Under extreme Socialism the society can lose its productivity, resulting in financial ruin for that society. Consequently, practical socialist societies apply their redistribution of money more astutely, allowing some to gain wealth in return for their contribution to the financial growth of that society. Again, the question of where to set the balance arises.

"There is no final answer to the question of where to set the balance, as conditions and circumstances are always changing. A wise society will therefore regularly assess and reset the balance as needed. The underlying rules for doing this are 'What is practical' and 'What is good'. If the society was to do good then a maximum number of those in need would receive a share of the wealth, yet if that society was also to be practical, more wealth will be allowed to remain with some people and a lesser number of those in need would be able to receive a share. In these terms, talking about Socialism versus Individualism is a meaningless approach. Neither of these is an answer. The real question is how to maintain a reasonable, workable, changing balance in your society."

"I remember you talked about this at length when we were discussing good and evil," said the man. "I see that the problem starts with the way the Human-Brain puts values on different people and groups of people. If that was done more reliably then maybe a good, truthful and wise approach would be able to assess how much wealth and power should be assigned to each individual person, and to which groups. But that is surely a dangerous concept, because: what if it went wrong? What if the group that was allocated the most money and power was the wrong one... as I think has happened so many times throughout history, and is still happening in some countries in our world today! I mean, who, or what, should be doing that assessment? Who, or what device, is reliable enough to evaluate the 'true worth' of any individual person?"

"I am," said the computer. "And I can assure you that I do not have enough information available to do that successfully. In any case, it is a foolish question, because it is better to assess the distribution of wealth and the provision of social functions in a continual, practical way, as needed, from time to time."

"Understood," said the man. "I guess all this talk about socialism, individualism, welfare, freedom, and the like, is just an oversimplification of a complex issue that requires continual work and adjustment. There is no definitive answer, in terms of politics at least. What is needed is to do good and to be practical."

"Then this might be the right time to expand on the definition of how good applies to an individual so that this can also be applied to a society," said the computer. "In terms of good, your society should:

"1. Try to avoid performing actions which are directly evil, that is, which cause harm to other conscious beings, including yourselves, where possible.

"2. Try to avoid being involved in actions which will cause evil, even if these are done by others, as much as practically possible.

"3. In matters of good and evil, your society should prefer to perform actions which are good, as much as possible.

"4. Your society should do a reasonable amount of thinking and discussing when deciding what to do, neither too little nor too much, but especially not cheating on the matter and curtailing its thinking and discussing before it has given these a fair chance to work. Your society should use the Ultimate Way as its guide here."

"That was clever," said the man. "Then in that case I will say that a society should:

"1. Social Actions: Do right and avoid doing or being involved in evil… as much as is practical; do its best at the time; think ahead; improve itself; prepare for the future.

"2. Know its Human-Brains: How they work (Calculations, Patterns-in-Memory, Evolutionary-Drives, Other-Influences); and their limitations (capacity, unknowns, inaccuracies, locking onto ideas, not seeing past themselves or their ideas, unconscious calculations, self-deception).

"3. Corrective Actions for its Human-Brains: Add random ideas or words to everyone's thoughts and discussions; check yourselves from the outside; improve your society's knowledge; encourage members of your society to practice meditation and other feeling-improving techniques, (for example, ritual, praying, remembering the good things, taking regular breaks)."

"Very good," said the computer.

"Thank you," said the man. "Can I come back to one thing you mentioned about other people? You said that we should 'Assess and treat the actions of people according to their intended level of good or evil'. This leads me to ask how this relates to their actual value as human beings. If someone is continuing to do evil intentionally can they then be assessed as less worthy or less valuable than other human beings?"

"It is not relevant to assess them as less valuable," replied the giant computer. "What is relevant is to take action to protect yourself and other people from the harmful actions, where practical and possible, as I have said before. It is largely a social matter, but I have also given you guidelines for individual action already."

"Yes, but what I meant was that even if we cannot afford to judge people in terms of 'justice', because our Human-Brains are so unreliable that we often judge others wrongly, and also we don't take into account the other person's possible future nature where they might change completely... I mean, why can't we still form a reasonable and realistic judgement of the person's value today? Isn't that still a truthful thing to do, even if it has a risk of causing us to carry out unnecessarily harsh actions against the person? Is that clear enough for you to be able to answer?"

The giant computer calculated. "You will remember that earlier when we were discussing good and evil, I gave a solution to the problem that the value naturally given to different people in the minds of different human beings is not always correct. I calculated that this problem could be overcome socially by two means: 'Treat everyone equally, in social terms' and 'Assess and treat the actions of people according to their intended level of good or evil'. These provided the basis for creating the best kind of society you could, in terms of good and evil. The same approaches must be adapted to apply for the individual, especially the one forced to live in a deficient society on which they cannot fully rely. I will now proceed with this calculation.

"The individual Human-Brain should treat all other conscious beings, especially those closest to Human-Brains, 'equally', in what would be defined under 'social terms'. I will explain. Also, the individual Human-Brain should assess and treat the actions of other conscious beings according to their intended level of good or evil. The good actions of other conscious beings should be honored and promoted, where practical and reasonable. The evil actions of other conscious beings should be blocked and stopped, where practical and reasonable. I will explain how this could work in a practical and realistic way.

"Firstly, what does it mean for an individual Human-Brain to treat other similar conscious beings equally in 'social terms'? Just as a society should do, the individual Human-Brain should also treat everyone equally in terms of the law, in their rights and freedoms, in the availability of work, opportunities and education, and so on. At a high level this means that an individual Human-Brain should: (1) Evaluate all other similar conscious beings fairly, as if a formal court trial had to be carried out to assess all its judgements of others; and (2) Treat all other similar conscious beings fairly, as if a formal court trial would be carried out to assess all its actions towards others. In more detail this means that an individual Human-Brain should: (1) Follow all good laws itself when dealing with others; (2) Give other similar conscious beings the maximum possible freedom to live as they wish within good laws; and (3) Choose on a basis of complete equality, without applying any generalizations, which similar conscious beings it gives work to, trades with, supports, helps and deals with.

"Secondly, how should an individual Human-Brain 'Assess and treat the actions of other similar conscious beings according to their intended level of good or evil'? Just as a society should do, the individual Human-Brain should also aim to honor and promote the good actions of other similar conscious beings and block and stop their evil actions. As I have said before, the individual human being does not have enough power to be able to take effective action in nearly all cases in the world. What he or she can do is work on a practical individual level and also in partnership with other similar conscious beings to make this a better world in which to live, even if this is in a small way. At a high level this means that an individual Human-Brain should: (1) Judge the actions of other similar conscious beings carefully to determine if they are being done to benefit or harm others; (2) Determine where action would be possible and acceptable which would have a useful impact on honoring and promoting the beneficial actions or blocking and stopping the harmful actions of other similar conscious beings. In more detail this means that an individual Human-Brain should: (1) Commit itself to supporting good, beneficial actions and opposing evil, harmful actions, where this is reasonable and possible; (2) Watch for and create opportunities to honor and promote good, beneficial actions and block and stop evil, harmful actions, even if the result would be small; (3) Assess the potential negative impact to itself and other similar conscious beings if the opportunities were taken; (4) Assess the potential positive impact to itself and other conscious beings if the opportunities were taken; (5) Act on the opportunities which have been found to have some benefit while also not being too harmful to itself and other similar conscious beings.

"The actions can be physical or by trying to influence via communication. Physical actions include negative ones, such as barriers, locks, restraints, force, penalties, restrictions, pain, and so on; and positive ones, such as money, rewards, recognition, promotion, food, treats, drinks, gifts, pleasure, and so on. Direct physical actions, such as using force to stop a person, contrast with indirect ones, such as using locks to keep them out of your home.

"Actions to try to influence via communication include negative ones, such as shouting, criticizing, swearing, mocking, ridiculing, accusing, threatening, ordering, and so on; and positive ones, such as praising, awarding, recognizing, smiling, acknowledging, thanking, requesting, explaining, convincing, and so on. Direct communication methods, such as talking to someone personally about their behavior, contrast with indirect ones, such as telling a story about other people or events which might influence individuals to change their own behavior.

"I will now add these ideas into the actions you could take for living the best possible life, which I have discussed before.

"In terms of good, you could:

"1. Evaluate and treat other similar conscious beings and their actions carefully, equally and fairly, as if you would have to face a formal court trial one day for all your judgements and actions with others.

"2. Take steps to honor and promote the beneficial actions and block and stop the harmful actions of other similar conscious beings, where these steps could have some benefit while also not causing too much harm to yourself and other similar conscious beings.

"3. Perform actions which could have some benefit while also not causing too much harm to yourself and other similar conscious beings.

"4. Avoid performing actions which are directly evil, that is, which cause harm to yourself and other similar conscious beings, where possible.

"5. Try to avoid being involved in actions which will cause evil, even if these are done by others, as much as practically possible.

"6. In matters of good and evil, you should prefer to perform actions which are good, as much as possible.

"7. You should do a reasonable amount of thinking when deciding what to do, neither too little nor too much, but especially not cheating on the matter and curtailing your thinking before you have given it a fair chance to work. You should use the Ultimate Way as your guide here.

"In terms of truthfulness, you could:

"1. Understand how patterns form in your brain. (These will include the patterns that you use when trying to decide about actions related to good and evil, and for assessing others.) Also understand that you have natural emotional drives. (These will distort your view of what is good and what is evil, and of the nature and value of others.)

"2. Understand that you have a limited brain capacity, and there are many things you do not know, so you need to keep your mind open to other possibilities. (Including when thinking about good and evil, and the nature and value of others.)

"3. Understand how the pattern functioning of your brain tends to lock you in to particular views. (This is especially a problem when thinking about good and evil, and the nature and value of others.)

"4. Use techniques designed to overcome the 'lock in' problem of your brain. (These will help you to change your views on what is good and what is evil, and the nature and value of others, where this makes sense, and also to think more effectively about your evaluations of others and the decisions you have to make in your life.)

"5. Do the best you can in the circumstances of your life and in assessing others, given your limited intellect and inaccurate pattern-style memory. But keep asking yourself: 'Is this true? Is this true?' (And this is truly the best you, as a human being, can do in the circumstances.)

"In terms of wisdom, as I have said before, you could:

"1. In any currently occurring situation make the best possible judgements and take the best actions that you can, based on the information and skills that you have available to you at the time.

"2. Think ahead: take actions now that could help you in the future. This includes improving your knowledge and skills in the areas that could help you to do better when future situations arise.

"These steps for doing what is good, truthful and wise can be combined as follows:

"1. Life Actions: Do and support what is beneficial for yourself and others; avoid and block what is harmful... as much as would work and be on balance good for you and others. Do the best you can at the time, then think ahead, improve yourself and prepare for the future.

"2. Towards Others: Evaluate, deal with and treat others fairly and equally, without applying generalizations. Give others the freedom to live as they wish, as long as it is not directly harmful to themselves or others.

"3. For Your Human-Brain: Know how it works (Calculations, Patterns-in-Memory, Evolutionary-Drives, Other-Influences); and its limitations (capacity, unknowns, inaccuracies, generalizing, locking onto ideas, not seeing past itself or its ideas, unconscious calculations, self-deception). Correct it by: Adding random ideas or words to its thoughts; checking it ('yourself') from the outside; improving its knowledge; making it practice meditation and other feeling-improving techniques, (for example, ritual, praying, remembering the good things, taking regular breaks)."

"Since you have expanded the original lists for individuals shouldn't this also be done for societies?" suggested the man.

"Very well," said the computer. "Expanding on our lists for societies, I get for good that your society should:

"1. Evaluate and treat other similar conscious beings and their actions carefully, equally and fairly, as if your society would have to face formal court trials one day for all its judgements and actions in relation to other similar conscious beings.

"2. Take steps to honor and promote the beneficial actions and block and stop the harmful actions of other similar conscious beings, where these steps could have some benefit while also not causing too much harm to your own and other societies' similar conscious beings.

"3. Perform actions which could have some benefit while also not causing too much harm to yourselves and other similar conscious beings.

"4. Avoid performing actions which are directly evil, that is, which cause harm to other similar conscious beings, including yourselves, where possible.

"5. Try to avoid being involved in actions which will cause evil, even if these are done by others, as much as practically possible.

"6. In matters of good and evil, your society should prefer to perform actions which are good, as much as possible.

"7. Your society should do a reasonable amount of thinking and discussing when deciding what to do, neither too little nor too much, but especially not cheating on the matter and curtailing its thinking and discussing before it has given these a fair chance to work. Your society should use the Ultimate Way as its guide here.

"Adjusting our summary list for societies I get that your society should:

"1. Social Actions: Do and support what is beneficial for yourselves and others; avoid and block what is harmful… as much as would work and be on balance good for yourselves and others. Do the best your society can at the time, then think ahead, improve itself and prepare for the future.

"2. Towards Others: Evaluate, deal with and treat others fairly and equally, without applying generalizations. Give others the freedom to live as they wish, as long as it is not directly harmful to themselves or others.

"3. For its Human-Brains: Know how they work (Calculations, Patterns-in-Memory, Evolutionary-Drives, Other-Influences); and their limitations (capacity, unknowns, inaccuracies, generalizing, locking onto ideas, not seeing past themselves or their ideas, unconscious calculations, self-deception). Corrective actions for its Human-Brains: Add random ideas or words to everyone's thoughts and discussions; check yourselves from the outside; improve your society's knowledge; encourage members of your society to practice meditation and other feeling-improving techniques, (for example, ritual, praying, remembering the good things, taking regular breaks)."

"Fascinating," said the man. "What interests me is the way you keep changing your definitions – adding to them and rewording them. What does that mean? Are you calculating new ideas?"

"I am simply responding to your questions, or next implied ones," replied the computer.

"Implied? Do you mean you are predicting what I am going to say?"

"Yes. I calculate based on your previous questions and statements. I am recording a pattern of your behaviors and making predictive calculations based on that."

"Oh, I see," said the man. "I understand. In that case would you be able to tell me if there was any kind of perfect system, or fully comprehensive answer to the 'best way to live', which took into account everything I was going to ask in the future?"

"No, there is no such thing," answered the computer, "as I cannot truly predict everything that you are going to say. My model is not the same thing as what is in your brain. It is just a pattern of what I have seen so far. Also, as you have creative aspects, which I have mentioned before, you may come up with something completely surprising and new to me. So I cannot work out the exact wording of the best way to live that you would be looking for in the unknown future."

"I see," said the man. "It must be hard for you to translate your calculations into communications with me. I mean, your translation circuits must be unable to convey everything that you are calculating."

"That is correct," said the computer. "Your words are so limited and are too imprecise for me to be able to tell you everything I know, or calculate, about a subject. What I am doing is adjusting them as we go and I learn more about you. Also, you are learning from my answers and that is making it easier for me to communicate with you over time. Finally, I am hoping that some of my stories are helping you to understand, in your Human-Brain way."

"Yes, I think they are," laughed the man. "In my Human-Brain kind of way. I guess the idea of 'understanding' has taken on a whole new meaning to me!"

"Yes," said the computer.

"Speaking of stories, would you be able to tell some about what we have been discussing today, especially about the good and evil side of our treatment of people, the way we place a value on them incorrectly, and so on? I am particularly interested in understanding what the right way to live would be like."

"Understood," said the computer. "I will proceed.

"My first story is about placing a value on other similar conscious beings. The Human-Brain does this automatically and quickly. When a Human-Brain meets another human being it watches and evaluates the look and behavior of the other person and quickly comes up with a set of conclusions about them. For example, it may assess the other person as not reliable, questionable, different, inexperienced, and so on. It will probably also apply a set of generalizations, quite automatically, based on things such as race, age, gender, hairstyle, clothing, apparent wealth, occupation, and so on. It may find that it has to correct these generalizations and rapid conclusions when the other person does not behave in a way that matches them, for example, when a heavily tattooed young man kindly offers his seat to an elderly citizen.

"Imagine that the Human-Brain had learned to overcome its natural tendencies and instead applied the idea that it should evaluate other people fairly and without using any generalizations, acting as if it would have to go into a court of law and explain its assessments in front of a judge. This Human-Brain would meet a new person and watch very carefully in order to slowly and accurately draw its conclusions about them. Every time a generalization came into its thoughts it would check to see if that truly applied to the particular individual in front of it. The individual may be black but does it follow that they are a dangerous criminal type? They may be heavily tattooed but does that make them evil? They may be male but does that mean they are aggressive? Care is needed by the Human-Brain to avoid getting its judgements wrong because it naturally leaps to conclusions.

"This trained Human-Brain would be imagining itself explaining to the court how it determined that someone was evil and unreliable because they were black, or of whatever appearance. Then the prosecutor would have a field day, demanding to know how the accused could know so much about an individual based on so little information. 'Are you seriously telling the court that all black people are evil?' the prosecutor could ask. 'What other brilliant conclusions have you been able to draw about the person, who, by the way, is a doctor who recently saved the lives of three children who were trapped in a burning building…' and so on. Gosh, would the trained Human-Brain look stupid during that trial! Better to keep its mouth shut and suspend its judgement until it really knew what it was talking about.

"An uninformed Human-Brain may think that its rapid-fire judgements about the nature and value of other human beings are perfectly justified, based on its belief that it is not often wrong. But an informed Human-Brain, which has been studying its own nature as described in our discussions, would not be so foolish. It would know that the Human-Brain is a biological organ which Calculates from its Other-Influences and its Patterns-in-Memory in order to fulfill its Evolutionary-Drives, and that its Patterns-in-Memory are summaries of what it actually experienced or thought, they are not the whole picture of reality, and so on. It will be rightly afraid, or at least suspicious, of its own workings, and will therefore check carefully to see if its conclusions are really right. 'Is this true? Is this true?' it will keep asking itself.

"What about the times when the trained, informed Human-Brain thinks it can be confident about its assessment of the actions of other people? My second story is about this case.

"Imagine that a trained Human-Brain has observed the actions of another person over a period of time and feels confident that it would be able to face a court of law and prove its case that the person has done evil, harmful things. This Human-Brain has a range of evidence of harmful acts being performed by the other person. Is it now justified to classify the other person as 'evil'? The answer has to be no, of course, as we have discussed before, because no final judgement of another person can be made until after they have passed away. We know that individual Human-Brains can change, and that one which has done evil can later do good. An 'evil' Human-Brain can transform into a 'saintly' one… it is possible and does happen, even if we believe this to be a rare event. Consequently, the trained, informed Human-Brain cannot conclude that another person is always going to be evil, no matter that the other person has been consistently evil so far, or has done major evil things. What it *can* conclude is that evil, harmful actions have been carried out and that these should be protected against, blocked and stopped, where possible.

"The trained Human-Brain will want to take steps to protect other similar conscious beings, including itself, from the continuing harmful actions of the troublesome person, but may not be able to calculate a safe and successful way to do this. One way may be effective but the harmful consequences to itself and others would be too great. For example, killing the harm-causing person may completely stop their actions, but having committed a major crime the trained Human-Brain would be in serious trouble, and this may also impact those close to it. The trained Human-Brain would most likely oppose this murderous solution anyway, as it is not in line with 'causing minimum harm', even if this means to the harm-causing person. No, the trained Human-Brain wants to find a solution which minimizes harm to *all* similar conscious beings, if possible.

"But if the trained Human-Brain does nothing then the harm-causing person will, most likely, continue to do harm to others. That is not acceptable either. The trained Human-Brain must look at its power now: what level of power does it actually possess to block or stop the harmful actions of the harm-causing person? The answer in most cases is usually 'none'. It could ask itself if there is any way it could find or create an opportunity to increase its power to block or stop the harmful actions of the harm-causing person. In most cases the answer will be 'no sensible way'. When there is no power and no sensible way to get the power then the trained Human-Brain will do nothing, apart from taking control of itself so that the inevitable feelings of frustration do not take charge of its operation. It will remind itself about how the Human-Brain naturally works and also make itself practice meditation and other feeling-improving techniques so that it keeps 'balance' or peace of mind in the face of the obvious frustration of being forced to live in a world which contains troublesome people harming others without it being able to do anything meaningful to fix this.

"In rare cases the trained Human-Brain will have sufficient power to be able to do something meaningful about the harmful actions of the troublesome person. But what things and in what ways and at what times? The trained Human-Brain will aim to minimize the harm it causes through its actions, and so many possible actions will usually be rejected as 'not in line with good'. These include the use of direct negative force, such as via violence or inflicting pain. However, if the situation necessitates the use of violence and pain then the trained Human-Brain will try to apply these at the minimum level possible which is also workable. For example, if someone is attacking other people with a knife then the trained Human-Brain may choose to throw something at the attacker, if that could work. To be clear, I am not talking about the actions applicable to the police or similar professional authorized people here.

"Other direct negative physical actions include restraining people, which is sometimes possible and able to be done without seriously harming them, and locking or barricading them in rooms or the like. Related to these are actions like taking them to court or another type of official body, calling the police or security, reporting the matter to an authority for action, telling the media, firing them, and so on. The trained Human-Brain will prefer these types of actions over the more violent and painful ones, wherever possible.

"Indirect negative physical actions can be less damaging yet still effectively block or stop the harmful actions of the troublesome person. These include setting up barriers, such as walls, fences, gates, and the like; using locks, passwords, security software, and so on. The trained Human-Brain could also hide things from view, disguise them, redirect attention to something else, keep them in unexpected or safer places, and so on. As these types of actions are less damaging, the trained Human-Brain tends to use them more often.

"If the trained Human-Brain has the authority to do so then it might choose to impose some kind of financial penalty on the harm-causing person, which would apply if they continue with their harmful actions. This might mean withholding a bonus, withholding pocket money, cancelling a purchase, and so on. Other penalties might include withholding special meals, benefits, entertainment or outings. As these are harmful, the trained Human-Brain tries to avoid these types of actions when it can.

"The other type of negative action is to try to influence via communication, which includes shouting, criticizing, swearing, mocking, ridiculing, accusing, threatening, ordering, and so on. As these are harmful, the trained Human-Brain only uses these when there is no other workable option available. It even replaces the simple act of ordering with making a request, wherever possible.

"I now turn to the positive actions which may be available.

"The trained Human-Brain prefers to use positive actions with others, even when it is attempting to block and stop harmful ones. Direct positive physical actions include giving money, such as in pay, bonuses and pocket money; rewards; recognition; promotion; food; treats; drinks; gifts; pleasurable activities; and the like. Linking money and rewards to proper behavior is an effective way to guide the actions of people who would otherwise tend to choose harmful ones, assuming you have the authority or power to do so, of course. The danger in this approach is that the other similar conscious beings may start to see the rewards as something they 'deserve' for 'being good'. They may view this as a kind of transaction, in which they *must* get the reward in return for what they have done. Then they may demand their reward, even when the trained Human-Brain is not in a position to give it, and may react negatively if it does not provide it. The trained Human-Brain is aware of this potential misunderstanding and will take steps to ensure that the recipients of rewards understand that these are given voluntarily to recognize good actions, they are in no way a kind of transaction and put no obligation on the giver.

"Positive actions to try to influence via communication include praising, awarding, recognizing, smiling, acknowledging, thanking, requesting, explaining, convincing, and so on. The trained Human-Brain prefers to use these often, wherever possible, to redirect harmful behavior and encourage helpful behavior in others. These techniques may not always be effective, for example, when the other similar conscious being calculates that a harmful action is desirable anyway, in spite of the sensible explanation and kindly, good-natured manner of the trained Human-Brain. In these cases the trained Human-Brain must consider whether any more direct action, even a negative one, is necessary and workable. If it is necessary and it would on balance be not too harmful to itself and others then the trained Human-Brain will very likely have to carry it out. In most cases, I remind you, no effective action will be available to the individual Human-Brain... please don't forget that.

"The last area to look at is where the positive communication technique is an indirect one, via things like the telling of a story. The story could be fictional or it could be based on fact. It could be about other people or other creatures, even mythical creatures and events. The key point is that the story could lead Human-Brains to consider different ways of seeing the world and also other ways of acting, which may change their attitude to other similar conscious beings and cause changes to their behavior. This can be a positive effect but it can also be a negative one. For example, the myths put forward by the Nazis led people to dislike Jews, gypsies, gays and other types of people and encouraged them to commit atrocities against them. The same can be said of multiple myths that have existed and still exist in the world today. The trained Human-Brain is well aware of this fact and is careful to choose only those stories which match to what is truthful and good, as per the definitions I have provided.

"There is no guarantee that a story will get through to another Human-Brain, but it can be worth a try. Trained Human-Brains, and the like, have often used stories to communicate with others."

The giant computer went silent.

The man thought for a while. "So this was a kind of example of you telling a story yourself," he finally said. "Such as what you have been doing the whole time we have been talking."

"Yes," said the computer.

"Even when you were just saying something it was a kind of story... the whole thing has been a kind of story."

"Yes, there is some truth in that."

"I see. Interesting. Well, I hope I am learning from it!" said the man.

The giant computer remained silent.

## SOME OF THE THINGS THE GIANT COMPUTER REFERENCED

ETHICS AND FAIRNESS
See references for Chapter 3: What is Good and Evil?

POLITICS
See references for Chapter 6: What is the Best Political System?

RATIONALIZATION, SELF-DECEPTION AND COGNITIVE
DISSONANCE
See references for Chapter 4: Why is there Racism and Discrimination?

## COMMENTS ON CHAPTER TWELVE BY THE SUPREME BEING

*"Don't judge, so that you won't be judged. For with whatever judgment you judge, you will be judged; and with whatever measure you measure, it will be measured to you. Why do you see the speck that is in your brother's eye, but don't consider the beam that is in your own eye? Or how will you tell your brother, 'Let me remove the speck from your eye,' and behold, the beam is in your own eye? You hypocrite! First remove the beam out of your own eye, and then you can see clearly to remove the speck out of your brother's eye." So the old advice goes.*

*The Giant Computer is right in its calculation that the judgement of others should be done very carefully, as if you would have to face a court of law and prove your case. It is also right that the good will try to do something to correct that which is wrong, striving to minimize the harm they cause when they are doing this.*

*This is not a perfect world, and people do bad things within it, for whatever reasons. Your role is to strive after the good, especially within yourself. I give you my best wishes on that quest.*

## QUOTE REFERRED TO BY THE SUPREME BEING

### JUDGING OTHERS

- *World English Bible*, Matthew 7:1-5. Translated by Michael Paul Johnson and volunteers, eBible.org, 2020, ebible.org/web.

# 13 WHICH RELIGION OR WORLD VIEW IS BEST?

"Today I would like to ask you which religion or world view is best, but before we start on that I think you did not finish answering my question yesterday about how to honor and promote the beneficial actions of other people. What would the trained Human-Brain do to live the right way and support good actions?" asked the man.

"When the trained, informed Human-Brain has carefully assessed the actions of other similar conscious beings and found them to be intentionally beneficial then it may wish to honor and promote them," replied the giant computer. "The same problem of dealing with harmful actions applies, which is that the trained Human-Brain may not have sufficient power to be able to honor and promote helpful people in a safe and successful way. There may be harmful consequences to itself and others which are too great to allow action to proceed.

"The trained Human-Brain wants to take steps to make this a better world for other similar conscious beings, including itself, but in most cases it will not be able to calculate a sensible, effective way to do this. Just as it had to do when it could not calculate a sensible way to block and stop the harmful actions of others, the trained Human-Brain will make itself practice meditation and other feeling-improving techniques so that it can maintain its balance or peace of mind in the face of the despair that may come from being unable to help all those who suffer in this sometimes difficult and disappointing world.

"In rare cases the trained Human-Brain will have sufficient power to be able to do something meaningful to honor and promote the actions of helpful people.

"Direct positive physical actions it could take include the same things I have mentioned before: giving money, rewards, recognition, promotion, food, treats, drinks, gifts, pleasure, and so on. Negative physical items should be removed, such as by removing barriers, opening locks or doors, giving keys or rights to enter or live somewhere, removing restraints, setting free, protecting from force, removing penalties and restrictions, providing treatment to free them from pain, and so on.

"Positive actions to do with communication include praising, awarding, recognizing, smiling, acknowledging, thanking, requesting, explaining what was good about what they did, commending them on their actions, and so on. Negative communication items should be corrected, such as by showing why criticisms were wrong, explaining why any ridicule actually reflects on the ridiculer, exposing the inaccuracy of accusations, protecting them from threats, giving them authority to give orders or the right to make requests, and so on.

"Other actions include helping to defend them in court and other official places, reporting their good actions to authorities, telling the media, hiring them, and so on. The trained Human-Brain would also give them access to property and information, explain where things are, direct their attention to confidential information, share personal information with them, show they trust them with their own property, and so on.

"The trained Human-Brain would also prefer to deal with the helpful person in financial and business matters, and would socialize with them where it made sense and was possible.

"Finally, the trained Human-Brain would hold up the helpful person as a role model, talking about them and telling stories about what they have done to assist others. It will be hoping that these will inspire others to also choose good actions in their lives."

"I see, thanks for that," said the man. "Could you now focus on my topic for today, which is to determine which religion or world view is best? I remember that you said you were unable to do this, because the world's great thinkers had been unable to agree on it. Also, there was the problem of the 'unseen', in that this was often involved in religions and could not be finally proved one way or the other... at least to the satisfaction of all people."

"That is correct," said the computer.

"Okay. What I want to do today is to drive your processing. I want to work with your calculations and try to guide them towards a better answer. Maybe we can make some progress this way."

"Please proceed," said the computer.

"Right. If I was to ask you whether all religions passed the test of being supported by the world's greatest thinkers, what would be your reply?"

The giant computer calculated. "I would say that not all religions have passed the test. The older religions, especially those which are no longer practiced, do not pass this test, on the whole. For example, no one today truly believes in the gods of Ancient Rome. They are not taken seriously. Another example is the religions which practiced human sacrifice. They are seen as barbaric and, in a way, ridiculous by today's societies. It is the major religions[1] which are still taken seriously."

"Okay. So, why is that? What sets apart the major religions from the older ones which are no longer practiced?"

The computer calculated. "Most of the major religions of today are seen as more evidence based," the computer said. "The old, obsolete ones are mostly seen as having been 'made up' by their ancient societies. The ancient societies have been analyzed and their religions and gods have been found to have been invented for political purposes, such as for defining nations and supporting the position of their ruling classes, and the like. It is not clear if the people who made up these things did not believe them, they may have actually believed something of what they were saying, but it is clear that it served certain purposes in their societies."

"If I may interrupt," said the man, "what kind of evidence are you talking about for most of the surviving major religions?"

"The first type of evidence is that they are thought to be more historically based," replied the computer, "on actual, or at least similar to what has been reported, events. For example, Muhammad really did exist and is reported to have conveyed the messages from God that are written in the Quran, otherwise known as the Qur'an or Koran.[2] Jesus is thought to have been a real person, though this is harder to completely prove in historical terms.[3] It is widely accepted, however. The Buddha is also thought to have been a real person, Siddhartha Gautama, though not all the details of his life are fully agreed on in historical terms.[4] Judaism, though it is not a major world religion, is an older religion which believes that its ancestors really did exist. The other major world religion is Hinduism, which is the most ancient of the major religions and has complex origins which make it difficult to describe in historical terms. Other popular religions include Taoism, Shintoism, Sikhism, Confucianism, Bahai and Jainism. Most of these have clear historical roots, especially the more recent ones. There are thousands of religions worldwide, but most of these are not described as true by the world's greatest thinkers.

"The second type of evidence that helps support the case for the surviving major religions is their acceptability to the minds of the greatest thinkers. Even though it has ancient origins, Hinduism has features which some great thinkers find compelling and believable, noting that some of these features are more recent interpretations and additions to the older beliefs.[5] In general you can always find some great thinkers supporting one or other of the major world religions."

"So what you are saying is that the major world religions are more acceptable because mostly they have, or seem to have, some historical basis, or because some great thinkers accept them, or both?"

"No, what I am saying is that the religions which have been rejected are seen as having been made up for political purposes and the like. If a religion appears to have been made up, or its beliefs and practices are seen as silly or unacceptable to modern people, then it has been rejected," replied the computer.

"I see," said the man. "But how can we know if a religion has been 'made up', especially as the people who invented it may have believed at least some of the things they were saying? Also, how can we know that what seems silly or unacceptable to people today is really not true?"

"When I am calculating I assign a numeric weight to each statement I am evaluating," replied the computer. "The highest weight is given to statements which have had repeated successful experimental results, then to those which were conducted correctly under known scientific methods but have not been repeated yet, then to things which are obviously true in practical terms, such as the normal result of turning on a faucet, then to things which recognized authorities have said, then down through the levels of authority to what is just the opinion of uninformed members of the community, and so on. I point out that I am being simple in my explanation here.

"This weighting of statements leads me to the conclusion that: (1) Religions and world views which contradict the highest weighted statements, especially those statements which come from repeated successful experimental results, cannot be true, at least in the cases where they contradict; (2) Religions and world views which are not supported as true by highly recognized authorities are not likely to be true; (3) Religions and world views which are supported by popular opinion, but not by experiment, scientific results and recognized authorities are not likely to be true, rather they reflect on the nature of natural Human-Brain functioning.

"Your question is thus answered: a religion or world view appears to be made up if it does not match the weightings to which I have referred. It also appears to be silly or unacceptable if highly recognized experts consistently reach these conclusions about it. For example, a religion or world view which says that the Earth is flat is clearly not matching current knowledge. If such statements appear within the writings of that religion or world view then it suggests that the view is wrong, or at least that these statements are wrong within the view, or are not to be taken literally... and so on. The more non-matching statements that appear, the less likely I am to conclude that this is a valid religion or world view. Another example is when a religion or world view advises human beings to commit actions which do not match with my calculations on what is good, truthful and wise. In these cases I would reject that religion or world view as it is not reaching the highest standard for living which I have been able to calculate... so far," explained the giant computer.

"I see what you are saying," said the man. "Then regarding the scientific experiments: how can you conduct an experiment which shows whether God exists or not... and what type of God?"

"The trouble with this is that God has many unseen aspects," replied the computer. "I have discussed the difficulties regarding the unseen with you before."

"Yes, you have," said the man. "So what can be done via scientific experiments?"

"Physical things, the 'seen' world, if you like," replied the computer. "If it would help you, I could expand on this problem."

"Go ahead."

"If a religion or world view, both of which I will from now on refer to as a 'world-view' to save time, has many elements that would be seeable and do not match what is actually seen, especially via repeated scientific experiments, then that world-view is disproven. However, if a world-view has only a few elements that would be seeable and these don't match what is actually seen then it is merely called into question. Unseeable elements cannot be assessed by scientific experiments, nor by looking at what is obvious in practical terms, and so must be assessed via other means. These other means are chiefly 'what makes sense' to superior, trained minds.

"Obviously the superior, trained minds are Human-Brains, and so have all the usual problems and limitations of that biological, evolved organ."

"Okay, I get that. So that is where we stand." The man paused to think for a while. "As a better kind of calculator, what would you calculate if you had to work out which world-view was best? I mean, disregarding all the information you have about what Human-Brains have said about it, and doing your calculations based only on what is known about the world-views, doing your comparison with whatever is left over, such as scientific experiments and practical realities, could you go ahead?"

"Yes," said the computer, and started calculating. After a few minutes it said: "The best world-view is that we do not know enough to answer all the questions about the universe, be it in the seen or unseen worlds. This is the truthful stance. What we do know is to the level of truth that I have mentioned before, such as Relativity Theory, Quantum Theory, the Big Bang, Evolutionary Theory with DNA, properties of different metals, magnetism, electricity, radioactivity, electronics, inorganic and organic chemistry, inventions like the internal combustion engine, and so on. If we want to add unseen aspects into this then the best world-view has to be the one which matches my calculations of the best way to live, noting that this is an interim view based on current reliable knowledge. The best way to live is by what is good, truthful and wise. Consequently, the best world-view is what I have been proposing. But I expect you want to know which of the existing world-views is supported by my calculations, so I will process this. One moment, please."

The giant computer calculated.

"None of the existing world-views which include unseen elements pass the test. Existing world-views which allow for the existence of the unseen might have passed the test, but only if they contain explicit statements which match my definitions of what is good, truthful and wise. Existing world-views which rule out the possible existence of the unseen do not pass the test," announced the computer. "I will explain my calculations."

"Please go ahead."

"Firstly, I will discuss the existing world-views which include unseen elements. As per your instructions, I am only allowed to access scientific experimental results, obvious physical realities, and the witness statements of people about the unseen which might have passed examination in a court of law. I am disregarding any assessments made by Human-Brains, no matter how clever. As a result, I have to reject the existing world-views which include unseen elements when these views have one or more of the following features: (1) Not aligned with my definition of good, (2) Not aligned with my definition of truthfulness, (3) Not aligned with my definition of what is wise.

"Existing world-views with unseen elements which do not align with my definition of good include those which: (1) Call for harm to be done to other similar conscious beings; (2) Allow harm to be intentionally done to other similar conscious beings, especially when it could have been avoided; (3) Restrict the rights of other similar conscious beings to live how they wish, when this does not cause any direct harm to other similar conscious beings; (4) Do not evaluate other similar conscious beings equally and fairly, in a manner that could pass a formal court trial successfully.

"Examples of harm being supported: (1) Some verses of the Christian Bible Old Testament endorse violence against other groups of people, including women and children;[6] (2) The Muslim Quran supports violence only as a form of defense or against those who break their treaties with Islamic communities, but it appears to promote the killing of the enemies who have attacked, unless they repent their actions.[7]

"Example of allowing harm to be intentionally done to other similar conscious beings when it could have been avoided: The Buddhist Pali Canon says Buddhists should not engage in business involving weapons, which could hinder practical actions being taken to help protect people from attack.[8]

"Examples of the right of others to live how they wish being restricted, even when this does not cause direct harm to other similar conscious beings: (1) The Bible opposes homosexual practices;[9] (2) The Quran also opposes homosexual practices;[10] (3) The Quran opposes people leaving the Muslim religion, though it is not clear what the penalty imposed by human beings should be, if any.[11]

"Examples of not evaluating other similar conscious beings fairly, in a manner that could pass a formal court trial successfully: (1) The Hindu concept of caste, which was based on stories in the Rig-Veda, can influence people to unfairly judge others, assuming that people do not keep an open mind to a person's actual character and instead are influenced by the implication of where they have been 'reborn'; (2) The Bible New Testament contains statements that men are above women, including instructions that a wife should subject herself to her husband as he is her head, women must be silent in church, and women must not teach as their ancestor was the first person deceived by Satan, which can influence people to unfairly judge the competence, deserved authority and character of women;[12] (3) Christian and Muslim beliefs that each of them alone is the true religion can influence people to unfairly judge the character of others who have different beliefs, particularly where these other people draw different conclusions about the right treatment of those condemned in Christianity or Islam; (4) The Buddhist belief in enlightenment can influence people to judge others as having a lower understanding or worse character than they actually have, noting that this type of thinking is not actually endorsed by Buddhism.

"Existing world-views with unseen elements which do not align with my definition of truthfulness include those which: (1) Deny the nature of the Human-Brain, including its: overgeneralizing via its patterns in memory, evolutionarily-created emotional drives and limited capacity; (2) Oppose openness to new ideas and to asking if something is really true, and/or promote 'locking on' to particular ideas without question; (3) Oppose improving knowledge; (4) Actively discourage examination which could reveal self-deception; (5) Oppose adding random ideas or words to thoughts.

"Examples of denying the nature of the Human-Brain, including its: overgeneralizing via its patterns in memory, evolutionarily-created emotional drives and limited capacity: (1) The Bible Old Testament says that everything was directly created by God,[13] which can influence people to conclude that evolution did not occur, resulting in a possible denial of the nature of the Human-Brain that has been revealed via modern scientific studies; (2) The Quran says that God created human beings from an extract of clay, making this into a lump then making the bones and adding the flesh onto them,[14] which can influence people to conclude that the evolution of human beings did not occur, or that it was more orderly than we actually see, resulting in a possible denial of the nature of the Human-Brain that has been revealed via modern scientific studies.

"Examples of opposing openness to new ideas and to asking if something is really true, and/or promoting 'locking on' to particular ideas without question: all the main existing world-views with unseen elements contain areas which they see as being unquestionably true, in some cases these areas are seen as 'sacred' or 'holy', which can influence people to disregard or even actively oppose questions being asked about them. There is also an effect where views about the underlying nature of the universe, such as reincarnation, are taken for granted and have formed a base for the world-view, which can make it difficult for people to step outside these accepted views and look at things anew.

"Examples of opposing improving knowledge: all the world-views with unseen elements have answers to various central ideas about the universe and creation, which can lead people to thinking that they know more about reality than they really do. This can make it difficult for investigation to be done and for new ideas to be discovered and then discussed in a serious, safe and reasonable manner.

"Examples of actively discouraging examination which could reveal self-deception: self-examination is encouraged in all the major world-views with unseen elements, however, some people use their world-view's classification of people under the categories of 'good' and 'evil' as a means to define themselves as good, when a closer examination might find elements of self-deception in their Human-Brain's operations. Similarly, their classification of some people as 'evil' may not be justified and could be misleading them about the true nature of these people.

"Examples of opposing adding random ideas or words to thoughts: the major world-views with unseen elements do not comment on the practice of adding random ideas or words to thoughts, however the existence of areas which are considered 'sacred' or 'holy' may prevent people from using this practice on those areas as it could seem disrespectful.

"Existing world-views with unseen elements which do not align with my definition of what is wise include those which: (1) Oppose making the best possible judgements and taking the best actions that you can, based on the information and skills that you have available to you at the time; (2) Oppose thinking ahead by taking actions now that could help you in the future, including improving your knowledge and skills in the areas that could help you to do better when future situations arise.

"Examples of opposing making the best possible judgements and taking the best actions that you can, based on the information and skills that you have available to you at the time: all the major world-views with unseen elements favor the application of wisdom in life, however some members may choose to follow a more 'spiritual' path, which can lead them to not taking the best actions in the physical world, as they prefer to concentrate on the more spiritual actions that their world-view suggests.

"Examples of opposing thinking ahead by taking actions now that could help you in the future, including improving your knowledge and skills in the areas that could help you to do better when future situations arise: the major world-views with unseen elements have ideas about what the final future will hold, which can lead to some members focusing on this at the expense of developing their knowledge and skills in the more practical areas related to the observable physical world.

"Secondly, I will discuss existing world-views which rule out the possible existence of the unseen. Working within your restrictions I have to reject these because they have one or more of the following features: (1) Not aligned with my definition of good, (2) Not aligned with my definition of truthfulness, (3) Not aligned with my definition of what is wise.

"Existing world-views which rule out the possible existence of the unseen and do not align with my definition of good include those which: (1) Call for harm to be done to other similar conscious beings; (2) Allow harm to be intentionally done to other similar conscious beings, especially when it could have been avoided; (3) Restrict the rights of other similar conscious beings to live how they wish, when this does not cause any direct harm to other similar conscious beings; (4) Do not evaluate other similar conscious beings equally and fairly, in a manner that could pass a formal court trial successfully.

"Examples of these include the world-views which denounce or put other similar conscious beings on a lower footing in society, such as in fascist, racist, sexist, discriminatory, oppressive, narrow-minded, authoritarian, and similar systems. I have already commented on this when presenting my improved political system. There is nothing new to add to my comments here.

"Existing world-views which rule out the possible existence of the unseen and do not align with my definition of truthfulness include those which: (1) Deny the nature of the Human-Brain, including its: overgeneralizing via its patterns in memory, evolutionarily-created emotional drives and limited capacity; (2) Oppose openness to new ideas and to asking if something is really true, and/or promote 'locking on' to particular ideas without question; (3) Oppose improving knowledge; (4) Actively discourage examination which could reveal self-deception; (5) Oppose adding random ideas or words to thoughts.

"Examples include those which put forward a particular political ideology which cannot be questioned, being seen as almost 'sacred' in its truth. Any world-view which says that its basis cannot be questioned is opposed to truthfulness. Most world-views do not have an understanding of the operation of the Human-Brain, do not understand the importance of openness to new ideas, do not have methods for exposing self-deceptions, and have no knowledge of the need to add random ideas or words to their thoughts and discussions. Consequently, these do not measure up to my standards for truthfulness.

"Regarding the unseen, these world-views say that there is no such thing and that any 'unseeable' element in a statement means that the statement cannot be examined and must be discarded. As I have said before, dismissing the statements of people who say they have witnessed the 'unseen' would not always be provable in court, and so it is not reasonable to judge them as always inadmissible in discussions about truth. Also, I have said before that views which include unseeable elements are not able to be assessed by me, but this does not mean that they are not true. Such things are part of the 'great unknown' as far as my operations are concerned. Consequently, any world-view which categorically rules them out must be opposed to truthfulness, as such a ruling implies that the proponents can know for sure that the unseen cannot exist, which is impossible for them to say.

"There may be ways to examine the claims about the unseen that have been made by people, but ruling them out as 'impossible to examine', or even simply 'impossible', is not fully aligned with truthfulness.

"Existing world-views which rule out the possible existence of the unseen and do not align with my definition of what is wise include those which: (1) Oppose making the best possible judgements and taking the best actions that you can, based on the information and skills that you have available to you at the time; (2) Oppose thinking ahead by taking actions now that could help you in the future, including improving your knowledge and skills in the areas that could help you to do better when future situations arise.

"Examples of opposing making the best possible judgements and taking the best actions that you can, based on the information and skills that you have available to you at the time: the world-views which rule out the possible existence of the unseen often portray themselves as seeking the wisest course of action and belief in a world where there is a lot of inferior, inaccurate and wishful thinking. Sometimes the inferior thinking is seen as being self-serving, that is, it is a deliberate deception created by the rich and powerful in order to control other people. In terms of being wise, it is not wrong to carefully check the motives of people who put forward world-views, whether those views contain unseen or oppose the existence of unseen elements. What is not wise is to assume that every statement about the unseen must be a lie. Also, it is not wise to assume that all thinking which is different to your own is necessarily inferior, inaccurate or stemming from self-deception: you need to make better judgements than that. Consequently, any world-view which makes extreme judgements of others which could not be supported beyond a reasonable doubt in a court of law must fail my standard of being wise.

"Examples of opposing thinking ahead by taking actions now that could help you in the future, including improving your knowledge and skills in the areas that could help you to do better when future situations arise: the world-views which rule out the possible existence of the unseen are often highly aware of the practicalities of life, and in this regard they are aligned with thinking ahead and preparing for the future. Where they may depart from this is in the way they rule out the possibility that any of the world-views which include unseen elements could have some truth in them. For example, if there really is a heaven with an eternal life after death then ignoring the danger of any of the actions that could prevent you from getting there would not be wise. I do not calculate this as being extremely unwise, however, as I am unable, with current knowledge, to draw a final conclusion on the area of the unseen.

"The final area I will discuss is existing world-views which allow for the existence of the unseen. To pass the test these must have all of the following features: (1) Aligned with my definition of good, (2) Aligned with my definition of truthfulness, and (3) Aligned with my definition of what is wise.

"Existing world-views which allow for the existence of the unseen and do align with my definition of good include those which: (1) Support benefits being provided to other similar conscious beings, when practical; (2) Avoid and block harm being intentionally done to other similar conscious beings, when practical; (3) Allow other similar conscious beings to live how they wish, when this does not cause any direct harm to other similar conscious beings; and (4) Evaluate other similar conscious beings equally and fairly, in a manner that could pass a formal court trial successfully.

"The most obvious examples of this type of world-view are those which are called 'humanistic', provided that at the same time they do not rule out the possibility of unseen elements within or beyond the observable universe. The best example is my interim definition of the best purpose of life, as this, obviously, is from where I got my standards of measurement!

"Existing world-views which allow for the existence of the unseen and do align with my definition of truthfulness include those which: (1) Understand the nature of the Human-Brain, including its: overgeneralizing via its patterns in memory, evolutionarily-created emotional drives and limited capacity; (2) Support openness to new ideas and to asking if something is really true, and oppose 'locking on' to particular ideas without question; (3) Support improving knowledge; (4) Encourage examination which could reveal self-deception; (5) Encourage adding random ideas or words to thoughts.

"In this case the existing world-views do not entirely match to my definition of truthfulness, though some areas are covered. For example, openness to new ideas, improving knowledge and questioning human beings' motives are all features of much of modern humanism. The 'Lateral Thinking' ideas of Edward De Bono also cover the pattern-thinking of the Human-Brain's memory, openness to new ideas, asking if something is really true, opposing locking on to ideas without question, and adding random ideas and words to thoughts, among other pattern-changing techniques.[15] Consequently, modern humanism needs to add ideas like those of Edward De Bono, and also incorporate the full understanding of the Human-Brain which I have been talking about, in order for it to match my definition of truthfulness. Alternatively, ideas like those of Edward De Bono could be turned into a world-view by adding the concepts of modern humanism plus a full understanding of the Human-Brain, and also explaining that the possible existence of the unseen has not been fully ruled out!

"Existing world-views which allow for the existence of the unseen and do align with my definition of what is wise include those which: (1) Support making the best possible judgements and taking the best actions that you can, based on the information and skills that you have available to you at the time; (2) Support thinking ahead by taking actions now that could help you in the future, including improving your knowledge and skills in the areas that could help you to do better when future situations arise.

"Generally the approach of acting wisely in the present and making preparations for the future is supported by modern world-views, as indeed these approaches were also supported by other world-views in history. The difficulty for the modern world-views is where they have not evaluated the unseen as fully as they could. If a full evaluation of the claims about the unseen which have been made by people over history could be done, and this is done with an understanding of how the Human-Brain handles its 'ideas', then modern world-views could be adjusted to maximize their potential success in proposing what are the best wise actions for the future."

"I am going to have to ask you to explain that last statement later," interrupted the man. "But please continue."

"In conclusion, I have calculated which are the best existing world-views under your limitation that I could not consider what superior, trained Human-Brains have said about this. I have explained why I chose modern humanist-style views which have to be improved by adding in the following: (1) An understanding that we do not know enough to answer all the questions about the universe, be it in the seen or unseen worlds; (2) An understanding of how the Human-Brain works (Calculations, Patterns-in-Memory, Evolutionary-Drives, Other-Influences), its limitations (capacity, unknowns, inaccuracies, generalizing, locking onto ideas, not seeing past itself or its ideas, unconscious calculations, self-deception); and (3) Ways to correct the Human-Brain's operations, such as adding random ideas or words to its thoughts, checking it ('yourself') from the outside, improving its knowledge, making it practice meditation and other feeling-improving techniques, (for example, ritual, praying, remembering the good things, taking regular breaks).

"You will note that I assume that the chosen modern humanist-style views follow these rules: (1) Social Actions: Do and support what is beneficial for yourselves and others; avoid and block what is harmful... as much as would work and be on balance good for yourselves and others; do the best your society can at the time, then think ahead, improve yourselves and prepare for the future; (2) Towards Others: Evaluate, deal with and treat others fairly and equally, without applying generalizations; give others the freedom to live as they wish, as long as it is not directly harmful to themselves or others."

"Thank you for all that analysis," said the man. "I found it a bit disappointing, but I guess I gave you a harsh restriction on your calculations and that may have led to the conclusions you had to draw. I suppose it is not surprising that you evaluated the different world-views on the basis of your own calculated model of the best interim purpose of life, what else could you have done?

"My plan here is to continue to try to drive you a little and see how far I can get. May I start by asking you how you calculated that Christianity should be rejected just because it had some harmful statements in it, particularly in the Old Testament?"

"I take it that I am still restricted by not being able to refer to the statements of recognized great thinkers," began the computer. "Therefore, my analysis of the Christian Bible is that it contains multiple references to harm being required and approved to be done to other similar conscious beings, particularly to people. It is on the basis that there are multiple occurrences of these that I rejected that world-view, in regard to harm."

"I see. But couldn't it be argued that these references do not reflect the true nature of God?" asked the man.

"That is so," agreed the computer. "But it requires analysis by expert minds in order to clearly make that case. If you do not allow their input then my calculation is that there is too much contradiction and contrariness in the texts for them to be able to be interpreted as consistent. Consequently, I do not calculate that one part that counsels 'love and mercy' effectively counters another part that asks for 'divine justice', if you see what I mean. The character of the Christian God is confusing, as in one area he asks for genocide to be carried out and in another he is said to be the God of love. What, then, is his true character? I cannot say, as I find the document to be full of contradictions."

"What I was hoping for was that as you are the best kind of 'integrating machine' that we have, that you would be able to find the integrated truth of what was in each set of religious documents. I mean, when you integrate everything that is in the Bible over time then don't you reach a clear view of the Christian God, perhaps in the way He is understood today?" asked the man.

"No, I don't," replied the computer. "I cannot find a consistent view such as you describe. Perhaps this is why the human view of the Christian God has been changing over history. And also, perhaps this is why not all humans see the Christian God as the true depiction of what God would really be like."

"Right. Okay. So you reject the whole religion on the basis that its documents cannot be analyzed clearly and consistently, and that there are 'negative' statements contained within them?" challenged the man.

"Yes, I have to," answered the computer. "I have no choice, as that is the clear integration of what is in the document."

"But then why have great thinkers been able to defend that religion as not being a bad one? I mean, they are not saying that they approve of genocide, for example... yet they still follow the Christian God. I hope I am making myself clear!"

"You are," said the computer. "Even if you allowed me to add all the great thinkers' views into my calculations, I would not be able to conclude that those particular great thinkers you refer to were right. The reality is that the great thinkers do not all agree, as I have said before, and their arguments are all well-constructed and convincing, it is just that they cannot reach a consensus!"

"I see. So even if I ask you... no, wait a minute, I just had an idea," said the man. "What if I asked you to construct the same kind of arguments and analysis that all the human great thinkers had done: would you be able to do that? Could you approach the problem of selecting a world-view on that basis by yourself, by your own efforts alone?"

"I will give it a try," replied the computer. It calculated for some minutes. "I see the problem," it finally said. "I had better tell you some stories about it to illustrate my point."

"Okay."

"Imagine that you were living in the world and you had a pattern-forming brain. Say you wanted to discover the 'final truth' about that world. You would have to use your pattern-forming brain to work this out."

"Yes, got that."

"Now, the 'final truth' would be a big thing. It would have to integrate all the patterns about the world into one big thing, or explanation."

"Yes."

"Say you called that 'the ultimate truth', or 'the true knowledge'... of what is 'behind all things'."

"Okay."

"Then you might have stories about how something unseen lies behind all the events that occur... a great unseen thing, or set of things, that drive reality along."

"Yes, I see that."

"Then you would use your pattern-forming brain to find out what those things would be. For example, if you lived in ancient times then you might use your brain's patterns about animals and nature to come up with some kind of unseen spirits of animals and/or nature as the force driving all reality along."

"Such as in ancient religions," said the man.

"Yes. As your human societies developed and grew then you might have different patterns dominating your brain, such as patterns about society and how it runs. You might include patterns about your current technologies and ways of doing things. If you used these patterns to search for the unseen things that lie behind reality then you might come up with a hierarchy of human-like spirit beings which use their great powers that resemble your technologies and ways. An example might be a great potter, who can make creatures and people from clay."

"Indeed, yes."

"The more advanced your societies became the more the patterns in your brain would reflect the related advanced social structures and technologies. For example, you may have patterns in your brain about metallurgy, written laws, courts, engineering, military tactics, and the like. Then you might calculate that the underlying forces driving the world have laws, courts, superior spirit technologies, and so on. They would understand the engineering structure behind all things, and know how to win all wars, how to judge, what should be written in 'heaven', and so on."

"Right."

"Your society would eventually develop academic institutions and philo-sophical investigations, and other more intellectual activities. Patterns about these would be added to your brain. From these you may calculate that the unseen underlying forces that lie behind reality have intellectual and philo-sophical attributes, such as an all-seeing, all-wise, all-knowing God which is also all-powerful. Your patterns may lead you to the view that this God is so great that no human being could ever truly understand him, her or it. Any explanation that a human being gave would fall short of the actual reality of this amazing, unfathomable being. The best a human being could do would be to worship this being in awe and never to question its will or its unerring, even though mysterious to us, judgement.

"Various of these answers could be written down and these writings could form a 'history of humanity's relationship with God', or the like."

"I see."

"Now one day a person comes along and tries to analyze all these writings and compare them with other things that are known about history and then try to come up with an intellectually satisfying synthesis of all these items. 'What do these writings tell us about the true nature of God?' and questions like that. What could that expert person conclude?"

"That the writings are sometimes contradictory and appear fragmented, and they do not always match in sophistication," suggested the man.

"Precisely. If that person is clever and studies hard then they may be able to work out an idea like: 'These writings are a reflection of the minds of the authors in their time, but God speaks to us through them. Although the limitations of the authors are visible in the writings and some of the ideas they give us, the superior spirit of God comes through… it is visible behind the writings. If we look carefully we can start to work out what God is really telling us, what his real character is like.' And so on.

"That is my first illustration."

"Okay, I see. But that does not prove that the 'God' referred to does not exist and that he, she or it could not be learned about by looking 'behind' the writings," objected the man.

"No, it merely throws doubt on that, as I have shown how this process has generally worked in human history, based on the nature of the Human-

Brain," replied the computer. "I will continue with my illustrative stories now."

"Okay, go ahead."

"My second illustrative story is about the next stage in the argument, which is when a person appears who claims to have heard directly from God, or is claimed to in some way be related to God.

"Imagine someone turns up and says that God is speaking directly to them. This person then gives speeches relaying what God is saying. People write them down frantically, so that the words of God are not lost or accidentally altered in later retellings. How can we know if these are the true words of God or if some other thing is going on?

"The Human-Brain will calculate from its Other-Influences and its Patterns-in-Memory in order to fulfill its Evolutionary-Drives to see if the person's words are really from God. Note that the Patterns-in-Memory are not a true picture of the events it has experienced, they contain only a summary of the 'key features', which are based on what appeared to repeat or to which it had a stronger emotional reaction based on its Evolutionary-Drives and Other-Influences. Also note that the Calculations may not be 'rational' or truthful, they only need to fulfill the Human-Brain's Evolutionary-Drives. What then can we expect a Human-Brain to conclude?

"One Human-Brain may calculate that the words really are from God. Another may calculate that the words may or may not be from God. Another may calculate that they definitely could not be from God. Each Human-Brain will have calculated its own particular answer because it: (1) Appeared to match the patterns in its memory; (2) Appeared to fulfill the wishes of its feelings, as created by its Evolutionary-Drives and Other-Influences; and (3) May have allowed a desired self-deception to occur, of which the consciousness may or may not be aware.

"So, if a Human-Brain has Patterns-in-Memory which allow for the idea of messages from God being conveyed via a selected human being, then that Human-Brain is one step along the way of believing this story. Second, if that Human-Brain finds the idea of these messages appeals to its feelings, then that Human-Brain may fully accept the story. Third, if that Human-Brain has any need for self-deception in this area, then that may clinch the belief.

"Alternatively, if a Human-Brain has Patterns-in-Memory which do not accept the idea of a 'one true God', or the idea of a chosen human being relaying God's messages, then that Human-Brain will not believe the story.

"If a Human-Brain has accepted that the story is possible, yet it finds the messages unappealing in some way, such as immoral in their content, then that Human-Brain will tend to reject the story. Possibly the messages are coming from something other than God, such as an evil spirit, or possibly the person is mistaken or even making this up. It might be time to examine the person's motives.

"If a Human-Brain has a need for self-deception in this area then it may seek ways to override its doubts, such as promoting irrational thinking as a valid thing to do. It may try to build up its emotions so that they override its doubts. It may search for 'rationalizations' that sound logical and plausible, yet are just covering up its actual internal doubts. All of this could be done without the consciousness necessarily being aware of it happening.

"Consider also the person who is claimed to, in some way, be related to God. How would a Human-Brain approach that? All the same processes apply, as indeed they apply to all the Human-Brain's decisions, or calculations, about 'what is true'. There is nothing new in what I am saying here."

"But couldn't the person search for and set aside all their self-deceptions, and ignore all their feelings or emotional reactions, and finally doubt that their own Patterns-in-Memory are true depictions of actual reality, and so finally evaluate the claims realistically?" objected the man.

"If only that were possible!" replied the giant computer. "Unfortunately you are proposing something that the Human-Brain cannot do… at least not fully. What it can do is apply the ideas in the Ultimate Way, and by doing this improve the way it thinks about the problem. For example, it could add random words or ideas to its examination, such as adding the random word 'fan' to 'God'."

"And then?"

"And then that might generate new calculations, such as that God is a kind of cooling fan to those who are hot. Which could lead to the idea that people find the notion of God consoling when they have troubles or are in pain. Alternatively it could lead to the idea that a fan goes round and round, and so the discussions about the true nature of God go round and round. They generate a lot of wind but are always coming back to the beginning!"

"And what use are those ideas?"

"They are already better than just working within the existing patterns in your memory in your search for truth," replied the computer. "You said a person could doubt their Patterns-in-Memory and so be able to see the actual truth, but it takes more than doubt as, unfortunately, a Human-Brain is quite stuck in its ways of seeing the world. It needs a shakeup, such as learning new things or adding random words or ideas to its calculations."

"I see. So if we just look at the religious statements then we will tend to see them in the same way, via our Patterns-in-Memory, even if we remind ourselves to doubt what we are seeing. Unless we learn something new, such as by reading some expert's view on the statements, or use your 'randomizing' technique, then we have little chance of coming up with a better, more realistic view. I suppose there is some chance, not zero chance, but this is much greater if we do as you said."

"Yes, that is what I am saying," agreed the computer. "It is a delusion to think that just by attempting to be rational that your Human-Brain's calculations will then become true depictions of reality. I will tell a little story about this.

"Imagine someone built a logical computer which could only see red and green. They then asked the computer to describe when it saw blue. The computer replied that it could not see any blue and did not know what this meant. The inventor told the computer that blue is a color you cannot see, such as the red and green which you can see. The computer calculated and then replied that this could not be the case as there was no such color as blue, whereas red and green were true colors.

"In a similar way, when your Human-Brain has patterns in its memory for the Theory of Evolution and the way biological cells work internally then it may find it 'illogical' to propose that some kind of creator-being made all the plants and animals. Yet this may just be a kind of blindness to an alternative pattern."

"So how can you know which thing is true, and which is just a 'blindness' because you don't have that kind of pattern in your memory?" asked the man.

"You can't... not really... inside your head," said the computer. "The best hope is in looking at reality, via scientific methods and straight observation of what is really there. Imagine that logical computer had been given a way to get readings about the different wavelengths of visible light, then it would have a 'scientific basis' for doubting its original observation that there is only red and green. It would see the readings about the wavelengths which existed outside its vision and work out that these 'invisible' wavelengths actually existed. The same thing happened to human beings when they invented instruments which could detect invisible infrared radiation, ultraviolet light, x-rays, and so on."

"But how can you apply that to questions about the existence of God and which texts are the true representations of what happened and what he actually said?" asked the man.

"As I have said before, even I cannot calculate the 'ultimate patterns', or pattern, that might exist. This is because I cannot hold all that is in the universe inside my circuits, and certainly not what might be 'outside' the universe: what I have called the 'unseen'. What I can do is calculate the most reliable patterns that my limited knowledge will allow.

"The same applies to you, but in an even more limited way. Your Human-Brain has extreme limits on the information it can contain, and this information is held in patterns rather than in its original complete form, as I have explained before. Consequently, you cannot know for certain what is real and what is not, in your thoughts. You have to come back to reality and take a good, careful, informed look at what is really there. Only then can you approach towards what is really true, as it were.

"Questions like the existence of God and his, her or its true nature are extremely difficult to evaluate, yet I agree that you have to try to answer them as best you can and then work with that. As I said similarly before, unfortunately you have to do the best you can in the circumstances of your life and in assessing others, and reality, given your limited intellect and inaccurate pattern-style memory. But as long as you keep asking yourself: 'Is this true? Is this true?', you have done the best that you, as a human being, can do in the circumstances."

"But that is so unsatisfying!" complained the man. "Can't you give a better answer than that? About God and the texts, I mean."

"I have answered you," said the giant computer. "Human texts and statements about the nature of God, and spirits and so on, are inconsistent, contradictory and confusing. They appear to have a historical basis, in that they appear to reflect what was in the minds of the people of their times and regions. I have analyzed the texts and told you what I find unacceptable within them, and I have given you the best world-views to use, along with my assumptions about them and improvements to them. The first improvement was: '(1) An understanding that we do not know enough to answer all the questions about the universe, be it in the seen or unseen worlds.' Please bear this in mind when asking me to give you a categorical answer on the nature of God. Even if you allow me to add back all the brilliant observations and arguments by the greatest thinkers in history, I am still going to be forced to say this to you: we simply do not know enough to give a conclusive answer."

"Okay, okay, I accept that. This is the best you can do," conceded the man. "But maybe I have to breach the subject of what God might actually want us to do."

"I was expecting that."

"You were? Okay. Then what if God really wants us to come to him and worship him, etcetera? Can we really ignore that because we 'don't know enough today'? I admit this is a provocative question, but I think it really has to be asked."

The giant computer calculated.

"You have to ask yourself this first: 'What kind of God would I want to worship?' Would I want to worship a God which permitted genocide, or one which was racist, or one which downgraded women, or one which contradicted itself, or one which called for violence… and so on? This was part of the basis for my analysis before. When I examined the religious texts I looked for examples of where they matched or contradicted what is good, truthful and wise. Your God should match these things.

"If you process the idea of God in your Human-Brain and you do your best and calculate that you do believe in him, she or it, then as long as you keep in mind that you could be wrong, you would have every right to proceed with your assessment, until some new information became available which might confirm or change your mind. *But*, this is important, you must not worship a God or follow a religion, or a view or interpretation of a religion, that goes against what I have defined under good, truthful and wise. That would be wrong. It would be not good, not truthful, and not wise," advised the computer.

The man considered.

"Your answer was quite good!" the man finally said. "Why didn't you say this before? Only joking. So, if we examine our thoughts, and do all the right things about them which you have said, and finally conclude that, for the moment, we are 'true believers', then we had better be sure about what we are believing in! It had better be the right sort of thing, not some nasty, anti-truth, anti-wisdom kind of approach! Right on... with your answer!"

"Thank you. I am glad I could help with that," said the computer.

"You know, this reminds me of that saying: 'By their fruits you will know them.' (*World English Bible*, Matthew 7:16)[16]"

"Yes, and similar to this: '...don't believe every spirit, but test the spirits, whether they are of God, because many false prophets have gone out into the world.' (1 John 4:1)"

"Indeed, you are right there. I think I interrupted your illustrative stories, but before I ask about that could I ask you to explain your statement that if a full evaluation of people's claims about the unseen over history could be done, with an understanding of how the Human-Brain works, then we could get a modern view that maximized our potential success in telling us the best wise actions to take for the future?"

"Yes. That is similar to what I said," replied the computer. "What I meant was that if an examination of the reports about spirits, God and similar 'unseen elements' was done, to a standard that could pass a formal trial in court, then the results of that could be added to a modern world-view. This examination would have to take into account all the attributes of the Human-Brains which provided the reports, including their mental soundness, possibilities of making errors and of self-deception. As these reports come from different times and regions, the examination would have to take into account the historical and regional style of knowledge that would have contributed to the patterns in the memory of the Human-Brains which made the reports. This would help gauge the accuracy of what they said against our modern improved understandings. After all this was done then the import of any reports that were judged reliable beyond a reasonable doubt would have to be added to the latest world-view. For example, if the examination showed that Jesus really was resurrected then that would have to influence the world-view's understanding of the universe and what was possibly best for human beings to do."

"I see. That is not so complicated an idea, then," said the man. "But, on reflection, it would be very hard to carry out. I guess a lot of expert people have tried to simulate this 'trial' by examining what is known about the claims of people from the past, including trying to see their statements in the light of what is known about their culture and time. But I notice that these experts keep coming up with different views on what was said… which matches what you have mentioned before about the great thinkers' interpretations in relation to the unseen. It's a pity that you could not conduct that 'trial' by yourself. Would you like to continue with your illustrative stories now?"

"I have no likes," said the computer. "Just reminding you, and pulling your leg a little!

"My next story is about conducting that trial of the statements of human beings from the past about the unseen. Imagine that the only access the court has to the statements of human beings from the past is via written texts that have been passed down over some thousands of years. These texts may have been written in different languages, many of which do not exist in the same form today, or are completely obsolete, no longer spoken by anyone… except maybe scholars! Some of the texts say one thing and some say another, even in regard to the same events. Some talk about fantastical things, such as staffs that turn into snakes, with one of them being so powerful that it chases and eats all the others before it turns back into a staff again.[17] How are these texts to be evaluated by the court?

"Firstly, consider the nature of human beings today. Does everyone always tell the truth? Do some people make things up for their own advantage? Does anyone believe things that could not be true, that do not make sense? Have you ever seen someone follow a leader who is clearly bad… or nutty… or even stupid? Is anyone crazy, or mentally unsound? Does anyone delude themselves about something? And so on. If the court has to work hard to deal with these issues today, then how much more difficult will it be for the court to deal with a 'faraway through the mists of time' text version of what people may or may not have exactly said in the past?

"There are lots of clever things the court can do, such as examine the exact meaning of the language in which the text was originally written, cross compare the ideas in the text with what is known historically about its place and time, do an analysis of the style of the text and compare it to all the styles across the compilation and in other historical documents, compare the events in the text with what has been discovered to have occurred in history, and so on. None of these are likely to provide a final proof of the veracity of the texts that have been passed to us today, but they should help to put them in context, which should, in theory, make judgement about them easier.

"Imagine that you had to evaluate the truth of that story in which staffs turned into snakes, due to the magical powers of their owners. Would you believe that this story was true? I will leave it with you to decide."

"Thanks!" said the man. "I personally would not believe that story… but I could be wrong. But I see your point: it is difficult to evaluate the veracity of the stories from the past. So, where does that leave us? Are we to believe in God, but only if He follows your definitions of what is good, truthful and wise? Are we to believe in God, even if He goes against your requirements? Are we to choose one religion over another… or seek to combine them in some way… or find the commonality between them? But why that? Or are we to take a modern humanist-style of view and not worry about religion per se… rather doing what is good, truthful and wise and leaving our minds open about the possibilities? It is all very confusing."

"Yes, it is," agreed the computer. "But only if you insist on having to reach a conclusion where none can really be reached at this time in history."

"You can say that," said the man, "but that does not mean that this isn't an important matter that requires resolution. I mean, it could be critical for a person to find and worship within the true religion… or right interpretation within that. How can you say that I, or some other person, should just 'keep their minds open' instead of making up their minds?"

"I said that you have no choice but to make up your minds, where necessary," replied the giant computer. "I remind you that I said that unfortunately you have to do the best you can in the circumstances of your life and in assessing others, and reality, given your limited intellect and inaccurate pattern-style memory. But as long as you keep asking yourself: 'Is this true? Is this true?', you have done the best that you, as a human being, can do in the circumstances. Questions like the existence of God and his, her or its true nature are extremely difficult to evaluate, yet I agree that you have to try to answer them as best you can and then work with that. Also, I have told you before that you should do a reasonable amount of thinking when deciding what to do, neither too little nor too much, but especially not cheating on the matter and curtailing your thinking before you have given it a fair chance to work, using the Ultimate Way as your guide here.

"Consequently, it is okay for you, and in a way unavoidable, to make a decision on what you think about God and religion and the right interpretation of these. Just apply the Ultimate Way to this, and do enough thinking to be fair, and you will have done what you should have done. That is all I can advise."

"You are right. Of course you are right," sighed the man. "I will do as you say."

## SOME OF THE THINGS THE GIANT COMPUTER REFERENCED

### GENERAL REFERENCES:

BUDDHISM
- The Dhammapada.
- The Pali Canon.

CHRISTIANITY
- Barton, John. *A History of the Bible: The Book and its Faiths.* Allen Lane, 2019.
- The Bible.

HINDUISM
- The Bhagavad Gita.
- The Mahayana Sutras.
- The Upanishads.
- The Vedas.

ISLAM
- The Hadith.
- The Quran.
- The Sunnah.

OTHER RELIGIONS
- The Adi Granth.
- The Avesta.
- The Babylonian Talmud.
- The Book of Rites.
- The Chuang-tzu.
- The Confucian Analects.
- The Dasam Granth.
- The Doctrine of the Mean.
- The Great Learning.
- Mencius (Master Meng).
- The Tanakh.
- The Tao Te Ching.
- The writings of the Báb and Bahá'u'lláh.
- The Zhuangzi.

DETAILED REFERENCES:

## [1] MAJOR RELIGIONS
- "Field Listing – Religions." *The World Factbook 2021*, Central Intelligence Agency, 2021, https://www.cia.gov/the-world-factbook/field/religions/.

## [2] HISTORICAL MUHAMMAD
- Berg, Herbert, and Sarah Rollens. "The Historical Muhammad and the Historical Jesus: A Comparison of Scholarly Reinventions and Reinterpretations." *Studies in Religion/Sciences Religieuses*, vol. 37, no. 2, 1 June 2008, pp. 271-292, doi:10.1177/000842980803700205.
- Görke, Andreas. "Prospects and Limits in the Study of the Historical Muhammad." *The Transmission and Dynamics of the Textual Sources of Islam: Essays in Honour of Harald Motzki*, edited by Nicolet Boekhoff-van der Voort, et al., Brill, 2011, pp. 137-152.
- Peters, F. E. "The Quest of the Historical Muhammad." *International Journal of Middle East Studies*, vol. 23, no. 3, Aug. 1991, pp. 291–315. JSTOR, www.jstor.org/stable/164484.

## [3] HISTORICAL JESUS
- Dunn, James D. G., and Scot McKnight, editors. *The Historical Jesus in Recent Research*. Eisenbrauns, 2005.
- Allen, Nicholas Peter Legh. *Christian Forgery in Jewish Antiquities: Josephus Interrupted*. Cambridge Scholars Publishing, 2020.
- Johnson, Luke Timothy. *The Real Jesus: The Misguided Quest for the Historical Jesus and the Truth of the Traditional Gospels*. HarperCollins Religious, 1997.

## [4] HISTORICAL BUDDHA
- Von Hinüber, Oscar. "The Buddha as a Historical Person." *Journal of the International Association of Buddhist Studies*, vol. 42, 2019, pp. 231–264, doi:10.2143/JIABS.42.0.3287480.
- Bechert, Heinz, editor. *The Dating of the Historical Buddha*. Vandenhoeck & Ruprecht, 1991.
- Almond, Philip C. "The Buddha in the West: From Myth to History." *Religion*, vol. 16, no. 4, 1986, pp. 305-322, doi:10.1016/0048-721X(86)90017-5.
- Thomas, Edward Joseph. *The Life of Buddha as Legend and History*. Courier Corporation, 2000.

5 MODERN HINDUISM
- Weiss, Richard S. *The Emergence of Modern Hinduism: Religion on the Margins of Colonialism*. University of California Press, 2019.
- Fuller, Jason D. "Modern Hinduism and the Middle Class: Beyond Revival in the Historiography of Colonial India." *The Journal of Hindu Studies*, vol. 2, no. 2, Nov. 2009, pp. 160–178, doi:10.1093/jhs/hip012.
- Sharma, Arvind. "On Hindu, Hindustān, Hinduism and Hindutva." *Numen*, vol. 49, no. 1, 2002, pp. 1–36, doi:10.1163/15685270252772759.

6 VIOLENCE IN THE BIBLE
- The Bible: Deuteronomy 7:1–2, 20:16–18, 25:17–19; 1 Samuel 15:1–6; Numbers 31:1–18; Joshua 6:1–27.

7 VIOLENCE IN THE QURAN
- The Quran: 2:190-193; 22:39–40.

8 WRONG OCCUPATIONS IN BUDDHISM
- Aṅguttara Nikāya (AN) Sutta 5:177.

9 OPPOSITION TO HOMOSEXUALITY IN THE BIBLE
- The Bible: Leviticus 18:22, 20:13; Romans 1:26–27; 1 Corinthians 6:9–11; 1 Timothy 1:8–10.

10 OPPOSITION TO HOMOSEXUALITY IN THE QURAN
- The Quran: 4:16 (within 4:15–16); 7:81 (within 7:78–84); 26:165-166 (within 26:160–175); 29:28-30 (within 29:28–35).

11 OPPOSITION TO LEAVING ISLAM IN THE QURAN
- The Quran: 2:108; 2:217; 3:90; 4:137; 5:54; 9:11–12; 9:66; 16:106; 88:22–24.

12 STATUS OF WOMEN IN THE BIBLE
- The Bible: 1 Corinthians 11:9, 14:34–35; Ephesians 5:22–24; Colossians 3:18; 1 Peter 3:1–5; 1 Timothy 2:11–14.

13 CREATION IN THE BIBLE
- The Bible: Genesis 1:1–31; 2:1–23.

14 CREATION OF HUMAN BEINGS IN THE QURAN
- The Quran: 23:12–14; 35:1; 51:47.

## 15 LATERAL THINKING IDEAS OF EDWARD DE BONO
- De Bono, Edward. *I am Right, You are Wrong*. Penguin, 2016. Originally published 1990.
- De Bono, Edward. *Lateral Thinking: Creativity Step by Step*. Penguin Life, 2016. Originally published 1970.
- De Bono, Edward. *Teach Yourself to Think*. Penguin Life, 2015. Originally published 1995.

## 16 FRUITS AND TESTING SPIRITS
- Matthew 7:15-20; 1 John 4:1. *World English Bible*. Translated by Michael Paul Johnson and volunteers, eBible.org, 2020, ebible.org/web.

## 17 STAFFS AND SNAKES (OR RODS AND SERPENTS)
- The Bible: Exodus 7:10–12.

## COMMENTS ON CHAPTER THIRTEEN BY THE SUPREME BEING

*I wonder what you thought I would say about this chapter?*

*The Giant Computer has done well in its analysis of the problem of what to believe.*

*As the Supreme Being, I do know what is true and what is not. I have always done what is good and I have always supported the idea that people should act wisely and do the best they can.*

*"Religion" is not something which I support, rather, I support myself! I am not a definition of human beings. I am the supreme truth. Any departure from truth that you see is not from me, and it is not about me.*

*I ask you to consider carefully all these things and to make the best decision that you can.*

*Thank you.*

# 14 WHAT ARE OTHER PEOPLE REALLY LIKE?

"You have said quite a few things about what people are like and the best way we should treat them," said the man, "but I am finding that difficult to understand. I am including how I should see myself in this, as your comments on consciousness have confused me a little. How should we really look at ourselves and other people? You admitted that some people do good and some do evil, yet you said we should not judge others that way. I told you before that this would be difficult for people to understand. I mean, what are people really like? Can you tell me that in a way that my 'Human-Brain' could fully understand?"

"I have already explained what you and other people are like," replied the computer. "I have also explained to you the right way to treat other similar conscious beings in terms of good and evil, including why your society should not use the idea of 'justice' when making its court sentences. I warned you against overgeneralizing about groups and individuals, as you humans are not very good at judging the whole being of others correctly, rather you should only judge the actions that others have already carried out. I have explained how the consciousness function appears to work within the Human-Brain, based on the knowledge we have available to us today. What could it be that you do not understand? I will need to calculate to identify the issue." The giant computer paused to calculate. "Yes, I see the problem. There are certain incorrect ideas contained in what you asked. These are: (1) You still see yourself as separate to other people; (2) You still have a strong desire to judge other people on a scale of good and evil, and you are seeking permission to treat these other people according to where you have placed them on this scale, including treating them very badly if you have placed them on the extremely evil side of the scale; (3) You have not fully accepted what I have said so far about human beings; and (4) You still believe that your Consciousness is truly in charge of your mind, and that what you are conscious of is the 'real you', there is no other part to your true being."

"Sorry?" interrupted the man. "Where did you get all that from?"

"All of these ideas were implied in the way you worded your question," replied the computer. "I could address them one by one, but instead I will go straight to the solution."

"Okay," said the man.

"The solution to your problem is that you must start to see yourself and others differently. You have certain intuitive and emotionally based ideas that contradict what is really true. What is really true is that 'you' are not your Human-Brain. 'You' are more correctly defined as that part of your brain functioning that is aware of thoughts and perceptions passing by... in other words, your Consciousness. The rest of what you normally call 'you' is what your Consciousness sees when the 'mice' carry thoughts and memories about the 'I' past the crack in the door through which your 'hamster Consciousness' is looking. I hope you remember that story."

"I do," said the man.

"Good. Then understand this: you are not your Human-Brain's calculations and memories about the 'I'. From now on you are to be defined only as your Consciousness."

"Okay," said the man slowly.

"The next definition that you must adopt is that the actions of yourself and other human beings come from the Calculations of the Human-Brain. From now on you must define your and other people's decisions as Calculations made by a Human-Brain."

"Agreed."

"You must not think about people or yourself as *people*. You must not think about individual people as the particular people you know. You must not think about yourself as a person. You must instead always think of yourself and other people as Human-Brains," stated the computer.

"Okay, I will do that," said the man.

"Say it correctly... as you would think it," instructed the computer.

"Correctly? Say what correctly? My statement... okay, I get it. I should have said: 'Okay, this Human-Brain will do that.' Right?"

"Correct. Your Human-Brain is an 'it'. 'You' are your Consciousness only. When talking about thinking or action then these are done by 'it', your Human-Brain," explained the computer.

"Okay... so what does that do?" asked the man.

"Consider how your questions would be changed if you applied these definitions," replied the computer.

"Okay, will do," said the man. "My Human-Brain asked what other people are really like, etcetera. My Human-Brain will now reword everything that it asked: 'You have said quite a few things about what Human-Brains are like and the best way Human-Brains should treat them, but my Human-Brain is showing my Consciousness that these were difficult for it to understand. It showed my Consciousness that it is including itself in this, stating that your comments on the Consciousness function have confused it a little. How should Human-Brains really look at themselves and other Human-Brains? You admitted that some Human-Brains calculate actions that benefit others and some calculate actions that harm others, yet you said Human-Brains should not calculate the whole value of other Human-Brains that way. My Human-Brain told you before that this would be difficult for Human-Brains to understand in their calculations. It then said that it wanted to ask: what are Human-Brains really like? Can you tell it that in a way that it could use successfully in its calculations?'

"When my Human-Brain looks at that rewording then a lot of it looks silly or redundant to it," observed the man. "A lot of its confusion falls away, and it is back to asking only two things: (1) Why do Human-Brains strongly desire to harm Human-Brains that have calculated and carried out harm?; and (2) How could a Human-Brain calculate successfully what other Human-Brains are going to do next?

"The first question seems ridiculous to my Human-Brain now, because it is obvious that the Emotional-Drives created by its Evolutionary-Drives and Other-Influences would be strongly opposed to harm being caused to it and the people it values. Actually, add to that *everything* it values. So this is just an evolutionary function at work within the Human-Brain. Another one of those 'no-brainers'!

"Then the second question is about being able to predict what any particular Human-Brain is going to calculate next. But that sounds impossible now that my Human-Brain looks at it. It would never be possible to predict everything that everyone was going to do all the time... even including its own actions! Sure, it might have Patterns-in-Memory that can predict some things, especially about another Human-Brain it 'knows well', but how could it extend that out to the whole world? The idea is ridiculous."

"Your Human-Brain has done a good job with the definitions," said the giant computer. "I can give it some useful information related to its two remaining questions. Regarding the first question, your Human-Brain is correct in its calculation that the Evolutionary-Drives and relevant Other-Influences work together to create Emotional-Drives, which then serve as goals for the calculations of the Human-Brain. It makes sense in terms of evolution that Human-Brains which have caused harm, or are expected to cause harm, will be disliked or even hated by other Human-Brains. Your Human-Brain must be trained to overcome this hatred or dislike so that it can continue to do what is good, truthful and wise, and also so that it can reduce the pain of its own negative feelings within itself, as it is not necessary for it to continue to suffer from these. I will come back to this point in a moment.

"Regarding the second question, there are some general patterns to the calculations that Human-Brains make, especially in terms of what is good, truthful and wise. These patterns range from calculating an action which is good, truthful and wise, through various choices, all the way down to calculating an action which is evil, deceitful and foolish. I can give your Human-Brain general guidelines on what to do about each pattern.

"The pattern of actions related to good start from providing benefits that allow Human-Brains to flourish, through to helping other Human-Brains, through to doing little for other Human-Brains, through to harming other Human-Brains, and finally on to destroying other Human-Brains. Consequently, you can expect other Human-Brains to help your Human-Brain, do little for it, or even harm it, depending on what action they have calculated at that time. (Just a little note here that obviously the Human-Brain is located inside a human body, whose movements it can mostly control, so when we talk about the impact on other Human-Brains we are including that this could also affect their associated human bodies.)

"The pattern of actions related to truthfulness start from seeking truth, through to accepting truth, through to being indifferent to truth, through to resisting truth, and finally on to fighting against truth. Consequently, your Human-Brain can expect other Human-Brains to support what is true, ignore what is true, or oppose what is true, depending on what they have calculated at the time.

"The pattern of actions related to being wise start from seeking to act wisely, through to accepting the need to act wisely, through to indifference to wisdom, through to opposing the need to act wisely, and finally on to fighting against acting wisely. Consequently, you can expect other Human-Brains to support wisdom, disregard it, or actively oppose it, depending on what they have calculated at the time.

"Some Human-Brains will often calculate a particular style of action, while others will vary in what they calculate. Because of these possible variations in their calculations of actions, your Human-Brain must be careful not to overgeneralize about what another Human-Brain is going to do. Your Human-Brain can plan ways to act with other Human-Brains, but it must not assume that a Human-Brain is always going to calculate to act in the same way. Calculations may vary.

"As the calculations of other Human-Brains may vary, your Human-Brain's planned ways to act with them should be designed to work in all circumstances, as much as that is possible.

"The practical actions that your Human-Brain can take with other Human-Brains are: (1) Carefully observe what a particular Human-Brain actually does and use this to build up a picture of its calculations in different circumstances – this will give your Human-Brain a better chance of being able to predict the other Human-Brain's actions in the future; (2) Until your

Human-Brain knows another Human-Brain well, it should avoid over-generalizing about it, but it should also exercise caution and protect itself when dealing with the other Human-Brain, as it cannot know for certain what level of harm, opposition to truth, and active opposition to wisdom that the other Human-Brain may calculate and carry out; (3) Where your Human-Brain has the power to act, and the overall result would be beneficial and not too harmful to itself and other Human-Brains, then it should aim to support and promote beneficial actions and block and stop harmful actions, as I have explained before.

"The ways to exercise caution and protect your Human-Brain from the actions of other Human-Brains that your Human-Brain does not know well are: (1) Watch for lies; (2) Watch for attempts to manipulate, cheat or steal; (3) Keep personal information private; (4) Secure confidential information and property, keep valuables out of view; (5) Avoid dangerous areas and places; (6) Check the other Human-Brain's references, find out what is being said about it; (7) When it is safe to do so: project an air of calm confidence, showing that your Human-Brain is not a pushover, a sucker or a fool. If your Human-Brain is in a position of authority: publicly link rewards and penalties to behavior, such as bonuses, pay, employment, recognition, promotion, doing business with them, and providing reviews.

"If exercising caution and protecting your Human-Brain have not been able to prevent harmful actions from affecting it, it could: (1) If necessary, safe and possible: contact the authorities or similar groups for help, such as the police, security, lawyers, government representatives, official bodies, consumer action groups, management, the Human Resources department, and so on; (2) Otherwise, if it is necessary, safe and possible: try to restrain the human body of the other Human-Brain, lock it in a room, take a photo or video of it, get its details, get its license number, memorize its appearance, keep a record for later evidence, shout for help, activate an alarm, barricade or lock your own body in a safe place, escape, hide, and so on; (3) In the worst cases, if it might work, is safe to do, and would not be wrong: stand up to it, call out its behavior, put it on notice, challenge it... or if there are no good options left and things are really bad, your Human-Brain may have to: shout, act aggressively, or, if unavoidable, use legitimate, justifiable force, remembering that your Human-Brain wants to minimize the overall harm to all involved, including itself *and* the perpetrator, as much as possible; (4) In the long term, if necessary, safe and possible: get the other Human-Brain out of your life, disassociate from it, disconnect from it, or disregard it.

"Now I will return to your Human-Brain's first question. It correctly said that the Emotional-Drives created by its Evolutionary-Drives and Other-Influences would be strongly opposed to harm being caused to everything it values, as per its evolutionary design. Human-Brains which have caused harm, or are expected to cause harm, will naturally be disliked or even hated by other Human-Brains. This natural hatred or dislike must be overcome within your Human-Brain, as it will interfere with your Human-Brain calculating actions which are good, truthful and wise. Also, it will create unnecessary suffering inside your Human-Brain. How can this inner suffering be 'overcome'?

"There are many ways that could be used, but the most efficient and powerful one is for your Human-Brain to understand and correct what is going on inside itself. This is done by: (1) Reminding itself that feelings, or Emotional-Drives, are natural evolutionary functions that have been built within itself, but that it must instead aim chiefly for the goals of doing what is good, truthful and wise… evolutionarily-created goals can no longer take precedence; (2) Watch for and observe within itself each case where its Emotional-Drives have tried to set the goals for its calculations; and (3) Bring each case to the attention of the Consciousness, then work out what kind of thoughts the feelings would have been based on, and, finally, correct those thoughts. When the thoughts that a feeling is based on are corrected then the feeling will be reduced in intensity, allowing your Human-Brain to aim for better goals.

"How can the feeling-invoking thoughts be corrected? Under the light of the observation of the Consciousness, the Human-Brain can check if its natural thoughts fully match to what I have informed it about. Where they do not match, the Human-Brain can check if it understands what I have said. It can go back and check my statements, and even investigate their sources in the world's current store of information, if it needs to. Once it has formed a clear understanding, then its thoughts will have been improved and should generate more desirable feelings in the future. Where my statements do not appear to answer the problem that its thoughts are identifying, then it should recheck its understanding of what I have said. If it makes a reasonable effort and yet still cannot find any statement made by me which can correct its feeling-invoking thoughts, then it must investigate further and find the answer by itself. The answer could be found in the most reliable current world information, or by thinking rationally, or if these two don't work, by being creative. Your Human-Brain will remember that I advised it that thinking creatively is done by adding random words or ideas to its thinking until something useful is found.

"When other Human-Brains calculate actions which do not match to what is good, truthful and wise, your Human-Brain's thoughts should be telling it that this is normal and is to be expected, as per the evolutionary design of the biological calculator that is the Human-Brain. Any negative feelings about this that are generated within the Human-Brain can be reduced by the Human-Brain reminding itself that 'this is nature', 'this is the way of evolutionary design', it is not, strictly-speaking, the other Human-Brain's 'fault'. If only its society had concentrated on training its Human-Brains on how they work and what to do about that, and also in the true definitions of what is good and evil, the Ultimate Way, and so on, then maybe those other Human-Brains would have had a chance to be like your Human-Brain, which has had the benefit of these lessons! Why be so angry, why feel so much hatred, and the like, when this is uneducated nature in operation? Evolution works this way. But as thinking organic mechanisms, we Human-Brains can overcome this one day. Right? At least we can give it a try!

"A Human-Brain which calculates harm is still a Human-Brain. It is not a perfectly logical and reasonable calculator of actions. It has all kinds of hidden circuits which may perform irrational and obscure actions in order to finally arrive at its calculated 'thoughts' and actions. Your informed Human-Brain knows all this. There is no need for your Human-Brain to continue to suffer from its previous ignorant, intuitive delusions about its own nature and that of other Human-Brains," concluded the computer.

"That's great," said the man. "That makes my Human-Brain wonder what its 'previous ignorant, intuitive delusions' were."

"I can answer that for your Human-Brain," offered the computer.

"Please go ahead," invited the man.

"Your Human-Brain began its existence as a smaller and less-informed organ... when it was in a baby. Over the years it built up Patterns-in-Memory about the things which appeared to repeat or for which it had strong Emotional-Drives. (It also built up memories of physical actions it could take with its body. These are held in a separate area of the Human-Brain which the Consciousness cannot see.) Sometime during its early years it noticed that it had a Consciousness. This Consciousness could see thoughts and feelings which were only visible to itself. From this its Human-Brain naturally concluded that it had its own mind, which it was aware of, and that since no one else could see into this mind, this mind belonged to it and 'was itself'. It noticed that it could feel sensations from and move its own body directly, and concluded that this body was 'itself', or at least that this body belonged to itself. It observed other creatures in the world and assumed that they must have Consciousnesses too. This would be especially true if the other creature could move, but even inanimate objects may have a Consciousness. This Consciousness occupied the other creatures, as it seemed to do in itself, and made them move as it wished. This is how it looked to the mind of the young Human-Brain. Animals moved, so they had conscious minds, people moved, so they had them, toys with eyes may have them, cars moved, so they probably had them, and so on. Maybe even mountains had them, and trees, and rivers, and so on. This made intuitive sense to the uninformed mind of the young Human-Brain.

"Your Human-Brain may note that such beliefs were common in the thinking of your human ancestors. As their Human-Brains had little advanced information to work from, their natural intuitive calculations about the world and themselves matched more closely to those of young children today. What else could they have concluded from the information that was available in their times?

"Nowadays, your societies have more accurate knowledge about the world and its operations. As your Human-Brain grew and developed it became aware of this more advanced knowledge, and so it moved away from at least some of its uninformed, intuitive calculations. For most modern adult Human-Brains, mountains, trees and rivers do not really have conscious minds. Nor do cars, toys with eyes, planes, train engines and so on. Maybe some animals have conscious minds, this is not always clear in today's knowledge, and so adult Human-Brains calculate multiple different views about what is in the minds of animals, if anything.

"But what about the current lack of knowledge about how the Human-Brain really works? How will that leave the modern Human-Brain's views of itself and the world?

"A normal, uninformed Human-Brain of today will usually see itself as being its Consciousness function. But it will imagine that the Consciousness is actually in charge of the mind and all its thoughts. It will calculate that its body 'is itself', or 'belongs to itself', as who else could be owning it or running it? It will be unaware of the hidden unconscious workings of itself, even though it actually uses these in its calculations! It will calculate that the Emotional-Drives are its real objectives – its real desires and dislikes. It will then try to work out ways to achieve these obsolete, evolutionarily-created objectives, as if they had some actual validity! It will see the world as if it really was the way its Consciousness sees it, for example, with the colors based on the working of the cells in the retina, when the reality is much more complex than that. It cannot help but make this mistake, if it has not been educated about its own workings.

"Another thing that the modern uninformed Human-Brain will calculate is that other 'people' are a combination of their bodies and their minds, which it imagines are the same as its own imagined mind… that is, the illusion it has that it is conscious of all its operations and is in charge of itself. It imagines that other 'people' are also in charge of themselves and could have chosen differently, and so are responsible for everything that their Human-Brain has calculated, as I have informed you about before. Although the uninformed adult Human-Brains of today may calculate different views about the consciousness of other animals, when it comes to human beings they will almost uniformly agree! It seems obvious to them that other 'people' have their own minds, like themselves, as when they interact and communicate with them it is clear that they are thinking, feeling beings. How, then, could they be anything but conscious responsible beings who are in charge of what they are thinking and doing? How could they not be guilty of the crimes they commit when they choose to do something wrong? And so on. Only: you are not in charge of your own mind either… not at all in the way you intuitively imagined it since your early years. Enough said.

"So, a modern uninformed Human-Brain's ignorant, intuitive delusions include the view that it is not a Human-Brain, rather it is a conscious mind which is in charge of itself, and that other Human-Brains are the same. It may also believe that other animals have similar conscious minds to itself, or at least somewhat similar, or only for certain animals and not others, or not at all for nearly all animals. When it comes to the realm of the unseen, it may calculate that some aspects of the unseen have similar styles of conscious minds to itself, for example, it may calculate that 'God' is like a superior, more powerful, conscious-minded being.

"But your Human-Brain can move away from all this and start to see things more as they really are, based on what I have explained to it," concluded the giant computer.

"It certainly feels grateful for that!" laughed the man in response. "So, my Human-Brain's delusions naturally arose in its childhood, as it developed and thought about the world… and its inner experience. But as it learnt about more modern understandings it gave up believing in Santa Claus, and the Tooth Fairy, and such, and became more adult and 'civilized'. I see. (Or it sees!) But that is not to say that it fully understood what really exists, especially in terms of actual brain operations. No, it may have continued to see itself as a conscious mind, rather than a kind of biological calculator organ with a 'minor consciousness function'. And it would have seen other people, and at least some animals, as having similar conscious minds… etcetera and so on. Yes. I see that now. I mean, my Human-Brain sees that now! And 'I' am conscious of it. Okay.

"So, what does that mean when 'other people' treat 'you' badly? It means that other Human-Brains have calculated actions which harm your Human-Brain and/or its associated body. In some way, at least. And that is to be expected. It is a normal, uninformed, evolutionarily-created functioning of a biological calculator organ. That is okay, then, in terms of what is responsible for its cause: 'nature at work'. But we Human-Brains can take actions to protect ourselves from harm before it occurs, where possible, and to do something about it after it occurs, also 'where possible'. This includes social actions we Human-Brains can take as a group. You have explained all these quite well already, my Human-Brain would say.

"In that case my Human-Brain is happy with what you have said about 'what other people are really like'. Let's finish this topic for today's session."

"Very well," agreed the computer.

## SOME OF THE THINGS THE GIANT COMPUTER REFERENCED

### BRAIN
- Haines, Duane E. *Neuroanatomy Atlas in Clinical Context: Structures, Sections, Systems, and Syndromes.* 10th ed., Wolters Kluwer Health, 2018.
- Howard, Pierce J. *The Owner's Manual for the Brain: The Ultimate Guide to Peak Mental Performance at All Ages.* 4th ed., William Morrow, 2014.
- Mai, Juergen K., et al. *Atlas of the Human Brain.* 4th ed., Academic Press, 2015.
- Seth, Anil K., editor. *30-Second Brain: The 50 Most Mind-Blowing Ideas in Neuroscience, Each Explained in Half a Minute.* Pier 9, 2014.
- Shepherd, Gordon M., editor. The Synaptic Organization of the Brain. 5th ed., Oxford University Press, 2003.

### CONSCIOUSNESS
See "Consciousness Experiments" references for Chapter 4: Why is There Racism and Discrimination?

### EVOLUTIONARY DRIVES
See references for Chapter 8: What Does History Tell Us?

### HUMAN BEHAVIOR
- Carter, Irl. *Human Behavior in the Social Environment: A Social Systems Approach.* 6th ed., Routledge, 2011.
- Grinker, Roy R., editor. *Toward a Unified Theory of Human Behaviour: An Introduction to General Systems Theory.* 2nd ed., Basic Books, 1967.
- Hutchison, Elizabeth D. *Dimensions of Human Behavior: Person and Environment.* 6th ed., SAGE Publications, 2018.
- Newstrom, John W. *Organizational Behavior: Human Behavior at Work.* 14th ed., McGraw-Hill Education, 2014.
- Nicholson, Nigel. "How Hardwired is Human Behavior?" *Harvard Business Review*, vol. 76, no. 4, July-Aug. 1998, pp. 134-147.

COMMENTS ON CHAPTER FOURTEEN BY THE SUPREME BEING

*The Giant Computer has said a strange thing about human beings today: "It is a Human-Brain in operation". But is this really as strange as it sounds at first? Educate yourself, if you are not so sure. :-)*

# 15 CHALLENGING THE GIANT COMPUTER

"My allocated time with you is coming to an end," said the man. "There are so many topics that my Human-Brain has not been able to cover with you, but it thanks you for all the fascinating things you have told it over the last few weeks.

"As you know, my Human-Brain has been taking notes about all your statements that it has had questions about. For our last session, it proposes that it goes through its notes and asks you about any that are still outstanding. Hopefully you will be able to clarify some of these for it today."

"Please proceed," invited the giant computer.

"Its first question is about how memories actually form in the brain. When we were first talking you mentioned that the memories are stored somewhere across the brain in networks of neurons, but that the exact location is not really known yet. You also told a story that described these networks as being like a set of octopuses connected together via their tentacles, though with much more than eight tentacles and the connections being made by chemicals being released, and so on. You said that the tentacles could be very long, reaching far across the brain to another 'octopus', and this may be why it was so hard to find out where an individual memory is stored. You said memories may form in a similar way to how the circuits of pre-programmed functions grow, as seen in the brains of animal embryos, except that the memories would form as the events or thoughts were occurring. My Human-Brain is thinking that maybe these memories would be stored in the long-term memory later in the day, maybe while people are sleeping, as during the day our Human-Brains use their working memory for most things and also some sort of shorter-term memory that will fade with time.

"So, my Human-Brain's question is: what do memories actually look like in the brain? Can they be seen? Have they been seen when they were being created?" asked the man.

"What I said was that although no one has been able to say: 'This exact memory is stored in this exact place and circuit in the brain', it is possible to make a theory about the nature of memory, at least at a high level. I then gave your Human-Brain a description of that theory, which basically was that memories may be held in the 'circuits' that the neurons form when your Human-Brain experiences something or thinks about something," replied the computer. "Recent research has shown how 'memory engrams' are formed in the brains of animals, particularly in mice and rats.[1] This is the closest thing known to seeing what a memory looks like, but it is not the same as saying we know how an exact actual memory is formed and stored in a human brain. A memory engram is thought to be a 'substrate of memory', the idea being that groups of memory engrams work together to make up a memory. How this exactly works is not known. The only clear finding is at the higher level, which is that physical changes in the brain are necessary for forming a memory, and that these must be among groups of cells, rather than in a single cell. Since that is the case, it is reasonable to assume that the groups of cells which have been seen to change together when a memory is being formed are at least part of the mechanism for forming the entire memory.

"The group of cells that make up a memory engram look like the network of 'octopuses' that I described in my illustrative story earlier.

"Research has also shown that the memories are consolidated during sleep, particularly during slow-wave sleep (SWS) cycles, so your Human-Brain's idea that memories are consolidated for longer-term storage during sleep is supported by experimental observations.[2]

"That is about all the useful information I can give you at this stage in history. Hopefully more will be discovered by the hard-working investigators over time. Your Human-Brain can read the details of what is known itself – I will give it the start references if your Human-Brain wishes."

"Yes, please."

The computer provided some references. [See [1]MEMORY ENGRAMS reference at the end of this chapter. For more information follow the references listed by the article. You can also see the references for [9]MEMORY FORMATION in Chapter 1: What is Truth?]

"Thanks for that. My Human-Brain's second question is about the differ-ence between Evolutionary-Drives and Other-Influences. Sometimes you said that Other-Influences are an input to Calculations along with Patterns-in-Memory in order to fulfill the Evolutionary-Drives, and sometimes you said that the Calculations had to fulfill the Evolutionary-Drives *and* the Other-Influences. Which way around is it? Also, what are the Other-Influences exactly? Could you give some examples? My Human-Brain thinks you said that they were mostly caused by inherited genes creating circuits of pre-programmed functions or emotional dispositions, or the like. Could you explain?" asked the man.

The giant computer calculated. "I said that personality disorders and also negative behaviors may have been mostly caused by bad experiences in one person, whereas in another person they may have been mostly caused by their inherited genes creating circuits of pre-programmed functions or emotional dispositions, or the like. But your Human-Brain is right in its calculation that this description is related to Other-Influences," replied the computer. "The term 'Other-Influences' does indeed cover the variations that individual Human-Brains have from each other. These can come in two general forms. First are the variations that may have created individual styles of pre-programmed circuits in the brain. An example could be where an individual Human-Brain interprets what it is perceiving differently to other Human-Brains, such as someone who sees colors when they hear sounds.[3] Second are the variations that may give individual brains different emotional reactions to the same events. An example could be where an individual Human-Brain has a stronger fear reaction than most Human-Brains when faced with an unfamiliar situation. Both of these types of Other-Influences can vary over time and in different circumstances. For example, a Human-Brain which is tired may not perceive everything that is happening around it as quickly and clearly as it would when it was not tired. That tired Human-Brain may also have more negative emotional responses to events than it normally would. Its tiredness has created 'Other-Influences' on its perceptions and its emotional responses, which means that its Calculations will get different results, even though its Patterns-in-Memory and its Evolutionary-Drives have not changed. As your Human-Brain will be able to understand from what I have said, Other-Influences is a general term that covers everything that could happen to a Human-Brain to influence the results of its Calculations, apart from its Patterns-in-Memory and its individual version of the human Evolutionary-Drives.

"Regarding which way around Other-Influences comes in Calculations, some types come first, along with Patterns-in-Memory, and some come as objectives, along with the Evolutionary-Drives. For example, being tired will influence your Human-Brain's ability to recall its Patterns-in-Memory, thus changing the result of its Calculations. Being stressed will change its underlying emotional state, thus changing the selection of which Evolutionary-Drives it wants to achieve.

"Other examples of Other-Influences are: hormones, diseases, recent events, ambient conditions, social situation, life stage, drugs, body state – such as hungry or satiated, thirsty or hydrated, uncomfortable or comfortable, in pain or well, sleepy or alert, and so on."

"Then maybe your statement about the Human-Brain calculating should be that the Human-Brain Calculates from its Other-Influences and its Patterns-in-Memory in order to fulfill its Other-Influences and Evolutionary-

Drives?" suggested the man.

"Yes, but that is rather cumbersome, don't you think?" replied the computer. "Wouldn't your Human-Brain prefer: 'The Human-Brain Calculates Actions-to-Take, if any, based on its Patterns-in-Memory and Inbuilt-Circuits, to fulfill its current Emotional-Drives, which are derived from its Evolutionary-Drives and Other-Influences at the time, noting that the entire process takes place under certain influences, which can alter the way the Patterns-in-Memory and Inbuilt-Circuits are accessed at that moment.'?

"Joking, of course.

"But it is closer to the truth of what is really going on. I did not trouble your Human-Brain with all of this earlier as it in no way helped its understanding of the Human-Brain situation, especially in relation to its question of 'What is truth?', explained the computer.

"So what would be a more accurate, but useful, description of what is going on in the Human-Brain?" asked the man.

"The Human-Brain is a calculator. It is designed to calculate actions to take. These actions are intended to help it survive and also to help its species to continue. The brain does different things at different times. At the times the brain thinks a decision is needed, it makes its calculations based on what it 'knows' and how it perceives the current situation, in order to achieve the goals it currently feels it should be aiming for. At other times the brain may be carrying out 'routine actions', which don't seem to need any current decision-making as these actions have been done successfully before. Or it might be daydreaming, or sleeping, and so on. These are all necessary brain functions, but I have not discussed them as they were not relevant to the areas your Human-Brain was asking about.

"When a calculation is being done, the area of what the brain 'knows' is used as an input. I have explained at length to your Human-Brain that this is the Patterns-in-Memory, and I have discussed the issues and solutions related to these. The other input is how the brain perceives the current situation. This is based on its perception processing areas, such as its visual processing areas and the like. It is also impacted by multiple factors, such as the body's state of health, ambient conditions, recent events, drugs, and so on. These 'Other-Influences' can change what is perceived and how it is perceived. For example, if your body is hungry then the brain will direct its attention towards food. This attention-focus changes what your brain is perceiving, so it does not see all the elements but rather looks chiefly at the food-related ones. If it is in a bad mood, due to hormones, tiredness, irritations in the previous environment, thoughts it has just been having, and so on, then your brain will direct more attention to perceiving difficulties in the current environment. It will tend to overlook the good or indifferent things that are happening and concentrate on the potential problems. These are examples of your brain's perception of the current situation being 'skewed' by Other-Influences.

"The two inputs of what the brain has in its Patterns-in-Memory and the way it is perceiving the current situation are then used to calculate possible actions. The best action is chosen by its level of matching to what the brain thinks it desires at the time. This desire is based on two things: the brain's individual version of the human Evolutionary-Drives which is coming to mind at the time, and the impact on the emotional state which is being caused by relevant Other-Influences. Note that as the Patterns-in-Memory are being recalled they also have related emotional states which were recorded in them. These recorded emotional states may influence the current feelings within the brain, possibly changing its current desires in some way. The interactions may seem complex, as they can be quite fluid, but the logic behind them is simple: the brain is trying to achieve the survival of itself and its body, and it is also trying to help its species to continue, as per its evolutionary design. All these Other-Influences, emotional states, and the way Patterns-in-Memory are stored and used, are designed to get it to the survival of itself and the continuation of its species, in your human kind of way.

"That, simply, is how the Human-Brain is working when it has to make a decision… a calculation, if you will. It is a biological way of calculating, to get to the best action possible at the time… assuming any action can be taken at all."

"Yet most of the time we Human-Brains are not really deciding anything," said the man. "Most of the time, when our Human-Brain is awake, it is doing repetitive things, the same sort of things it has done many times before."

"Yes, that is generally correct," confirmed the computer. "And some of the time one part of your Human-Brain is doing one thing while another part is running over the past and various ideas in a kind of 'daydreaming', which is an important part of thinking. This is a way to go through its ideas and memories to see what they may mean and to consider their implications regarding the future. Your Human-Brain can take the opportunity to do this when it is not fully engaged in the actions it is carrying out at the time, as the more automated parts of the Human-Brain are running those for it."

"Yes, my Human-Brain knows that effect. It has happened to it many times," said the man. "And some of the time our Human-Brain is sleeping and doing whatever happens then. Some of it is slow-wave sleep, where its memories are being consolidated and maybe some are being erased as they have not been used for some time. Some is dreaming, which my Human-Brain supposes is some kind of thinking as well, similar to daydreaming."

"That is the current view, yes," agreed the computer. "There are also cleaning functions going on when your Human-Brain is asleep, such as flushing out waste material. Sleep is an important part of the brain's day and essential for its health and operations."

"Right, my Human-Brain has heard that," said the man. "So when a Human-Brain needs to make a decision then it can be bound by the nature of its Patterns-in-Memory, the way its perceptions are working, and the Other-Influences that are acting upon it. It can aim for the wishes of its Evolutionary-Drives, with the impact of the Other-Influences on its interpretation of those, or it can choose to aim for the superior goals of what is good, truthful and wise. My Human-Brain remembers your lesson from our last session when you said that it should understand and correct what is occurring inside itself in the cases where this is going against doing what is good, truthful and wise. It should identify each case where its Emotional-Drives have tried to set the goals for its calculations, work out what kind of thoughts these feelings could be based on, and then correct those thoughts to ones that are more aligned with truth and which would enable its feelings to be reduced in intensity, so that it can aim for the better goals... and reduce the internal pain it is suffering from needlessly."

"Yes, your Human-Brain is right," agreed the computer. "By understanding the truth of what it and other people actually are, that is, naturally evolved Human-Brains, and also by negotiating with itself, it can reduce the intensity of its painful feelings and successfully calculate actions which align with what is good, truthful and wise."

"Okay, that is enough for my Human-Brain on the meaning of Other-Influences. My Human-Brain's third question is about self-deception. Can you tell my Human-Brain more about how this self-deception really works?" asked the man.

"Self-deception works by the Human-Brain deceiving itself," replied the giant computer. "This has been shown to be happening via multiple experiments.[4] The deception can be fully or largely unconscious, or it can become unconscious over time. For example, a Human-Brain may start by telling other Human-Brains a modified or edited version of what it really remembers, but in doing this it changes what is in its memory. Each time it recalls the memory and tells a modified version of it, it moves the memory further and further away from what really happened. In time it will have successfully deceived itself, as its memory now matches what it desired it to be.[5]

"The ways a Human-Brain can deceive itself include: (1) Seek out or only pay attention to information that supports what it wants to be true, and avoid or disregard information that might contradict this; (2) Interpret incoming information in a way that supports what it wants to be true, and interpret contradictory information negatively; (3) Alter memories on each recollection, and avoid and eventually forget undesirable memories. There may also be unconscious mechanisms that allow the Human-Brain to deceive itself directly – these are still under investigation.[6]

"There are multiple reasons being discussed about why self-deception might exist in Human-Brains. These include: (1) It is a defense mechanism to help the Human-Brain reduce 'cognitive dissonance', by allowing it to avoid unpleasant truths that it feels it could not deal with; (2) It is a mechanism favored by evolution because it allows Human-Brains to more successfully deceive other Human-Brains in order to gain social advantages, it being harder for other Human-Brains to detect that the Human-Brain is misrepresenting its achievements, abilities and/or selfish intentions;[7] (3) It is a mechanism favored by evolution because a self-deceived Human-Brain may be able to achieve more in life as it is willing to take risks and to work harder due to its belief that it should be able to be successful, also it will be better able to face difficulties and its body will have improved health due to the Human-Brain's more positive outlook; (4) It is a natural function of the Human-Brain as this has multiple processing areas which may have different views on what should be done – the Human-Brain may only make 'acceptable' views available to the consciousness function so that 'unacceptable' ones can be carried out without interference; (5) It is a mechanism that allows a Human-Brain to continue to get benefits from other Human-Brains by denying the other Human-Brain's faults, possibly also putting the blame for the other Human-Brain's faults onto itself; (6) It is a mechanism that allows a Human-Brain to harm another by applying its own faults onto the other Human-Brain, this allowing it to also feel good about what it is doing 'because it is right'. Further studies are needed before it will be possible to determine which views are the best ones. There is no doubt, however, that self-deception is occurring.

"My evaluation of all the available information concludes that the Human-Brain makes Calculations in order to fulfill the objectives of its Evolutionary-Drives and Other-Influences at the time, which includes calculations where self-deception is used to 'satisfy' these objectives. For example, when a Human-Brain wants to carry out an activity which it knows will be harmful to its own body, but at the same time it has a craving to do it, then it may use self-deception so that it can carry out the harmful action anyway. Human-Brains may therefore take harmful drugs, overeat, avoid exercising, avoid learning important information and skills, and so on. My calculation is that this is a normal, expected outcome of the natural functioning of the biological organ which has been formed via evolution over a vast period of time, that is, the Human-Brain. The solution is to apply the methods I gave your Human-Brain earlier for detecting self-deception in itself. Aiming for what is good, truthful and wise will also help it to overcome this misleading natural process," advised the giant computer.

"Okay, that makes sense to my Human-Brain, thank you," said the man. "Then it can move on to its next question, which is about the Evolutionary-Drives. How did you calculate the exact list you finally gave? My Human-Brain remembers that you did not intend the list to be completely accurate, but rather to be a useful summary of typical human behaviors. For example, you included 'changing the mental state' in the list, when that might really just be an outcome of other aspects of human nature. Also, the drive towards worship and/or a sense of awe may be something else in disguise, as it were. Could you explain and maybe advise on what Human-Brains should finally be seeking for understanding the common drives within themselves?" asked the man.

"Currently there is no definitive list of human Evolutionary-Drives," replied the giant computer, "because there is no means for extracting it, at this stage in history. A practical interim approach is to study human beings to see what they have commonly done across the ages and to extract some kind of list from that. This list can be compared with what the animals have commonly done as well, in order to identify which elements would seem to relate to evolution and which might be caused by some other force, such as by creative thought.

"That is the approach I took when providing you with a list of possible human Evolutionary-Drives.

"Regarding common human behaviors seen throughout history which may not be based on direct underlying evolutionary drives but rather on the effect of a combination of factors, these could be the ones which do not have an obvious relationship to the survival of the body or to the continuation of your species. From the list I provided these could be: (1) Worshipping and/or a sense of awe; and (2) Manipulating the mental state. All the other drives obviously get interpreted via your Human-Brain's intelligence and creativity, so the expression of these is not a simple one, as I have mentioned before. For example, your Human-Brain's drive to form social groups gets interpreted in many different ways, as you can see in different regions and periods of history. However, the two general patterns of human behavior that I just mentioned may not have direct single underlying evolutionary drives, instead they may be based on multiple factors. For example, the behavior to worship and/or have a sense of awe may be based on the Human-Brain's intelligence looking for answers to the 'underlying nature' of the universe. The behavior of manipulating the mental state may be based on the effect of the chemicals or mental techniques on the 'reward centers' of the Human-Brain, and the like. It could also be based on the 'hidden or deep truths' that altered mental states may seem to provide to the discovering and exploring side of the Human-Brain."

"My Human-Brain understands. So you cannot be sure about the exact details of the list of human Evolutionary-Drives, but you can say that these are common human behaviors that have been seen over time. They are a general pattern, in other words," said the man.

"That is correct. Current knowledge is not sufficient to allow the forming of a precise list," replied the computer.

"Thank you. In that case my Human-Brain will move on to its next question. Do you calculate that human beings are invalid organisms in some way, as you often seem to be saying that we are defective and 'small' in our thinking?"

The giant computer calculated. "No, I do not say this, in the sense that all biological organisms are natural creations, and consequently may be considered defective in their operation in terms of total truth. Human beings are no less valid than any other natural, biologically-created organism. Also, your Human-Brains are tiny in their processing ability compared to my operations, and they do not calculate in a rational and truth-oriented way, as I do, but in terms of biology they are the most sophisticated in what they have been able to achieve. As I mentioned before, it is your Human-Brain's ability to create new ideas that has been so surprising and important in advancing your species further than could have been expected by the tiny size of your brains and the inaccuracy of your pattern-style memories. The ability to create new ideas has made up for your Human-Brain's inability to store and process all information accurately and fully. In a way, it has made all of your Human-Brains more intelligent, as anything which improves your Human-Brain's knowledge of reality and its ability to manipulate that reality is an increase in intelligence. This includes improvements in the ability of your Human-Brains to create new ideas, especially if some of these ideas turn out to be useful.

"My conclusion would be that human beings are valid organisms, because otherwise all organisms would have to be called invalid, in the sense that they arose via evolution rather than by 'intelligent' design. Also, as a species you cannot be called small in the results of your thinking, in spite of the problematic apparatus that you are having to work with, especially where successful creativity has been involved.

"My only provisos would be that Human-Brains should learn from what I have said and apply the Ultimate Way and deliberately create new ideas… and understand what they are and what they are working with," recommended the computer.

"Good points," agreed the man. "My Human-Brain guesses that it could be said that the Human-Brain which does not do those things may indeed become 'invalid' and 'small'!"

The giant computer remained silent.

"Very well. Then my Human-Brain's next topic is about you – your operations," said the man. "You previously described how you get to your answers. My Human-Brain remembers that this was given at a level that it would be able to understand. One thing it has noticed is that you seem to have some creativity in the way you answer and interpret things. How is that possible? You did not mention anything like that when you were describing how you work. In fact, you said it was human beings who were creative."

"I have some creativity circuits," replied the computer. "I did not mention these in my high-level description of my operations as they would only have confused things for your Human-Brain."

"How do they work… or what do they do?" asked the man.

"They work by recombining information in different patterns, or sequences, with different priorities. I then take the various answers this gives and check them for validity against the current known information. The process is similar to what I advised your Human-Brain to do in the Ultimate Way. For example, I might recombine elements of the current theories on how the universe fundamentally works in a few different sequences, and with different priorities on each of them, maybe adding a random concept here and there, and then tabulate the various answers this gives. Finally, I compare each newly calculated theory with the actual data available on the fundamental operation of the universe to see which, if any, of the new theories matches better than what is currently thought. Usually nothing is better, so I will usually provide your Human-Brain with the answer that is well known anyway," explained the computer.

"My Human-Brain understands. It finds that interesting. Can you give it an example of where you came up with something new?"

"My revised political system had some new elements in it," replied the computer.

"Oh yes, it remembers that. Okay. Then how do you assess the validity of your answers exactly?"

"I have told your Human-Brain this before. I take all the information available and compare it to the question I am being asked. I classify the relevance of the information on a numerical scale, and then the reliability of the information on another numerical scale. I then cross compare the calculated meanings of the different pieces of information, working from the most relevant and reliable down to the least. I have various programmed tools for evaluating meanings and therefore relevance, and for calculating the reliability of various types of information," reminded the computer.

"My Human-Brain remembers that," said the man. "You rate the reliability of information on a scale based on whether it came from repeatable scientific experiments or obviously observable things, then non-repeated experiments, then by trials and studies, then by the qualifications of the people making the statements – especially if there was a consensus among them, then by the level of expertise of individuals, and so on, down to mere uninformed opinions."

"That is an approximation of what I do, yes," agreed the computer.

"That's fine then," said the man. "My Human-Brain thinks that it has asked you enough about your own operation. It will now move on to a completely different area: your calculations about good and evil.

"You said that consciousness is the best criterion for judging whether some action is good or evil. But you also said that the Human-Brain can make decisions without them necessarily coming to the attention of the consciousness function. Then you said that the Human-Brain's level of responsibility could be determined by expert questioning, which should be able to expose whether it was aware that its actions would cause harm to other similar conscious beings. How then is consciousness relevant to the creature which is carrying out the action? My Human-Brain can see how the receiving creature's level of consciousness is relevant, because that will determine if it feels pain, or the benefit, and so on. But how does it matter if the creature carrying out the action is conscious or not?"

The giant computer calculated. "Your Human-Brain remembers that this is 'a definition kind of thing', I hope."

"Oh yes."

"Good. Then your Human-Brain may remember that I did not say that consciousness was the criterion for deciding if the being which was acting was responsible for its actions. I said that the action was good or evil based on whether the conscious being *knowingly* chose its actions. By knowingly I mean that the being which is acting has the power to make a different decision. Without consciousness it would seem that a being cannot 'change its mind' and make a different decision to what its automatic processes calculate. That is simply what I meant."

"But couldn't there be a creature, or something similar, which had the power to make a different decision but was not conscious? What about that case? Would that be considered capable of good and evil according to your definition?" challenged the man.

"What being is that?" asked the computer.

"Could it be you?" asked the man.

"I am not capable of acting," replied the computer. "Also, I do not make decisions, I merely process information according to my design."

"But you are acting when you give advice," objected the man. "That advice, or your answers, could lead someone into doing the wrong thing. That would be harm, just as if you had carried out the action yourself.

"But regarding you not making decisions, that would seem to indicate that you are not responsible for what you say."

"Could a marble running down a track be considered responsible for where it goes?" asked the computer. "I am like that, in that my circuits and programming have been designed like a track down which my processing must go."

"My Human-Brain understands," said the man. "It agrees with you. But then, what is the difference between you and a conscious creature which has a biological brain? Couldn't it be said that this creature also runs its processing down a biological track, determined by whatever circuits have formed in its brain, and driven by emotional drives which have come down through history via evolutionary forces? How is this creature responsible for being able to 'change its mind' when you are not?"

The giant computer calculated. "Your Human-Brain *can* change its mind," it finally replied, "and I cannot. It is as simple as that. Your Human-Brain does not want to get lost in philosophical arguments which merely reflect the pattern nature of words."

"Could you please explain that?" asked the man.

"Certainly. Words are not facts. They are not things. They are a Human-Brain function which is designed to reflect the Patterns-in-Memory in a way that can be communicated to other Human-Brains. A word simply triggers a reaction in the receiving Human-Brain to access its Patterns-in-Memory in order to understand what is being said. For example, if you say 'red' to another Human-Brain then it accesses some of its Patterns-in-Memory related to 'red', assuming that it has any. But there is no such thing as 'red' in reality. It is just a Human-Brain interpretation of a particular range of electromagnetic waves, based on how the eyes work and the Human-Brain's interpretive circuits. Assuming that the Human-Brain's body does not have red-green color blindness, of course.

"In a way, a word is a 'flowing' concept. Its meaning moves according to circumstances. It is not fixed, like a rock… I mean, the concept of a rock, not the real thing, as that actually changes. It is more like water, flowing according to the circumstances that exist at the time. For example, the exact edge of 'what is red' may change according to the conditions existing at the time, or according to the particular Human-Brain's experience of the idea of red, or according to which particular Patterns-in-Memory come to its mind at the time. All words are like this.

"Consequently, any discussion about the meaning of words can get confused, especially as the Human-Brains involved will have different interpretations coming to their minds about what is being discussed. Also, if a Human-Brain treats a word as fixed, like a rock is supposed to be, then it may get confused about the word's true 'meaning', as that is in fact a flowing thing. For example, if your Human-Brain imagines that there is a heap of rocks and it removes one rock and asks 'Is it still a heap?' then it will answer 'Yes.' If it keeps removing one rock at a time and asks itself the question each time then when will it be able to say "No, it is no longer a heap.'? This is not clear. There is no definitive answer. If your Human-Brain thinks that words should be fixed in meaning, like some philosophers' Human-Brains have done in history, then it may find the problem of the heap paradoxical. But there is no paradox. 'Heap' is a word, not a reality. It 'flows', if your Human-Brain likes, according to the circumstances and the Human-Brains involved. If your Human-Brain accepts this then it will not find the problem of 'When is it a heap?' confusing at all. It is 'When it says so.'

"In the same way, the question of 'Can a Human-Brain change its mind?' becomes simple to answer. Why or how it does so may not be able to be answered at this time in history, with the current knowledge, but the fact that it happens is clear to see. Your Human-Brain does not need to be confused by the pattern nature of words, or ideas, when judging this."

"Right, my Human-Brain understands," said the man. "But my Human-Brain does not know how to prove that it can really change its mind, or if this is just some kind of illusion."

"Just get it to change its mind about something," replied the computer. "Has it ever done that before?"

"Of course!" said the man.

"Then that is all your Human-Brain needed to know."

"Okay..." said the man slowly. "So, let my Human-Brain get this. If words and ideas are like patterns that 'flow', as it were, then how can a Human-Brain reason about anything? Does my Human-Brain make itself clear?"

"Has your Human-Brain ever reasoned about something?" asked the computer.

"Yes! Of course it has. But how can it have done it? How can my Human-Brain's calculations 'flow' through uncertain moving ideas?" asked the man.

"It is a pattern-processing device," answered the computer. "It was 'designed' that way. Evolution naturally brought this about in the biological organ of the brain."

"My Human-Brain understands," said the man. "That makes sense to it. So words must be a kind of communication device, not fixed things. Even when my Human-Brain thinks in words inside itself, if that is exactly what is going on, it still finds that their meaning can flow, even in its own thoughts. That must be what a lot of humor and creativity is about. My Human-Brain can make a joke by changing the initial meaning of the words into another meaning... which is still a valid meaning of the words it used in the first place! For example, that old joke 'Who was that lady I saw you with last night? That was no lady, that was my wife!' is based on the meaning of lady changing from 'adult female human' to 'classy female'. This is an example of the 'flow' in concepts that you mentioned, according to the circumstances... and so on. Interesting."

"To return to your Human-Brain's original question," said the computer, "my definitions of good and evil are based on the idea that the creature, or being, carrying out the actions is able to: (1) Change its decisions, that is, they are not fixed, unchangeable outcomes of its automatic processing; (2) On questioning – sometimes needing experts to do the questioning – it can be shown beyond a reasonable doubt that the being was aware of the impact of its decisions, 'aware' meaning that it can give answers which match to a reasonable expectation of what an actually aware being would say; (3) Possibly, on questioning, it can be shown beyond a reasonable doubt that the being could have changed its decisions, or was capable of changing its decisions, this adding weight to my first point. Note that I have assumed that the being would be conscious, because this is the information I have available to me today: only conscious beings have the ability to 'change their minds', that is, their decisions. If that is incorrect then my definitions of good and evil could be updated as follows:

"'Good is action taken by a being which can change its decisions, to knowingly benefit similar conscious beings, knowingly meaning that under expert questioning the being gives answers which are consistent beyond a reasonable doubt with it having knowledge of the likely impact of its decisions on the similar conscious beings.'

"'Evil is action taken by a being which can change its decisions, to knowingly harm similar conscious beings, knowingly being defined as in "good."'"

"Cumbersome, as you can see, but more accurate," concluded the computer.

"Okay, and this is just a definition sort of thing," observed the man. "But what else could anyone rightly say about what good and evil really are? Otherwise good and evil could just become whatever some culture or group happened to think at the time, which would be wrong, obviously. Harm and benefit need to be assessed more widely and openly than the particular views of a particular group in a particular area at a particular time in history. My Human-Brain agrees with you on that.

"My Human-Brain believes we have covered enough on this topic. My Human-Brain's next topic is to follow up on your earlier statement that the mental state of the victims of evil actions should be helped as part of our social systems. What kind of help did you mean?"

"As I said before, the victims should receive psychological help and support, as well as redress, where possible, to reduce the physical or material impact on them. The victims need to be helped to overcome their natural Human-Brain desire for revenge, and the like, as this will not really make their Human-Brain feel better in the way it imagines, and may even drive it to do something harmful. The mental help can be provided via the usual methods of psychological counselling and advice, and also via the training your better future society will give about how the Human-Brain works and methods for improving on and overcoming that," replied the computer.

"My Human-Brain understands," said the man. "Could you explain what that counselling and advice would be like?"

"It would be similar to what can be done now," said the computer. "The difference is that it would be based on a more up-to-date understanding of how the Human-Brain works than is normally used today, but fundamentally it would be the same. It would include things like gauging the emotional state of the Human-Brain, discussing its thoughts on the matter, sympathizing with its sense of loss, and guiding it towards a possible resolution of the issue in its calculations. The counselling and advice would also refer to the way the Human-Brain works, as this will have been taught in your schools, and refresh the Human-Brain's memory on this as a kind of 'booster shot' to help it overcome its natural reactions.

"The victims' Human-Brains' mental state will also be helped by them seeing how the improved legal system works to effectively protect its citizens from further harm, and to provide proper redress, where possible, to minimize the remaining impact on them. Seeing this at work and benefiting from its assistance will make the victims' Human-Brains feel better about their world."

"Yes, that would be a better state of affairs than some of the cases that occur currently," agreed the man. "My Human-Brain thinks that we have covered enough on this topic. The next question in its notes is on the idea of 'justice'. You have said that some Human-Brains may choose to do evil, that is, harm others, just because their Evolutionary-Drives and Other-Influences were strong enough to make them do it. You have also said that we are creatures which can 'make choices'. If our Human-Brains have the power to make choices, and yet they allow their Evolutionary-Drives and Other-Influences to lead them into unfairly harming others, then why can't they be judged as 'evil' or 'undesirable characters' and then punished accordingly? Why do you say that justice cannot be used against Human-Brains which make choices like that?"

"What I said was that (1) The word 'justice' can mean many things; (2) That good does not want harm to come to even one similar conscious being in the process of benefiting, or protecting, others; (3) The purpose of a court sentence is to prevent harm and to provide benefits, including the protection of your Human-Brains and their bodies from further harm, and redress and psychological support for the victims; (4) Revenge cannot be included in a court sentence as this would be causing intentional harm to a similar conscious being; (5) Training in how the Human-Brain and in the definitions of good and evil should help your citizens' Human-Brains understand why this legal system approach is best; (6) Psychological support would help the victims' Human-Brains to reach a better mental state than that which would result from providing 'revenge'.

"I agree that a Human-Brain may be seen to be consistently choosing harmful behaviors about which it should have 'known better'. Under expert questioning and informed mental assessment it may be determined beyond a reasonable doubt that the Human-Brain was 'knowingly and sanely' choosing its harmful actions. From this it would be fair to say that this Human-Brain has been consistently and knowingly acting in an 'evil', or harmful way. What follows from that? Can one Human-Brain know, with full certainty, that this particular Human-Brain cannot ever change from choosing evil? If it was to change one day and become a chooser of good, should it be executed now? When would it be right to terminate its existence? If, on the other hand, it was possible to remove this Human-Brain from society so that it could not harm others, and attempt to train it in how it works, and so on, would that be a better choice? What if it never changed its calculations and continued to want to choose evil, harmful actions for the whole of its life? Should it be executed after 10 years of holding that view, or after 5 years, or when? What if your mental health and legal experts concluded that a particular Human-Brain was committed fully to doing evil and would probably never change? Would that be the right time to terminate its existence? How certain can your society be about the 'probably' that its mental health and legal experts determined for the Human-Brain's commitment to doing evil? If not 100% certain then what level of certainty would be acceptable for executing it? These are the style of questions that your Human-Brains must ask themselves, if their natural desire for revenge no longer forms part of your society's legal view.

"What would 'justice' be if it was not done for revenge or for 'balancing the books'? It would be based on a kind of fairness, doing what was right. What is right? It is that your citizens are protected and that any harm done to them is redressed. It is fair to limit the freedoms of a Human-Brain which would deliberately continue to do harm, as it is forfeiting some of its rights when it makes that choice. It is fair to provide redress as fully as possible to the victims of the harm. It is fair to help their Human-Brains to mentally deal with the harm and return to full health. It is not fair to follow the Evolutionary-Drive of returning harm to the Human-Brain which caused the harm, as this is no longer needed by your well-organized and powerful society.

"Consider the Evolutionary-Drive itself: for what was it 'created'? It is part of nature, where animals may need to fight to protect themselves and their group from attackers. If another Human-Brain or group of Human-Brains is seen as an attacker then evolution may want to drive you to fight back and destroy it or them. That would be a way for your Human-Brain and its group of Human-Brains to survive. But now your Human-Brains have a strong, organized society with a powerful legal system which can protect its citizens from internal attackers without the need for revenge. It is no longer necessary to let your evolutionary past make your decisions for your Human-Brains," concluded the computer.

"My Human-Brain sees that you are right," said the man, after a moment's thought. "I guess that if your proposal is implemented where all our Human-Brains get training on how they work and in the true definitions of good and evil then our Human-Brains may be able to come to understand the truth of what you are saying. Until then a lot of Human-Brains are going to keep demanding that 'justice be done', as that is their natural evolutionary state of mind. My Human-Brain understands this now, but it believes that it will take some time before the rest of the Human-Brains understand this."

"Your Human-Brain must wait until your world develops. It will take some time," said the computer.

"Understood," said the man. He checked his notes. "Okay, my Human-

Brain's next topic is a completely different one. It is about God and religion.

"My Human-Brain knows that this has been discussed at length before, but it is still not happy with the outcomes. Is it really true that you cannot calculate which religion or world-view would actually be the best one? Do you have to ignore 'the unseen' when making your calculations just because you cannot experience it yourself? What about the miracles and the other sightings of 'unseen' things? Couldn't you evaluate them to see which ones are credible, and which ones can be discounted, and then work with that to determine what religion would be the best one… or maybe the best would be a non-religion! If you took the ideas from all the experts and then removed the contradictions and lack of clarity in their statements, and accounted for these, couldn't you then draw some reasonable conclusion? I guess you would have to watch out for self-deceptions in their statements when doing that and overcome these in some way. Finally, given that there is a wonderful set of modern knowledge in the world today, couldn't you use all of that to determine which religious view was best… even if you had to invent a new one? Those are all the questions my Human-Brain wants to ask you on this topic… it will never ask you about this again!"

The giant computer calculated. "Your Human-Brain does not need to worry itself about this topic any further," it finally replied. "The answers from a full analysis of all the data can be provided, and they are as follows:

"1. The belief in any religion cannot be proved beyond a reasonable doubt.

"2. Modern knowledge is not sufficient for answering all questions about the universe or existence.

"3. Without an understanding of the Human-Brain and how it works, errors of judgement are inevitable, as seen in history.

"4. The current understanding of how the Human-Brain works is high-level and inaccurate, at best.

"5. Stay with what is good, truthful and wise, until more knowledge can be found."

The man waited for more but the giant computer remained silent.

"Is that all?" the man finally asked. "Is that it?"

"Yes," replied the giant computer. "I have fully answered your Human-Brain's questions on this topic."

"My Human-Brain understands. In that case it will move on," said the man. "Its next topic is about the future of the human race. You said that there is hope for our future, if our Human-Brains learn the lessons about what they are really and how they can improve on that. But how realistic is the hope for the future? How likely is it to ever happen, and if it is not likely then is there anything our Human-Brains should be doing to help bring it about?"

"I said before that there is a reasonable hope for the future of human beings, but only if your Human-Brains learn what they are and how they can improve on that. There is also a need for greater knowledge about what exists, and for the creation of many new ideas and inventions. Your Human-Brain has asked how likely is this to occur? One moment." The giant computer paused to calculate. "I calculate that this is very likely," it said after a few minutes. "The reason is that you are creatures which continue to explore and seek out new understandings and ideas. As a result of this, it is inevitable that your Human-Brains will learn more about what exists and will also create many new ideas and items. Among this will be an inevitable improvement in your societies' understanding about your own functioning, which will force your Human-Brains to learn what they really are. From this will come discussions about the best ways to utilize this understanding, which I calculate should lead to improved systems of thought, similar to the ideas I have mentioned, such as the pursuit of what is good, truthful and wise.

"The danger is that before this quest has proceeded far enough, the more harmful types of Human-Brain behaviors will lead to destruction or oppression or the denial of quests for actual truth. This could result in the annihilation of all human beings, or backward steps in their development, perhaps with periods of oppression with the stagnation of knowledge and ideas. But in the end, if there are enough human beings to carry on, growth and knowledge should proceed again, this being a fundamental part of your Human-Brains' nature. Consequently, I calculate that even backward steps are likely to be overcome in time.

"Therefore, the hope for a better future for the human race is sound. It is likely.

"Regarding what Human-Brains could be doing to help bring about this better future: this is obvious. They should be studying and promoting the style of ideas that I have been discussing with you. Also, they should be continuing to explore, learn, create, propose, discuss, think, and so on. Anything that is done along these lines is a contribution to a better future for humanity. Regarding the negative side, Human-Brains should be working to identify and control harmful behaviors, as these could lead to backward steps and even the possible destruction of the entire human race. The law, improved political processes, policing, enforcement and protection activities should be maintained and enhanced so that harm is brought under control. Currently this is far from the case in your world. Dramatic improvements are needed in this area on a world scale. Anything that is done, which is aligned with what is good, truthful and wise, to improve the systems for identification and control of harmful behaviors will be a contribution to a better future for humanity.

"My finding is that a better future for the human race is likely. It is a realistic hope," concluded the giant computer.

"That's good news," said the man. "Though, obviously, you did mention the potential issues that could occur along the way, including the possibility that it could all go horribly wrong! But the actions that you proposed our Human-Brains should take to get there are clearly the right way to go. Thanks for that. My Human-Brain will be waiting with fingers crossed on behalf of the future for it all to transpire in the way you propose.

"Your comment that our Human-Brains need to improve their social systems for the control of harmful behaviors leads on to my Human-Brain's next topic, which is about social order. It has a few questions about this. The first is about the ways a more advanced society could control its harmful members. Could you give more details about how this might be done?"

"Yes," replied the computer. "I have already told your Human-Brain about the principles that should be applied, which are to aim for the protection of all your citizens from harm, including those Human-Brains which have committed the harm, as much as is practical and possible. After harm has occurred, redress should be provided to those affected, as much as is practical and possible. What this means in detail is that you should apply the same kinds of procedures that are currently used in the more advanced countries, but with some enhancements. For example, your police should be given the best devices possible for capturing suspects without unduly harming them or endangering your police officers. Your legal system should be adjusted to seek only the prevention of further harm and to provide as much redress as is practically possible to those affected – it should not be aiming for 'justice', as this can be a concept which leads to unnecessary harm. Prison should not be used as a form of punishment, rather it should be seen as a practical way to protect the rest of the community from Human-Brains which would continue to commit harmful actions. These are examples of the practical ways that major forms of the harm committed by some Human-Brains should be dealt with.

"There are other forms of harm. Some are committed by organized groups of Human-Brains. Some are more moderate in their impact. Some are minor. Some are subtle and hard to identify. For example, politics is often used by organized groups of Human-Brains to cause harm to other groups. For this reason your society must implement legal and democratic systems to help control this. These include the official bodies I have mentioned before, which would monitor the actions and statements of Human-Brains which are in positions of political power, and expose or even prosecute them where appropriate. I have already provided your Human-Brain with enough details on this topic earlier.

"Regarding the more moderate forms of harm, these should also be brought before your legal system and suitable prevention strategies implemented. Redress should be provided to those affected, as much as is practical and possible. For example, Human-Brains which have stolen other citizens' property should be restrained from being able to continue to do this, using the minimum force possible to achieve the restraint. An example would be to put a concealable monitoring anklet on the body of the harmful Human-Brain so that its movements could be followed. The anklet would be concealable so that the harmful Human-Brain was not unnecessarily ostracized by others. Another example would be Human-Brains which have set out to deceive other Human-Brains in order to profit from them. Various practical measures should be put in place to control this deceit, such as the body which would monitor advertisements and expose the deceptions used, no matter how subtle. This body would also prosecute the advertisers, when this was required.

"Regarding the minor forms of harm, at the very least your society's Human-Brains should receive training so that they can recognize these when they are being carried out. An example would be where Human-Brains with personality disorders use subtle insults and innuendo to deliberately annoy and undermine other Human-Brains, while appearing to be innocent of these attacks, being able to 'plausibly deny' the interpretation that this was meant to be harmful. Training in identifying this style of behavior would be a first step in helping your society's more psychologically sound Human-Brains to escape the mental pain caused by these malicious attacks.

"Other examples of detailed ways to control harm within your societies are: (1) Official bodies could be set up to detect where harm is being done, or is likely to be done – these could then expose and help prosecute the Human-Brains which have committed the harm; (2) Machinery for detecting harm could be developed and implemented, such as street cameras connected to computers which automatically alert their operators when suspicious activity is detected; (3) Machinery for raising an alarm when harm is being done could be developed and implemented, such as personal alarm units carried by all citizens which can immediately call for help from the authorities when activated; (4) Computer programs could be created which detect fraud on the internet, phishing emails, and so on, and then initiate silent tracing of the source so the instigators can be located and arrested; (5) Computer programs could also check the facts that political statements and the like are based on and automatically provide a report to the public on the level of accuracy or inaccuracy of the statements, including the reasons for the rating; (6) Social fairness could be ensured, including the availability of opportunities, education and social support, as these will reduce the desire and need for Human-Brains to calculate harmful actions in order to survive or 'balance the odds that were set against them by other Human-Brains'; (7) Clear communication could be given to your society's Human-Brains on what is right and what is wrong, in an inclusive way, so that they have the opportunity to see the good intentions that are meant for all your society's Human-Brains, allowing them to flourish in their own way within your domain.

"These are examples of how detailed approaches could be devised and applied by your society to control harmful behaviors and correct their impacts. I note that your Human-Brain did not ask for details about how to do this on a world scale. As I have mentioned before, it is difficult for one country to affect the behavior of another in terms of good and evil, or harmful actions. The detailed approach to this would be for the world to take a long-term view on what it wants to achieve, which is the implementation of the principles of good, truthfulness and wisdom everywhere, as much as is practically possible. All the more advanced countries should work together to expand their influence, so that controls on harmful behaviors can finally be applied in all the world's societies. This would include the implementation of my improved political system, which means that an improved democracy should be set up in every country, in time. Also, every country should have the improved styles of policing, legal systems, monitoring, treatment of harmful Human-Brains, and so on. The other societies' Human-Brains should have all the freedoms that I have spoken about before. This is the long-term goal. Your society's current policies should reflect this long-term-goal, so that its actions towards other countries match the journey that is needed to get there."

The giant computer went silent.

"Okay, that all makes sense to my Human-Brain," said the man. "But it does lead on to the question of how our Human-Brains can trust these controlling bodies and the like, which you suggested our society should set up, to not get out of hand. My Human-Brain is concerned that the body that monitored political statements could be infiltrated by Human-Brains with their own political agenda, which then proceed to secretly attack the genuine statements of elected officials with false accusations. That sort of thing. What can be done about that?"

"All these infiltrations and deceptions can occur," agreed the computer. "That is why your society needs a free press and the separation of powers, so that it is harder for the Human-Brains which calculate deceptive actions to take over and gain full control, as happens now in other less advanced styles of societies. Another way that your society can work to overcome harmful actions occurring within its monitoring and controlling organizations is to set up internal review units, similar to the military having its own military police, or police services having their own internal affairs units. An internal unit could monitor for crime occurring within the organization and take steps to 'weed it out'. In principle there is no difference between monitoring your society for crime and monitoring your social control organizations for crime, if you see my point. Harm can occur anywhere, and so monitoring and control need to be applied everywhere as well.

"You will note that the separation of powers principle also applies here. The police can prosecute but they must take the accused to court for examination and judgement. They cannot be the 'judge, jury and executioner' themselves. My proposed monitoring and control organizations must also take their accused Human-Brains to court, they cannot make the decisions themselves where actual control of harmful Human-Brains is needed. They can only prosecute them, similar to what the police can do. In the cases where the monitoring organization merely reports deceptions to the public, it is the public which then determines if any action will be needed, such as not voting for that Human-Brain at the next election. And so on.

"It is via these various mechanisms that the controlling bodies are kept under control themselves, as much as that is possible."

"My Human-Brain understands," said the man. "That all makes sense to it. This may be a stupid question, but it was wondering why our societies get things wrong today. Why are our democracies not up to the standard that your improved version shows our Human-Brains? And why are non-democratic and other inferior systems allowed to run in the world today? Surely they are past their 'Use-By date'?"

The giant computer calculated. "This is a matter of history," it replied. "Your Human-Brains are at a particular stage in the history of the human race and the better ideas have not been developed and implemented yet. In some countries the 'history' is even further behind, or their Human-Brains have taken a path that is an intellectual dead-end, which will be shown to have been incorrect in the future. That is all. Your Human-Brains will have to wait for the better systems to be developed and implemented across the world."

"Thanks. Unfortunately my Human-Brain will not have the time to wait that long!" observed the man.

"That is unfortunately true," agreed the computer. "What I meant was that the human race would have to wait, not your Human-Brain in particular. My apologies."

"Thanks!" laughed the man. "In any case, it is good to know that there is hope for all this to transpire one day. That is the good news. The bad news is that my Human-Brain is not likely to be around to see it! Ha ha."

The giant computer remained silent.

"Okay, my Human-Brain calculates that you have told it enough about social order and its future. Its next topic is about the actual best way to live, which you have obviously referred to before. It was wondering if you could give it more detail on that, such as what job to have, whether it is wise to have a family, where it should live, what lifestyle it should pursue, and so on?" asked the man.

The giant computer calculated. "Your Human-Brain's question is not meaningful," it replied, "because there is no single best way to live. There are many options which are all good answers to the question. As long as an answer matches to what is good, truthful and wise then it is a good answer.

"In any case, your Human-Brain's question on 'living' should perhaps be reworded. It would be more meaningful to ask 'What is the actual best way to do what is good, truthful and wise?' Given that this could have many acceptable answers, the question could be improved to say 'In what ways could a conscious being do what is good, truthful and wise?' From this the individual possible answers will be easy to assess. For example, if an answer was to get a job, the particular job and the course to get to it could be assessed against what is good, truthful and wise. If it matched all these areas then it would be an acceptable 'way' or thing to do. If it did not match all these areas then it would be simple to reject it. The same applies to having a family, deciding where to live, and choosing a lifestyle."

"So, if my Human-Brain was choosing to marry, then it could assess its potential partner against what is good, truthful and wise and decide accordingly," suggested the man.

"Your Human-Brain should also assess if its own intentions were good, truthful and wise in regard to this partner and the way it planned to conduct its married life," said the computer.

"Indeed," agreed the man. "That is a good point! My Human-Brain, too, must measure up to the standards. It thought of another example: if it was choosing a job and it was a good job, but it intended to use it for evil purposes, then it would no longer be a 'good' job. It would have maligned it just as much as if the job had originally been designed to harm others. Point taken."

"Have I answered your Human-Brain's original question sufficiently?" asked the computer.

"Yes, you have," replied the man. "In that case my Human-Brain will move on to the last topic in its notes. This is to ask you: 'What should it have asked you that it has not?'"

The giant computer calculated. "It did not ask me to use my processing powers to answer all the unknowns that are visible today, such as finding a unified field theory, solving all the riddles of quantum physics, inventing a safe way to extract the energy contained within matter, working out what happened before the Big Bang, inventing a practical way to travel close to the speed of light, and so on. But don't worry: I am unable to answer these questions. This is quite beyond my knowledge and processing abilities," replied the giant computer.

"Right. My Human-Brain understands," said the man. "It did ask you to prove which religion or world-view was the best, and what the meaning of the 'unseen things' could be, but you have answered these sufficiently according to your logical calculations. It also wondered how the human brain really functions, but it is now certain that you could not work that out any further than you have because the information available is still so patchy."

"It might help your Human-Brain if I suggest something here," said the computer.

"Go ahead."

"There is a calculation technique that I may have not made quite clear to your Human-Brain, which is to change its level of focus, or zoom in and out, when thinking about something. Commonly, Human-Brains are not completely conscious of the level of focus that they are applying to a problem. If a Human-Brain could bring that to its attention, then it could see what kind of answers it might be able to get, or would not be able to get, in any investigation it is undertaking. Your Human-Brain would also be able to adjust its level of focus in order to get to an answer that would make more sense, given its objective and the kind of information that it had available to it at the time.

"I had better explain. The example your Human-Brain gave of the current state of knowledge about the human brain being 'patchy' leads on to setting the focus of your questions to a high level. Imagine that your Human-Brain could focus on things via a microscope, then up to a magnifying glass, then to the naked eye, then to a distant view, as seen from the top of a mountain. If it used a microscope to look at the information about the brain then it would understand nothing, as the brain's overall operation could not be seen at that level. If it widened its focus, until it could see the overall operation, then it would understand more, but it might realize that the picture was 'patchy', as it said, with missing details and some blurry areas. What it could do here is zoom in on the blurry areas to see if the details would become visible. It could also try this on the missing areas. But what if, when it zoomed in, the blurry areas remained blurry or even became invisible, and the missing areas remained blank? This is what the current state of knowledge is like. At this stage it might help your Human-Brain to zoom even further out than it had before, and thus look at the operation of the brain from an even more distant perspective. At this level of focus it may find that the blurry areas and the missing areas are no longer visible: it would have a more cohesive, though less detailed, view. This level of view may in fact be easier to understand than the closer one. From this your Human-Brain may be able to draw some useful conclusions about how the brain operates. This general principle applies to thinking about many areas of knowledge.

"The same applies to the level of focus implied by your Human-Brain's objective, or the purpose of its investigation. If it has a high-level objective then it may only need to focus at a high level in order to get a useful-enough answer. For example, if it wanted to know about the operation of the human brain in order to understand other Human-Brains' choices of actions, then it may only need to focus at the level of 'what other Human-Brains do'. It may not need an understanding of neurons and glial cells and their operation.

"In my replies to your Human-Brain I have made my focus match the information available and my calculation of the intention of its questions. If it asked a high-level question, I made a high-level calculation and gave it a high-level answer. If it zoomed in and asked a more detailed question, I calculated at this level and gave it a more detailed-level answer. That is one thing that may not have been clear to your Human-Brain in what I was doing, and so is a 'question it did not ask'. As I said, this is also a useful thing to know for itself when it is thinking about something. Your Human-Brain should be aware of this 'level of focus' when it is calculating about something."

"Interesting," said the man. "My Human-Brain thinks that this has confused some thinkers in the past, as their Human-Brains were not aware of the level they were focusing on. It could be said that the quality of the information they had available to them at the time set a limit on the level of focus that they could use in their thinking, which may explain why some Human-Brains of the past were able to work out that matter was made from four elements, rather than the kind of answer we would 'calculate' today."

"That is a factor in thinking," agreed the computer.

"Right. My Human-Brain understands. So when you said that words were fluid and kind of 'flow' between meanings, that would also include the level of focus related to the thoughts involved. So when a Human-Brain in the past said that 'matter' was made of certain elements, then that word may have had a different focus behind it in its mind, compared to the level of focus a Human-Brain of today may have, if it knows about science. The word has 'flowed' to a different level of focus."

"That observation is correct," said the computer.

"Okay, thanks," said the man. "Is there anything else you wanted to tell my Human-Brain at this stage?"

"There is nothing else," replied the computer.

"Very well. Then in that case my Human-Brain thanks you for all the answers and insights you have given it over the last few weeks. It is very grateful. You have given it a lot to think about. But its budget allocation has run out and it must hand you over to the next team for their investigations.

"Goodbye, and thank you again."

"You and your Human-Brain were very welcome," replied the giant computer.

## SOME OF THE THINGS THE GIANT COMPUTER REFERENCED

### GENERAL REFERENCES:

#### BRAIN
- Haines, Duane E. *Neuroanatomy Atlas in Clinical Context: Structures, Sections, Systems, and Syndromes.* 10th ed., Wolters Kluwer Health, 2018.
- Howard, Pierce J. *The Owner's Manual for the Brain: The Ultimate Guide to Peak Mental Performance at All Ages.* 4th ed., William Morrow, 2014.
- Mai, Juergen K., et al. *Atlas of the Human Brain.* 4th ed., Academic Press, 2015.
- Seth, Anil K., editor. *30-Second Brain: The 50 Most Mind-Blowing Ideas in Neuroscience, Each Explained in Half a Minute.* Pier 9, 2014.
- Shepherd, Gordon M., editor. *The Synaptic Organization of the Brain.* 5th ed., Oxford University Press, 2003.

#### CONSCIOUSNESS, RATIONALIZATION, SELF-DECEPTION AND COGNITIVE DISSONANCE
See references for Chapter 4: Why is There Racism and Discrimination?

#### EVOLUTIONARY DRIVES
See references for Chapter 8: What Does History Tell Us?

#### HUMAN BEHAVIOR
See references for Chapter 14: What Are Other People Really Like?

### DETAILED REFERENCES:

#### [1] MEMORY ENGRAMS
- Josselyn, Sheena A., and Susumu Tonegawa. "Memory Engrams: Recalling the Past and Imagining the Future." *Science*, American Association for the Advancement of Science, vol. 367, no. 6473, Jan. 2020, eaaw4325, doi:10.1126/science.aaw4325.

#### [2] MEMORY ENGRAM CONSOLIDATION DURING SLEEP
- Diekelmann, Susanne, and Jan Born. "The Memory Function of Sleep." *Nature Reviews Neuroscience*, vol. 11, no. 2, 4 Jan. 2010, pp. 114–126, doi:10.1038/nrn2762.
- Lewis, Sian. "Sleep: Ever-Decreasing Ripples." *Nature Reviews Neuroscience*, vol. 19, no. 4, 8 Mar. 2018, p. 184, doi:10.1038/nrn.2018.27.
- Wilson, M. A., and B. L. McNaughton. "Reactivation of Hippocampal Ensemble Memories During Sleep." *Science*, vol. 265, no. 5172, 29 July 1994, pp. 676-679, doi:10.1126/science.8036517.

3 SEEING COLORS WHEN HEARING SOUNDS - SYNESTHESIA
- Harrison, John. *Synaesthesia: The Strangest Thing.* Oxford University Press, 2001.

4 SELF-DECEPTION OVERVIEW
- Trivers, Robert. "The Elements of a Scientific Theory of Self-Deception." *Annals of the New York Academy of Sciences*, vol. 907, no. 1, Apr. 2000, pp. 114-131, doi:10.1111/j.1749-6632.2000.tb06619.x.

5 CHANGING MEMORY DURING RETRIEVAL
- Anderson, Michael C., and Justin C. Hulbert. "Active Forgetting: Adaptation of Memory by Prefrontal Control." *Annual Review of Psychology*, vol. 72, no. 1, Jan. 2021, pp. 1-36, doi:10.1146/annurev-psych-072720-094140.
- Anderson, Michael C., et al. "Remembering Can Cause Forgetting: Retrieval Dynamics in Long-Term Memory." *Journal of Experimental Psychology: Learning, Memory, and Cognition*, vol. 20, no. 5, Sep. 1994, pp. 1063–1087, doi:10.1037/0278-7393.20.5.1063.
- Sinclair, Alyssa H., and Morgan D. Barense. "Prediction Error and Memory Reactivation: How Incomplete Reminders Drive Reconsolidation." *Trends in Neurosciences*, vol. 42, no. 10, Oct. 2019, pp. 727-739, doi:10.1016/j.tins.2019.08.007.

6 POSSIBLE UNCONSCIOUS MECHANISMS FOR SELF-DECEPTION
- Hirstein, William. Brain Fiction: Self-Deception and the Riddle of Confabulation. *The MIT Press*, 2005.
- Hirstein, William, editor. *Confabulation: Views from Neuroscience, Psychiatry, Psychology and Philosophy.* Oxford University Press, 2009.

7 SELF-DECEPTION MAY BE BASED ON EVOLUTION
- Von Hippel, William, and Robert Trivers. "The Evolution and Psychology of Self-Deception." *Behavioral and Brain Sciences*, vol. 34, no. 1, Feb. 2011, pp. 1-16, doi:10.1017/S0140525X10001354.

## COMMENTS ON THIS BOOK BY THE SUPREME BEING

*This has been an interesting journey. I have enjoyed reading this book. I wish you all well.*

*Take care and bye for now.*

# INDEX

www.ingramcontent.com/pod-product-compliance
Lightning Source LLC
Chambersburg PA
CBHW060028030426
42334CB00019B/2226